The Other John is a book that anyone with an inquisitive Biblical mind will not be able to put down. With profound respect but without fear, Fr. John Spencer addresses virtually every issue that has ever been raised regarding the authorship of the Johannine works.

Blending his theological training with his investigative training, Spencer takes us on a journey from the Biblical era to Patristic and Early Church heroes, scholars, and saints who grappled with the issue of authorship. Like an investigative reporter, he "interviews" a wide range of personalities from those who walked with Jesus, those who traveled with St. Paul, and those who with apostolic integrity shared the authentic oral tradition passed down from those who knew Jesus and His followers in Galilee and Jerusalem. Analyzing language and linguistic style in the Johannine texts, Spencer guides to ask questions that, perhaps, we have never asked before about authorship.

Without questioning the authority of Scripture as the Word of God, he takes us from Jerusalem to Ephesus to Patmos as we join in his search to discover "the other John." Written in a style that will challenge and engage everyone from Biblical scholars to Bible study class members, Spencer proves that asking questions without preconceived outcomes is the healthiest way to approach research. His ability to analyze, summarize, and suggest additional resources encourages his readers to take much more seriously the truths of Holy Scripture versus commonly held assumptions about authorship.

—The Rt. Rev. Keith L. Ackerman, DD
Eighth Bishop of the Diocese of Quincy

What a fascinating read is John R. Spencer's *The Other John: The Puzzle of the Fourth Gospel*! Spencer, a theologically adept Anglican priest, puts his experience as a trained criminological investigator to good use in drawing a somewhat iconoclastic conclusion on who exactly wrote the Gospel of John. Like Catholic scholar Raymond Brown, Spencer rejects the traditional theory that John bar Zebedee authored this gospel.

I'm intrigued by Spencer's proposal – and by his step-by-step "forensic analysis" of the gospel and early Patristic sources to try to identity who the *other* John was. Spencer presents a fascinating proposal that a man known as John the Presbyter, who was also an apostle but *not* one of the Twelve, wrote the Fourth Gospel, then digs further to suggest the possible identity of this other John and his close relationship with Jesus as "the beloved disciple."

Much like Spencer as an Anglican priest, I, as a Catholic priest, assume the veracity of the text from the authority of the Church that approved the text. Authorship is an entirely secondary matter to me – a matter of discussion I left behind upon graduating from seminary. However, Spencer's argument for the other John's authorship offers an intriguing payoff: if true, this John was almost certainly an eyewitness to events that took place in and around Jerusalem – *before* Jesus called the Twelve and before he began his subsequent Galilean ministry. And if this is true, Jesus' lengthy discourses recorded in John's Gospel by an early eyewitness deserve a great deal more respect than they presently receive from far-too-many contemporary scholars.

I hope his study gains widespread attention – and a point by point, scholarly response.

—*The Rev. Douglas Grandon, PhD*
National Chaplain, FOCUS
(Fellowship of Catholic University Students)

The Other John

The Other John

The Puzzle of The Fourth Gospel

A Reexamination of the
True Author of the Gospel of John

John R. Spencer

The Other John, The Puzzle of The Fourth Gospel
© 2007, 2024, John R. Spencer
All rights reserved.

First Edition
DeerVale Publishing,™ Trempealeau, WI, June, 2024

DeerVale Publishing thanks you for supporting Copyright of intellectual property by purchasing only authorized copies of this work.

No part of this book may be reproduced, scanned, stored in a retrieval system, transmitted or distributed in any printed, electronic, or audio form without the written permission of the author or his authorized representative.

All scripture quotations, unless otherwise noted, are from the Revised Standard Version of the Bible, copyright 1952 [2nd edition, 1971] by the Division of Christian Education of the National Council of the Churches of Christ in the United States of America. Used by permission. All rights reserved.

Scripture quotations noted "ESV" are from The ESV® Bible (The Holy Bible, English Standard Version®), © 2001 by Crossway, a publishing ministry of Good News Publishers. Used by permission. All rights reserved.

Scripture quotations noted as NASB are taken from the (NASB®) New American Standard Bible®, Copyright © 1995, by The Lockman Foundation. Used by permission. All rights reserved. lockman.org

Permissions and Author Contact information:
Email: deervale@mtco.com

The author and publisher have made every effort to provide accurate contact information at time of publication. Neither the author nor the publisher assumes any responsibility or liability for errors or changes after publication, or for any third-party websites or their contents.

ISBN 978-1-7365689-2-7 (Print)
ISBN 978-1-7365689-3-4 (eBook)

Cover design by *Images In Ink*
Cover images
Domenico Ghirlandaio (1448-1494)
Dom Prosper Guéranger OSB (1805-1875)

DEDICATION

For my wife Candice, whose love,
patience, and support
are boundless

TABLE OF CONTENTS

Introduction	1
Chapter One	5
Chapter Two	20
Chapter Three	40
Chapter Four	47
Chapter Five	68
Chapter Six	95
Chapter Seven	118
Chapter Eight	138
Chapter Nine	148
Chapter Ten	166
Chapter Eleven	172
Chapter Twelve	180
Appendix A Sequence and Location in John	186
Appendix B John the Evangelist in the New Testament	201
Appendix C The Evidence of Justin Martyr	206
Appendix D The Evidence of Tertullian	208
Appendix E The Supposed Letters of Ignatius	212
Appendix F Development of the Four Gospels	218
Bibliography	231
About the Author	235

Introduction

IMAGINE THAT A LARGE TREE stands in your yard just outside your front window. You've looked out that window every day for more than fifteen years, so you no longer really see the tree, just a tall shape obstructing your view of the street beyond. Then one night a violent windstorm brings the tree down. When you look out the next morning, you instantly *notice* the tree — for its absence. The tree is gone, but your mind's eye somehow still "sees" it. Your mind, long conditioned, rebels against the fact that the tree no longer stands where you expect it.

As with many things in life, we become so accustomed to seeing things in a certain way that it becomes next to impossible to even consider any other view.

Such is the case with the question of who wrote the five biblical books that carry the name "John." Who was this man? Did one man, in fact, write them all? Or was there more than one author?

Readers who have spent serious time studying popular New Testament commentaries may consider these questions silly, because they have already — perhaps uncritically — accepted one prevalent theory that all five books were written by "John the Apostle," meaning John the son of Zebedee, the brother of James, one of "the Twelve" apostles of Jesus. Long conditioned by this view, many readers may reject out-of-hand any different suggestion because they have been taught, by teachers they respect, this common, "traditional" view. In other words, they want to see that tree standing there — just as they have always seen it.

Serious students of the Fourth Gospel and the other Johannine books, however, know the answer is not that simple. For centuries, the authorship of the Fourth Gospel has puzzled readers and scholars, and a variety of theories of authorship have been put forward. It's uncertain relationship to the other four books, especially to Revelation, has been the subject of serious debate going back, as we shall see, to the earliest centuries of the Church. Commentators, interpreters of the Bible, and theologians have tried to discern a plausible answer to the apparently simple question of which "John" wrote each of these five books.

It would, therefore, be presumptuous of me to say I have found "the" answer. In the study that follows, I will lay out what I have uncovered over many years of detailed consideration of this question and let you, the reader, decide.

A caveat, here, is required. I have been a serious student of the Bible for over 50 years, since my seminary days. In fact, I began this particular study on the authorship of the Johannine books while in seminary. I do not, however, consider myself an advanced Biblical scholar. What I am is a trained investigator: I have formal investigative training and over 20 years of actual investigative experience in law enforcement, corrections, and the social service field. As an investigator, I was trained to uncover evidence, but more importantly to relate and compare pieces of evidence, even when they did not seem related or relevant to a particular investigation, or to each other. This has given me a rather different perspective in approaching biblical studies: I don't just read other previous work, but also look carefully at previous assumptions (and conclusions) and weigh them against the broader field of evidence.

That is the approach I have used in the present study. I began with an objective look at the "traditional" view about the authorship of the Fourth Gospel, and its relation to the other Johannine books. I have also considered its relation to the other three gospels, and to the Book of Acts. My goal was to conduct a "fresh" review of the scant evidence that actually exists, to "reassemble" that evidence, and, where necessary, to rule-out certain evidence that appears to be unreliable. My objective throughout has been to assemble a "working theory" about who actually wrote the Fourth Gospel, and then look at the connections (or lack thereof) to the three Johannine letters and Revelation.

I began this study with an open mind, examining both internal and external evidence relating to the Fourth Gospel. I ask the reader to read with an equally open mind, because I believe only that will enable him or her to make their own objective analysis of what I will suggest. If your only interest is to see that old tree standing where it has always been, you need not read on.

My goal is not to give a finalized or indisputable "case" about the authorship of the Fourth Gospel. Quite the contrary: I hope that what I present here may open new avenues for further inquiry by other students of Scripture, and more qualified scholars than I. Toward the end, I will suggest a summary framework of what I have come to believe is the relationship of the Fourth Gospel to the other Johannine books and the other three Gospels.

My conclusions must remain to some extent speculative, for the simple reason that we do not presently have — and may never find — absolutely conclusive evidence regarding these questions about authorship. Our earliest Christian ancestors, expecting the imminent return of our Lord, were notorious for their incomplete records about the origins of the New Testament books. We work with what we have. One of my objectives has been not to take every "traditional" assumption or conclusion at face value, but to consider them in light of other evidence which may run contrary to commonly accepted views. I did this in order to come up with a theory and framework that credits each bit of evidence and is also *consistent* across all the evidence.

The reader will not find here an "air-tight," indisputable answer to every puzzle raised by the Johannine books, because we have so little hard evidence on which to base conclusions. If you are looking for absolute certainty, you will be disappointed, and you might want to pursue some entirely different subject. I try to shed new light on a number of nagging questions that have pestered researchers over the ages. What I will suggest is not certitude but a reasoned, and in many ways *probable,* answer to the puzzle of the Fourth Gospel, and the other four books which have always carried the name John.

I will also diverge from what some may consider "established facts" about Johannine authorship. I have done so because I have found that too often in the study of Holy Scripture "facts" have become "established" simply because they relied on earlier "facts" that were, originally, only someone's suppositions. Then, oft repeated and passed down from writer to writer, those suppositions became "facts" merely by repetition.

C. S. Lewis once wrote that he took a low view of "climates of opinion." As Lewis rightly saw, discoveries are only made, and "established" errors are corrected, only when others are willing to ignore the climate of opinion in their field.[1]

Our minds, being essentially lazy, want to revert to what we "know" and see things as we have always seen them. So, the reader will forgive me if I have purposely disregarded the "climate of opinion" that has held sway about the authorship of the Johannine Books. I struck off down a different path to take an objective look at the evidence and seek a proposal which fits all the facts. I ask readers to keep both minds and eyes open. Getting around the perceived roadblock of "the climate of opinion" is always difficult, but will, in this case, be worthwhile.

Endnote

1. C. S. Lewis, *The Problem of Pain*, p. 134

One

WHO WAS THE AUTHOR of the Fourth Gospel of the New Testament? Was he John the son of Zebedee, the brother of James, as one long-standing Christian tradition maintains? If not, who was this John?

There follows from this a more complicated question: did the same person author all five New Testament books that carry the name "John"?

For centuries, many people have been taught the theory that John the son of Zebedee wrote the gospel that bears the name John. A good many students of Scripture leap from that assumption to the further assumption that one and the same John wrote all three letters that carry that name, and also the Book of Revelation.

If we objectively assess this traditional view, however, and take a deeper look, we will be quickly struck by a number of facts. The first is this: we have to acknowledge that nowhere in the Gospel of John, nor the three letters that bear that name, is the author ever identified by the name "John," or any other. (The same is true of the three "Synoptic" gospels, Matthew, Mark, and Luke: the author is never identified internally by name, only in the title.) In fact, the only book of the five Johannine works that includes the name of the author is Revelation. A cursory look at the Fourth Gospel shows that the only two Johns mentioned by name are John the Baptist (chapters 1, 3, 4, 5, & 10), and John the father of Simon Peter (1:42, 21:5-17).

Then we come to a more startling fact: in the gospel "According to John," as the manuscripts title it, John the son of Zebedee is *never mentioned at all*, except in one rather oblique reference in the last chapter (21:2) where the "sons of Zebedee" are mentioned. Even there, neither of their first names is given; and, as we will see, it is quite probable that this last chapter was an addition to the original gospel.

If we relate this strange fact to the Synoptic Gospels, it will strike us as more curious, because in Matthew, Mark and Luke, John the son of Zebedee, along with his brother James and Simon Peter, are *key figures* throughout those books and mentioned often by name. Indeed, these three men make up the inmost circle of Jesus' disciples within the inner circle of the Twelve.

Examining the Fourth Gospel more closely, another curious fact leaps out: while this gospel refers to "The Twelve" as a group (6:67-71, 20:24; and perhaps indirectly in 6:13, based on the number of baskets), only five of the Twelve are ever named: Peter, Andrew, Philip, Thomas, and Judas Iscariot. The Gospel of John speaks of another prominent disciple, Nathanael (who is not named in Matthew, Mark or Luke, even though he was from Cana in Galilee), but nowhere do we find "James and John," the sons of Zebedee, named in the Fourth Gospel.

Curious Details

If John the son of Zebedee (whom I will from here forward refer to as John bar Zebedee) authored this book, why is he never even mentioned in the main body of the gospel (chapters 1-20)? Indeed, after reading the many crucial events recorded in the Fourth Gospel, we would not even know there was a disciple named John bar Zebedee, let alone that he was one of the "Twelve."

These facts may at first unsettle some readers, but they are significant and should not be ignored, for this reason: if John bar Zebedee *was* the author of this gospel, why would he be so completely invisible? Some have suggested this could have been out of humility, but that hardly seems to fit with the man who, in the Synoptic tradition, was known as one of "the sons of thunder" (Mark 3:17).

Further, why would he not only exclude his name, but not even hint at his membership among the Twelve when he *does* refer to that group? This is even odder, considering this John's very prominent role in the other three gospels.

These oddities, however, are only the beginning of the curiosities. The details outlined so far are only the tip of the proverbial iceberg of intriguing facts about the Fourth Gospel that seem to be ignored by "the traditional view" that John bar Zebedee was its author.

The "Author"

Before digging further into the question of authorship, however, I want to make one of my primary goals clear, to cut away the weeds which might be introduced by others if I don't state this objective clearly: in searching for the identity of the "author" of the Fourth Gospel, I am not trying to identify the man — or men (or women) — who actually put the ink on the page. Rather, I am looking for the man who was the principle *authority* behind this gospel, regardless of who ultimately put pen to paper (or papyrus) to preserve this important record of Jesus for us. In searching for the primary "author," the "authority" behind the gospel, I am not seeking to debate (let alone resolve) how many hands may have later edited the work, up to and possibly including the addition of chapter 21.

My primary objective is to try to identify which "John" was the authoritative "source" behind this work, the one who reveals himself as a *reliable* eyewitness to the ministry of Jesus of Nazareth. I will not, therefore, enter the decades-long debates about exactly who wrote certain "odd" verses in John, verses that quite frankly stick out like sore thumbs in their contexts, or whether there developed a subsequent "Johannine Community" that had a hand in the eventual editing or "polishing" of the gospel. In short, I have not made it a goal to answer when, where, or by whom the original gospel may have been edited after its original, primary writing. Capable scholars have proposed a number of highly speculative theories about how the

Fourth Gospel came to be in its final (present) form, and where individual verses may have been added, deleted, or shifted about since its first writing. I don't tackle those issues here; that is not my primary purpose. Those theories of editorial development, while interesting and useful, do not help us answer the fundamental question of who originally wrote the essential body of this gospel: was it John bar Zebedee, or some other John? Further, while some of those scholarly theories are intriguing, they are — in my modest opinion — often convoluted, and confusing. Some writers seem to believe that because there may have been emendations in the text, or comments which clearly seem "inserted" (John 19:35 being an obvious example), that *the entire gospel* as we have it must therefore have been very late in composition (not finished until perhaps the very end of the 1st century or well into the 2nd). This leads to the suspicion by some that it is therefore thoroughly unreliable as to actual history.[1]

As the reader will see, the evidence I have assembled here will, in fact, suggest exactly the opposite.[2]

So, although I will touch by necessity on some "secondary" editorial issues, my primary purpose is to answer this question: who was the man who was the real author, the main *authority* behind this gospel? Whether or not he was the actual "writer" (which I believe he *may* have been), and whether he later edited his own work, or whether someone else edited it, perhaps after his death, are secondary issues I will not try to settle. The primary question I have set is, was *this* John, the man who gave us this stunning and very unique history of Jesus Christ, John bar Zebedee, or someone else?

This question is not new. From the earliest centuries of the Christian Church, readers of the New Testament recognized the obvious fact that the Gospel of John bears little resemblance to the three Synoptic gospels of Matthew, Mark, and Luke (called "Synoptic" because they can be "seen together," that is, read side by side because of their many closely-parallel passages). When we put John alongside the other three, and compare the "story lines," we see that there are few points of contact or even similarity in John, until we reach the passion narrative. Even there, we find significant differences in John's record, in part because John alone gives us a number of highly specific details of the passion account that the Synoptics do not.

The question is, why?

It has sometimes been argued that the main difference is that the Synoptics focus on detailing *events,* while John focuses on a more highly developed verbal *teaching and theology* from Jesus. This view, in my opinion, is weak on two counts. First, the Synoptics also contain passages of lengthy teaching and highly developed theology (for example, Matthew 6, Matthew 13, Mark 13, and Luke 6). Second, John often contains much more specific detail about a particular event than we find in the Synoptics, particularly in his passion narrative.

Unique Material In John Not Found In The Synoptics

A close examination of the Gospel of John reveals not only a significant amount of material unique in his record, but some very important events and specific details that are missing from the Synoptics. Here are just a few examples:

1. Multiple visits by Jesus to Jerusalem for Jewish feasts (2:13, for Passover; 5:1, for Pentecost ?; 7:1-11, for Tabernacles; 10:22-23, for The Dedication; 12:1-17:26, for his last Passover).

2. Visits to, and significant events in Cana of Galilee (2:1-11; 4:46-54; 21:2).

3. Water changed into wine at the Cana wedding feast (2:1-11).

4. Nicodemus, a member of the Jewish High Council, is involved with Jesus (3:1-21, 7:50, 19:39).

5. Jesus' visit to Samaria, the woman at the well (4:4-42).

6. Healing of the official's son at Capernaum when Jesus again visited Cana of Galilee (4:46-54), "having come from Judea to Galilee."

7. Healing of a man at the Pool of Bethzatha, or "Bethesda" (5:1-9).
8. The Bread of Life discourse (6:29-71).
9. Healing of the man born blind (9:1-41).
10. Raising of Lazarus from the dead (11:1-44).
11. Jesus washing his disciples' feet (13:1-20).
12. Jesus withdraws to Ephraim after raising Lazarus because his life was in danger (11:54).
13. The post-resurrection appearance at the Lake of Galilee (21:1-11).

Notable Details Not Found In The Synoptics

In addition to the events just enumerated, we also find in John these very specific details that are absent from the other three gospels:

1. John the Baptist's lengthier discourse about Jesus, "the lamb of God" (1:19-40).
2. Two of Jesus' first disciples were originally disciples of John the Baptist (1:35-41).
3. The "cleansing of the temple" (2:13-25) occurs near the beginning of Jesus' ministry rather than near the end, while the similar event reported in the Synoptics takes place during his final trip to Jerusalem.
4. Jesus only conducts major ministry activities in Galilee after his life was in danger in Judea, where most of the previous events, according to John, took place (7:1).
5. John contains significant "insider" details of the Jewish Council Meeting before Jesus' arrest (11:47-53).
6. Judas Iscariot is identified as "son of Simon" (13:2).
7. John supplies greater detail about the supper and anointing at Bethany (12:1-11).
8. The high priest's servant whose ear Peter cut off is identified by name (18:10).
9. One of Jesus' disciples (the "Beloved Disciple"?) was personally known to the high priest (18:15).

10. Jesus was taken first to Annas after his arrest, and only then sent by Annas to Caiaphas (18:13-24).

11. One of the servants who confronts Peter in the courtyard was a relative of Malchus, whose ear Peter had cut off in the garden (18:26).

12. Nicodemus assists Joseph of Arimathea in burying Jesus (19:38-42).

13. John reports that Peter and "the beloved disciple" followed Mary Magdelene back to the open tomb early Easter morning (20:2-10).

14. John records a unique Resurrection appearance to Mary Magdalene (20:11-18).

15. John includes the Resurrection appearance to the Ten without Thomas (20:19-25).

16. John also records the Resurrection appearance to the Eleven a week later, with Thomas present (20:26-29).

17. John shows much greater familiarity with Hebrew place names in and around Jerusalem: for example, Siloam, Bethzatha, Kidron, Gabbatha ("the Pavement") and Golgotha.

18. There are many fewer miracles reported by John, but most are followed (in contrast to the Synoptics) by a lengthy discourse by Jesus explaining the significance and meaning of the miracle.

Looking at this list of details, it becomes very difficult, in my opinion, to support the view of those commentators who claim that John's gospel was very late in composition, and unreliable as actual history. How does one square that theory with these many highly specific and seemingly *personal* details — details found only in the Fourth Gospel?

The Traditional View

As I have already outlined, the commonly accepted "traditional" assumption of many commentators since the 4th and 5th century (what Lewis would call "the climate of opinion") has been that the Fourth Gospel was written by "John the Apostle," meaning bar Zebedee.

A cursory look at various contemporary commentaries and study Bibles bears this out. One example (of many) is found in the *New American Standard Study Bible (1999 Edition)*.[3] Its Introduction to the Gospel of John says that the author of the gospel was "the apostle John, the disciple 'whom Jesus loved'" (p. 1513). The reference to "The apostle John" with no further specification surely means John bar Zebedee, brother of James. The writer of this Introduction then goes on to say that early writers such as Irenaeus and Tertullian "say that John wrote this Gospel." However, what this writer *fails* to say — and what we will see in much greater detail further on — is that *neither* of those ancient authorities identifies the "John" they are talking about as John bar Zebedee. Tertullian, for example, *does* refer to the author of the Fourth Gospel as an "apostle," but of course many disciples of the Jesus besides the Twelve were known as "apostles" in the earliest years of the Church: Paul, Barnabas, Timothy, Silvanus, and "The Seventy" of Eastern tradition being prime examples.

Interestingly, the writer of this *NASB* introduction does admit that John the Apostle is never mentioned by name in the Fourth Gospel; but he then makes a poorly-grounded leap: he leaps to the illogical but comforting conclusion that this omission of any mention of John the Apostle "would be natural if he wrote it, but hard to explain otherwise" (p. 1513). On any amount of reflection, the supposed logic of this claim simply vaporizes into thin air. There is *no* reason, natural or otherwise, to assume that because John bar Zebedee is not named in this gospel that he must therefore be its author. Suggesting the absence of his name as an argument for authorship is a classic argument from silence. Should we test this conclusion, the same faulty logic might compel us to also conclude that the other six members of the Twelve not named in John may also have written it; and, further, that every other known disciple of Jesus not named in the gospel might be its author.

Indeed, it is not clear in what way would it be "natural" for the author of a gospel to exclude himself from all mention. If we look at the Gospel of Matthew, for example, this argument crumples to its knees. For whether Matthew was the original writer of that gospel, or merely the authority behind it, he is mentioned by name several times, and clearly named among the Twelve.

It seems to me a great deal more likely — and natural — to conclude that John bar Zebedee is not named in the Fourth Gospel simply because — as an examination of the actual text clearly shows — he plays no significant role in the particular events recorded in this gospel, nor does his brother James.

Who Then Was *This* John?

Once we do that — look at the actual text of this gospel — and once we carefully examine the earliest historical references to its author, as I will in subsequent chapters, it is not at all clear how the commonly held tradition about John bar Zebedee being its author came to be so common.

In recent decades, some students of this gospel and the other Johannine books (the three letters, and Revelation) have come to the conclusion that it is, in fact, highly *unlikely* that John bar Zebedee was its author. One of the most respected scholars on the Gospel of John, and known to many American readers for his exhaustive research and commentaries on the Fourth Gospel and the three Johannine letters, was the late Roman Catholic scholar Raymond E. Brown. After analyzing the many theories and proposals about authorship alongside the text itself, Brown concluded that the author of the Fourth Gospel was indeed an eyewitness authority and a close disciple of Jesus from the beginning of his ministry, but was not one of the Twelve, and thus not John bar Zebedee.[4]

Having examined and considered a good many theories, I have come to agree with Brown. Briefly, these are my objections to the assumption that John bar Zebedee was the author of the Fourth Gospel:

1. Scholars have recognized that the Greek vocabulary and style found in the Fourth Gospel (as well as the three letters that bear the name John) are from an author who was not only well-schooled in the traditions of Judaism but was proficient in Greek, the common literary language of the Roman Empire in the first century. It is unlikely that John bar Zebedee, a Galilean fisherman, would have possessed the command of Greek style and vocabulary displayed in this gospel, and the three letters. Certainly, as a business man in "Galilee of the Gentiles," John bar Zebedee would have known and used the common *koine* Greek (the "street Greek" of his time) in his trade. But the Fourth Gospel shows a fine command not only of oral Greek but of Greek literary style. Of course, as some have suggested, and I will readily admit, John bar Zebedee could be the "author" (the source) of the gospel record but not the actual writer, while the actual writer could have been more proficient in Greek than he. So, this objection, by itself, cannot be decisive.

2. Much more persuasive is the fact that the author of John reports almost nothing about Jesus' ministry in Galilee, which seems not only odd but nearly incredible if the author was the Galilean fisherman who was, as we know from the Synoptics, a main witness and very central to the ministry of Jesus in that region.

3. The author of John, as I've noted, possessed very detailed knowledge about events and places in and around Jerusalem, including specific Hebrew place names; and he knew of several visits of Jesus to Jerusalem — including major teachings by Jesus — that are never mentioned in the Synoptics.

4. The Synoptics rely heavily on parable-style teaching to convey Jesus' message, which John bar Zebedee, as one of the disciples first called in Galilee, no doubt heard with his own ears. Those parables are all missing from John. Not some, but *all*. In fact, John's Gospel rarely records short

"parable" teaching and includes instead lengthy discourses by Jesus (most notably, the five-chapter discourse at the Last Supper, Chs.13-17).

5. As previously noted, "the sons of Zebedee" are mentioned only once in John, in the 21st chapter which, when considered in light of the "concluding" statements in 20:30-31, may well be an addendum to John's original gospel; and, as also mentioned, even in chapter 21, neither John nor his brother James is identified by first name, as they so prevalently are in the Synoptics. Further, although their presence is mentioned, the brothers Zebedee have no significant role in the events, or conversations, recorded in this final chapter.

6. While "the Twelve" *as a group* are mentioned four times in John (6:67, 6;70, 6:71, 20:24), seven of the twelve apostles — including the brothers Zebedee — are never named in this group, and those seven have no significant part in the events recorded in John, even at the Last Supper — unless one argues from silence, as some have, that John bar Zebedee is "the beloved disciple" who has a central role at the supper.

Glaring Omissions

Far more problematic for the "traditional" theory, and perhaps the most telling argument against John bar Zebedee being the author, is the fact that several significant events recorded in the Synoptics in which bar Zebedee was centrally involved do not appear in the Gospel of John at all.

The most remarkable and glaring of these omissions, if John bar Zebedee was its author, is the Transfiguration of Jesus.

In all three Synoptic accounts, John bar Zebedee is one of only three eye-witnesses to this absolutely central, and no doubt stunning, event. It is one of the most significant and memorable events in the Synoptic record, found in all three at a pivotal moment in the ministry of Jesus, just before his final journey to Jerusalem. It can be argued that this event in the Synoptics is on par with the raising of Lazarus from the dead in John (which, by the way, is *not* found in the Synoptics). Yet the Gospel of John makes no mention — not even an indirect mention — of the Transfiguration event. If John bar Zebedee was its author, why would that be?

Let us freeze the image, though, and go along for just a moment with the traditional view that John bar Zebedee authored the Fourth Gospel, but chose to hide himself and be anonymous. Even if that were the case (which I don't believe), *surely* he would have included the Transfiguration in his record. It would not only have made an indelible impression on those three disciples, but it foreshadowed the Resurrection which would become the core revelation of the entire Gospel message. The Transfiguration was the practical, experiential confirmation of Peter's profession of faith just six days earlier, that Jesus was indeed the awaited Messiah, "the son of the living God."

If John bar Zebedee had written this gospel, how do we explain such a major omission? Yes, it's true Jesus ordered them to keep it secret at the time (Matthew 17:9; Mark 9:9), but they certainly trumpeted the event loudly after the Resurrection — as he also instructed them to do — for it is recorded in fine detail in all three Synoptic gospels. If John bar Zebedee authored the Fourth Gospel, how can we credibly account for the absence of this truly "mountain top" event? That it could have been an *intentional* omission by bar Zebedee strains even the most fertile imagination.

When we unfreeze our frame, and return to the gospel text, we discover that the Transfiguration is just one of several omissions of important events described in the Synoptics which involved John bar Zebedee as a key participant that are *all* absent from the Fourth Gospel:

1. The healing of Jairus' daughter, where Peter, James, and John accompany Jesus into the house (Mark 3:37ff; Luke 8:51ff).

2. The dispute over who is the greatest (Mark 10:35ff; Matthew 20:20ff).

3. Peter, James, John, and Andrew questioning Jesus privately about the destruction of the Temple (Mark 13:3).

4. James and John asking Jesus if he wants them to call down fire on a Samaritan village (Luke 9:54).

5. The early events in the garden of Gethsemane (Matthew 26:37; Mark 14:33) where only Peter, James and John accompany Jesus to a private place to pray.

Now, it could be argued that the incident about "who is the greatest" might have joyously been omitted as an embarrassment to John bar Zebedee and his brother James. But that argument falters when we recall again that Jesus nicknamed these two *"Boanerges,"* the sons of thunder.

If, as tradition speculates, John bar Zebedee authored the Fourth Gospel, why are *all* these events missing? Not some, but all. Even if we were inclined to downplay these lesser events, how do we reasonably explain the missing Transfiguration account? Would one of only three witnesses to that event, in his own gospel (if it were his), omit such a theologically significant event? John's Gospel shines as a work of theology. The Transfiguration was a clear confirmation and revelation of Jesus' divinity as the Word Incarnate, the image with which John opened his gospel. Why omit it?

It is my view that this omission, added to many others, tells strongly against John bar Zebedee having been the author of this gospel.

Further Examples

If we compare John more closely with the Synoptics, where bar Zebedee is so central, we find even more details that are missing in John. In particular, we notice that the actual baptism of Jesus is missing in John. The baptism is certainly referenced when John the Baptist speaks of having seen the Holy Spirit descend like a dove and rest on Jesus (just as the event is described in the

Synoptic accounts), but the actual *event* of Jesus' baptism is not described by John.

Similarly, and perhaps more significantly, John makes no mention of Jesus giving his disciples the sacred bread and cup as his Body and Blood at the Last Supper. Of course, John had already recorded a lengthy discourse by Jesus about the importance of receiving his Body and Blood (6:51-59), which *presumes* the actions of the last supper to make sense. And John does not entirely *omit* the Last Supper event. But in John's account, the bread and cup, along with the words of consecration and promise that accompany them, are not mentioned. Notably, John adds something different here, of very different significance — something never mentioned in the Synoptics: his account of Jesus' indescribable humility in washing his disciples' feet.

What Can We Conclude?

The questions pile up quickly, and there must be a plausible answer to each. Take just one. Why would the author of John's Gospel have failed to report something as significant as the Transfiguration? The simplest answer may be the correct one: he didn't report it because he wasn't there.

In fact, as I will explore in the next chapter, it may well be that the Fourth Gospel is so very different from the Synoptics for one very simple reason: as an actual "eyewitness" to the ministry of Jesus, the author reported *only those events* at which he was present, or at least had some immediate knowledge. If that was so, this may lead us to another fairly simple reason for why this gospel is so different: where the author lived.

Endnotes

1. See, for example, Kieffer's summary in The Oxford Bible Commentary, pp. 960-61.
2. I agree with the view of some commentators that the Fourth Gospel has undergone at least some editing, and possibly development, since its

first composition. As mentioned, for example, all or a portion of chapter 21 was almost certainly a later addition, possibly added after the death of the Beloved Disciple, to explain why that disciple had died (unexpectedly) before Jesus' return. I do not, however, agree with elaborate theories that postulate complex "pre-gospel" documents upon which someone other than the Beloved Disciple actually based the *original* gospel. Nor do I agree, as some have proposed, that the original gospel was written by a group of disciples. As I will show in due course, I think it more probable that the original body of this gospel was composed by one man, the Beloved Disciple, and later editors simply clarified specific verses. An example would be John 19:35, where, after the gospel was written, an editor (or early commentator?) made a note to reinforce the authenticity and reliability of the particular incident, and the fact that it was based on actual eyewitness observation.

3. *New American Standard Study Bible* (NASB), Zondervan Press (1999 Edition). Overall, this is an excellent study guide in many respects.

4. In the final edition of his excellent *An Introduction to the Gospel of John* (see Bibliography), published posthumously, Brown draws a number of conclusions, including his view that the "Beloved Disciple" was indeed the author/source behind the Gospel of John. In the early stage of the developing Gospel tradition found in John, according to Brown, the Beloved Disciple was the source of the information and teaching, though not necessarily the one who put pen to paper. Brown carefully grounds his conjectures in the text of the Gospel itself: he suggests that the beloved disciple was formerly a disciple of John the Baptist (based on John 1:35-37) and so was a follower of Jesus from the start of Jesus' ministry, but was *not* one of the Twelve (p. 74). Brown suggests it was probably others who created and used the title "the disciple whom Jesus loved" rather than John himself since it might seem too "laudatory" for the author to use the title of himself (pp. 194-95). Brown's overall conclusion, however, is that the Beloved Disciple was the eyewitness behind the basic testimony and record of the Fourth Gospel, even though others may have been involved either in the original composition of the book, or in subsequent redactions (pp. 195-96). I will go further to suggest that the Beloved Disciple himself may have actually composed all, or most, of the original draft of the gospel.

Two

AS I HAVE SAID, I long ago became intrigued with authorship of the Fourth Gospel. Why explore it at all? For two central reasons. First, readers such as myself are naturally curious to know — if we can — who the author was. As soon as one ventures into reading this gospel, it becomes obvious that it is strikingly different from the other three.

Second, as I have discovered in teaching this gospel in a parish setting, it does not take long for the average reader to begin to doubt the traditional view that John bar Zebedee wrote it. With its fine command of ideas, language, and beautiful literary style, it seems difficult to see how this book could have been produced by a man who spent most of his early life as a fisherman in Galilee. Further, many readers quickly notice what I detailed in the previous chapter: very few events reported in John have anything to do with Galilee, which was John bar Zebedee's home. While Galilee is the central location of most the events reported in the Synoptics, in John, Galilee appears mainly as a side-trip destination.

Unfortunately, these oddities sometimes lead readers not only to doubt John bar Zebedee wrote it, but to begin to doubt or mistrust its contents, value, and authority. Their reaction is: *if I have been told John bar Zebedee, an apostle, wrote this gospel, but now it seems unlikely he actually did, how can I trust what it says?*

For that reason, among many, I felt compelled to pursue this study.

In doing so, one of the first questions I faced was, how did the "traditional" view gain such wide ascendency? Why was the

Fourth Gospel ever attributed to John bar Zebedee in the first place? From years of study, I can say the most honest answer is, "We really don't know." Several factors, though, no doubt played a role.

When we look at early Christian records, it appears the gospel "According to John" was well-known very early in the life of the church, no later than the end of the first century, and copies of it circulated to other churches by the early 2nd century. There also existed three letters, two of which bear a striking resemblance to this gospel in language, imagery and theology. These letters, too, were preserved under the name "John." Because they were preserved from such an early date, it is quite possible that the author may have been personally known to some members of those churches. (See the discussion later regarding Papias.) The Fourth Gospel, internally, seems to rest on an *eyewitness* testimony about the life, ministry, and passion of Jesus. It thus carried "apostolic" authority in at least some of the churches as a product of the apostolic generation.

It may well be, however, that this fourth gospel record was questioned by other churches, in part because its contents were so strikingly different from the other three known gospels that were also in circulation by the end of the 1st century, those we now call "the Synoptic gospels."

As time passed, the Church as a whole struggled to compile and preserve as many authentic apostolic writings as it could, as these writings gradually came to be recognized as the Holy Scriptures of the New Covenant (New Testament). For a book to be accepted as both reliable and authoritative, two conditions had generally to be met. First, antiquity, and second, "apostolic" authority. Since one of the known "apostles" of Jesus was John bar Zebedee, some second and third generation Christians may have simply assumed that he was the likely author of "John," even though the text of the gospel itself (they would have seen this as easily as we do) didn't lend much support to that view.

Another factor that came into play was the fact that the apostolic authority of Christian scriptures needed to be established to combat early heresies that were already spawning in parts of the Church. We know, for example, that the Fourth Gospel became a favorite, in the late second into the third centuries, of heretical groups knowns as Gnostics, who sought to transform Christianity away from is Jewish roots and remold it into a "more spiritual" religion more in line with popular Greek philosophers. The language in John, in particular his use of the term "logos" ("the Word") in his prologue (chapter 1), lent itself to this misuse.

So, the attribution of the gospel to John bar Zebedee may have come about in part to combat the Gnostics' penchant for adopting this gospel as their own. By insisting it was written by one of Jesus' first apostles, the church could hold ground in rejecting new "more spiritual" interpretations of the book from Hellenized Jews and Hellenistic gentiles. If it could be claimed this gospel was from "one of the Twelve," this would identify it an unassailable source of authentic, first-generation Christian faith.

The problem for the later church, however, was that beyond the close of the first century, no clear record had been preserved as to who this particular "John" was. Yes, later Christians in the 3rd and 4th centuries would fall back on bar Zebedee as the "safe," presumed source, although, as I will show, writers such as Irenaeus did *not* make a clear identification of the author with John bar Zebedee. Further complicating matters, the great disparities in both style and content between the Fourth Gospel and the Book of Revelation were as obvious to readers then as now; but one of the earliest Christian apologists, Justin Martyr (born around the year 100 AD) recorded that John bar Zebedee had indeed written Revelation.

So, while the *safe* route followed by the Church was to cling to the view that John bar Zebedee was the Fourth Evangelist — a view a good many people cling to today — it was never by any means a *certain* route. Still, as time passed, the "fallback" assumption that bar Zebedee, a member of the apostolic inner-circle, was the author of the Fourth Gospel apparently gained strength. Later writers and commentators either failed to take into account the fact that this apostle is not named in the main body of the Fourth Gospel, or they dismissed the fact as unimportant. They also seemed little concerned with the fact that another book also attributed to bar Zebedee, Revelation, seemed so entirely unlike the Fourth Gospel, and three letters. Indeed, Revelation contains seven letters of its own, but these are even more unlike 1, 2, and 3 John than Revelation as a whole is unlike the Fourth Gospel.

Over time, then, the seemingly simple assumption that John bar Zebedee wrote all five Johannine books gained broader acceptance. As we will see in later chapters, though, this assumption was by no means unanimous, and even in the earliest centuries some writers challenged the belief that Revelation and the Fourth Gospel could have come from the same author.

Complications and Implications

I recognize that some readers and students of this Gospel may believe that if we challenge the traditional view, it would call into question the "apostolic" authority of this gospel. As I will endeavor to show, however, the "apostolic authority" of the Fourth Gospel — or any of the other New Testament books — does not rest on its having been written by one of "the Twelve," particularly if we can demonstrate (as I will try to show) that the author *was* indeed an eyewitness authority. In other words, if we conclude that John bar Zebedee did not write this gospel, it in no way impugns the gospel's authority or impedes us from accepting its reliability. If we closely examine and credit the actual text of the book, there seems to me to be no serious question that this gospel was based on the authority of a close friend of Jesus who witnessed most, if not all, of the events this gospel records.

We are, however, still faced with the question of uniqueness: why so much in John is missing from the Synoptic record, and vice-versa. Those familiar with the history of commentary on the New Testament know that various creative suggestions have been made to explain why this is the case. It is an intriguing problem: why would those familiar with Jesus' ministry (directly, or indirectly) set down such very different accounts of his ministry, passion, death, and resurrection, or, in the reverse, leave so much out? This is a complex issue because the same question can be asked about the contents of the three Synoptics themselves when compared with one another.

Later on, I hope to suggest a broad framework of how I think the four gospels may have developed essentially alongside each other; but my intent is not to review or analyze the many theories that have already been suggested. My main focus, instead, will be on the question of the reliability of the Fourth Gospel in relation to the other three. On the whole, over centuries, the underlying facts recorded in the Synoptic gospels have not been challenged, at least among Christians. Some scholars have concluded that the Synoptics are more accurate as history. This, sadly, seems to grow in part out of the fact that they carry so many similarities. That is a dangerous approach, since it is clear that the similarities probably grow out of direct literary dependance rather than out of independent sourcing.

By contrast, other scholars, particularly since the 18th and 19th centuries, have taken a hacksaw to the "factual" basis of John — in large part because it does vary so much from the Synoptics. Some have reached the conclusion that John is essentially the work-product of a committee who assembled fragments of someone else's speculative work and theological ramblings. With this fact in mind, as I move through questions of the authorship of John, I have kept an eye on this question of reliability to see if such challenges to the historicity of John are warranted, or over-blown.

The tendency among some readers to credit the authenticity of the Synoptics over that of John may appeal purely on the "three against one" premise, the attitude that the numbers alone mean something, and that because three writers set out certain (very similar) events, those must be the more reliable or accurate. But as just mentioned, similarity cannot go far in proving reliability. Many scholars agree that all three Synoptic gospels are based on perhaps one or two primary (common) sources. That cuts deeply into the heart of this assumption that similarities in the Synoptics should be weighted as making them reliable.

Having examined some of the theories of the relationship of the Synoptics to John, I would pose what seems to me a rather obvious but rarely asked question: is it not possible that *both* traditions, the Synoptics and John, are equally old and therefore equally reliable, but simply come from very different sources? It seems to me the most solid footing from which to find a solution to this long-standing debate — and the one requiring the fewest mental gymnastics — is this simple fact: real eyewitnesses, if they possess basic integrity, will tend to report mainly what they themselves have observed, or can account for by direct information.

If that is the case, to allow for the possibility that the Gospel of John is just as old and reliable as the Synoptics we need only one reasonable explanation of why John's observations might have been so different; and when we look at the Fourth Gospel without preconceptions, the answer to this dilemma nearly leaps off the page.

A Possible Solution

If we look carefully and objectively at the actual data in the Gospel of John, we make a very intriguing discovery. What sets John so clearly apart from the Synoptics is not so much events, sequence, or theology, but *geography*. Whereas the whole focus in the Synoptics prior to the Passion is the ministry in Galilee, John could be called "The Jerusalem Gospel," or at least "The Judean Gospel," because nearly all of the key events it narrates, in very great detail, are centered in or near Jerusalem.[1] We can readily see from the differences between John and the Synoptics outlined in the last chapter that whoever wrote the Fourth Gospel possessed intimate, detailed knowledge of places and people in and around Jerusalem that is not demonstrated in the Synoptic accounts. As I have already highlighted, this would be peculiar indeed if a Galilean fisherman (bar Zebedee) was the author.

So, instead of looking for an author from among the disciples of Galilee, I suggest we should begin our search by looking for a well-educated resident of Judea or Jerusalem. This approach, as the evidence will quickly show, will go a long way toward solving the authorship puzzle.

The Beloved Disciple

Many readers and scholars have recognized that the cryptic figure in John called "the beloved disciple" (more literally, "the disciple whom Jesus loved") is very likely a reference to the author, who is in fact never named by his proper name. Who was this unnamed, enigmatic figure mentioned only in this gospel, who Raymond Brown and others suggest was likely its author (13:23, 19:26-27, 20:2-8, 21:7)?[2]

The appellation itself makes it evident that he was a close friend of Jesus who would therefore have been an eyewitness to at least part of Jesus' public ministry. He could, therefore, be a trustworthy source for the unique accounts found in the Fourth Gospel. If so, we begin from the acknowledgement that the account and teaching found in this gospel may certainly be just as accurate and trustworthy as any in the Synoptics, not only as statements of an eyewitness, but as those of a close, personal friend of the Lord.

A number of examples can be given. Statements such as "He who saw it has borne witness — his testimony is true, and he knows that he tells the truth — that you also may believe" (19:35) are clearly meant to assure us that the authority behind this gospel did in fact witness the events it records.

The same sentiment is expressed again in the statement, "Now Jesus did many other signs in the presence of the disciples, which are not written in this book; but these are written that you may believe that Jesus is the Christ, the Son of God, and that believing you may have life in his name" (20:30-31). This Gospel thus claims for itself apostolic authority: its "author" was a close friend of Jesus and one of the first generation of disciples, although not one of "the Twelve." Its readers' faith in Jesus is to be grounded in the fact that the author knows firsthand what he has reported, and that he himself was known to be trustworthy.

Having studied Raymond Brown's analysis of this question, I agree that the Beloved Disciple was the author (the "authority") behind the Fourth Gospel. If we accept him as author, we find in him a witness to *the central event* of the entire Gospel and the Christian Faith, alongside St. Peter: the Resurrection of Jesus. For it was this disciple who ran ahead of Peter to the tomb after they first heard the news of the Resurrection from Mary Magdalene. He beat Peter to the tomb but did not go in. After Peter entered the tomb, this disciple also went in, "and he saw and believed" (20:2-8). In that light, we ask: is his record reliable?

This same disciple was near the cross with Jesus' mother Mary (John 19:26-27) when Jesus commended her to his care (19:26-27). The Synoptics place none of the Twelve anywhere near the cross, and make rather painfully clear they had *all* fled into hiding (Matthew 26:56; Mark 14:50). Even Peter had fled the scene of Jesus' interrogation early that morning at cock crow (Matthew 26:75). That being true, it seems unlikely in the extreme that John bar Zebedee would have been at the site of the crucifixion just hours later. By contrast, if the Beloved Disciple was not one of the Twelve but a less-publicly-known disciple, it explains how he may have remained close by and actually stood at the foot of the cross with Mary.

Showing us the Beloved Disciple at the foot of the Cross, along with so many other unique details in John, was, I believe, meant to assure future readers that the information in the Fourth Gospel is true, historical, and reliable. We should pay close attention to this claim and not, as some have, simply dismiss it as an imaginary scene concocted by a later group of Christians writing about this man whom they clearly revered.

Indeed, for our study, this repeated insistence on the reliability of its main witness *in itself* weighs heavily against the argument that John bar Zebedee was the author, for surely the authority of John bar Zebedee's would have been beyond challenge among the early Christians. What we find here is something quite different: the Fourth Gospel's insistence that this particular evangelist is trustworthy and knows what he is talking about reinforces the view that he was not one of the Twelve. It would seem this author, or one who subsequently published or copied his gospel, is trying to demonstrate a level of authority that John bar Zebedee would have possessed without question.

If, however, the Beloved Disciple was not one of the Twelve, we come up against a rather large obstacle — for some — in letting go of the traditional view that bar Zebedee was the Fourth Evangelist: the question of which disciples, according to a rather widely-held assumption, were present at the Last Supper. So, we must tackle that question next.

What About The Last Supper?

Some readers may already be protesting that "the disciple whom Jesus loved" *must* have been one of the Twelve because he sat right next to Jesus at the Last Supper (John 13:23; cf. 21:20), and "everyone knows" that only the Twelve Apostles were present that night. Isn't that right?

Is it? Or is this one more example of the common wisdom, the "climate of opinion" that has come to be "true" by mere repetition?

Here, I must take an important side-track that is crucial to resolving the identity of the Fourth Evangelist: who was actually present at the Last Supper? If, as many have traditionally assumed, only the Twelve were there with Jesus, then clearly the "disciple whom Jesus loved" must have been one of those Twelve. But if our author John the Beloved Disciple was not John bar Zebedee, then we are quickly forced to the realization that others besides the Twelve *must* have been present. Can that be?

Not only *can* it be, it is in fact very likely. For despite da Vinci's famous depiction of the Last Supper — itself based on a long-held but unproven assumption that only the Twelve Apostles were present at this meal — the New Testament never says this. When we carefully examine the actual texts, the four gospels themselves do not support the view that only the Twelve were present.

First, and regardless of the debate over precisely which day of, or before, the actual Passover the Last Supper occurred, we recognize that this was Jesus' final Passover meal with his disciples. (Some commentators argue that it may not have fallen on the actual Passover day that week). This being a Passover meal, we must recall that ever since the Mosaic institution of the Passover, this sacred meal was typically celebrated by gathered families — a setting that always included the women and children who were part of the family (Exodus 12:3-4, 12:21). It continues to be celebrated as an extended-family meal in many Jewish homes today.

If the Passover supper remained similar in Jesus' day, the women and children of his disciples' families would not only have been permitted but would have been *expected* at this meal. Here, in particular, the younger generation learned the faith as they re-enacted the ancient traditions of God's salvation. Jesus himself, recall, had gone to Jerusalem for Passover when he was a boy (Luke 2:40-41) with his *extended* family, which is why he was thought to have been wandering among the family crowd once they started home.

If we look carefully, and without blinders, that is what we find implied in the gospels. When Jesus arrived at Jerusalem that last week, many disciples besides the Twelve had accompanied him from Galilee, including a number of women (Matthew 27:55-61), and his own mother. Indeed, some of these women were at the cross with Mary, and some were the first witnesses of the Resurrection (Matthew 28:1-5).

Knowing the Passover supper was a meal with one's "extended family," are we to believe that after so many disciples trekked all the way from Galilee, Jesus excluded most of them from the most important meal of the year, and — in this case —

the most important Passover of their lives? In particular, can we wrench our imaginations so far as to believe that after having celebrated 30 some Passovers with his beloved mother, and after she had once again traveled the long road to Jerusalem for this feast, that Jesus would exclude *her* from his most important Passover ever?

To my mind, this defies not only imagination, but reason. It would have been unbelievably strange, not to mention uncharitable, after their long journey together, for Jesus to send many of his closest friends — and his own mother — off to some other place in a city not their home to celebrate Passover without him.

It is much more reasonable and plausible to believe that many of his closest disciples, including his mother and those other women who had ministered to him for months, would have joined Jesus and the Twelve in the upper room that night. This would explain, by the way, the easily missed detail that the place Jesus sought for his last Passover was "a *large* upper room" (Mark 14:15; Luke 22:12).

Were there children and young people in the room, too? This, too, is likely. Parents routinely took their children along for Passover in Jerusalem, as Jesus' own parents did (Luke 2:41-42 again). Would this journey have been any different? Perhaps, for we know there was tension around this trip because Jesus expected trouble from the authorities in Jerusalem. If children of the disciples did accompany them on this journey, would they have been left sitting on the porch?

Since the Passover meal was always a family gathering, where did we get the idea that only the Twelve Apostles were allowed at this crucial Passover, the institution of the Lord's Supper? I cannot answer that with any certainty, but the traditional idea presupposed by da Vinci that only the Twelve were there may have arisen because of two simple mistakes.

First, when reading the gospels we easily forget that while the words "the disciples" sometimes refer to "the Twelve," but equally often they do not. "The Twelve" were selected out of a much larger group of disciples who followed Jesus throughout his ministry, which included a number of women (Luke 6:13, 8:1-3). In addition to the first recorded missionary journey of the Twelve (Luke 9:1), Jesus sent out 35 or 36 other pairs of disciples to preach and heal (Luke 10:1). Some of those other disciples, besides the Twelve, probably accompanied Jesus on his final journey to Jerusalem, because Luke mentions that along the way Jesus "took the Twelve aside" from the others to speak of his coming Passion (Luke 18:31). Also, the Fourth Gospel shows us that Jesus already had many disciples in Judea from his early ministry there (John 4:1-3).

The common assumption that only the Twelve were at the Last Supper is fueled by a second easy mistake. All three Synoptic gospels say that when Jesus sat down that night he "reclined" with the Twelve (Matthew 26:20; Mark 14:17; and Luke 22:14, where they are called the "apostles" rather than "the Twelve"). We should not, however, infer more from that statement than what it says; and then we should ask why the statement is there at all. The Greek in Matthew literally says "he reclined with the Twelve." A literal rendering of Mark runs "and evening coming, he comes with the Twelve, reclined with them and eating." And a literal rendering of Luke reads, "he reclined, and the apostles with him." None of these three writers say, or even imply, that others were *not* present. In fact, we might ask, *why* are we told at all that he reclined "with the Twelve" unless others were present and a description was being given about where, and with whom, Jesus sat?

What else do the gospels tell us about who was present? Contrary to da Vinci and other popular images, several passages actually imply that other disciples *were* present at the Last Supper. We know, for example, that before entering Jerusalem, Jesus sent some of the disciples ahead to prepare for the supper. Luke reports that the two Jesus sent were "Peter and John" (Luke 22:8). But Matthew and Mark give a different account. Matthew says:

> Now on the first day of Unleavened Bread the disciples came to Jesus, saying, "Where will you have us prepare for you to eat the Passover?" He said, "Go into the city to a certain one, and say to him, 'The Teacher says, My time is at hand; I will keep the Passover at your house with my disciples.'" And the disciples did as Jesus had directed them, and they prepared the Passover. When it was evening, he sat at table with the twelve disciples (Matthew 26:17-20).

How many went to prepare, and when exactly "the Twelve" arrived, are not certain in Matthew's account. It is clearer, however, in Mark:

> And on the first day of Unleavened Bread, when they sacrificed the Passover lamb, his disciples said to him, "Where will you have us go and prepare for you to eat the Passover?" And he sent two of his disciples, and said to them, "Go into the city, and a man carrying a jar of water will meet you; follow him, and wherever he enters, say to the householder, 'The Teacher says, Where is my guest room, where I am to eat the Passover with my disciples?' And he will show you a large upper room furnished and ready; there prepare for us." And the disciples set out and went to the city, and found it as he had told them; and they prepared the Passover. And when it was evening he came with the twelve (Mark 14:12-17).

Mark's account, in other words, suggests that the two unnamed disciples who went ahead to prepare were not of "the Twelve," for the Twelve only arrived that evening with Jesus. If so, would Jesus have sent those two ahead to prepare, and then excluded them from the Passover meal?

Some may be tempted to try to harmonize Matthew's and Mark's accounts by speculating that Mark's "Twelve" who arrived with Jesus were only "the rest" of the Twelve. It is an easy temptation, and can't be absolutely ruled out, but it's not what the text says. Moreover, when we look further at St. Luke's account, we find more compelling evidence that suggests others were present:

> And when it was evening he came with the twelve. And as they were at table [literally, "reclining"] eating, Jesus said, "Truly, I say to you, one of you will betray me, one who is eating with me." They began to be sorrowful, and to say to him one after another, "Is it I?" He said to them, "*It is one of the twelve*, one who is dipping bread into the dish with me (Luke 14:17-20).

On reflection, this point seems obvious: why would Jesus have any reason to say "It is one of the twelve" if no one else was present? This sounds as though he is addressing others besides the Twelve. Also, each table in the room would have its own "dipping dish," so by adding it was "one who is dipping bread into the dish with me," he excluded any disciple at another table.

A further detail in Luke strongly suggests that others besides the Twelve were present. When Jesus (according to Luke) sent Peter and John ahead to prepare, they are to say "The Teacher says to you, Where is the guest room, where I am to eat the Passover with my *disciples*?" (22:11). They will be shown "a large upper room." Then, when Jesus arrives, Luke says, "And when the hour came, he sat at table, and the *apostles* with him" (Luke 22:14). It is easily missed: Jesus wants a "large" room for a meal with his "disciples," but we are then specifically told he sits with his "apostles," those who will dip bread into the same dish as he. Is the distinction unnecessary, or an accident? Or, is it an intended clarification about who was present that evening?

We must then consider the women who traveled many miles for many days to come to Jerusalem with Jesus for this Passover, and who would witness the crucifixion the following day. They included Mary his mother (John 19:25), Mary Magdalene, Mary the mother of James the younger and of Joses, and Salome (Mark 15:40-41), and the mother of James and John the sons of Zebedee (Matthew 27:56). (Some commentators identify Salome in Mark as "the mother of the sons of Zebedee" in Matthew.) After this arduous journey to *the* major feast of Judaism, would Jesus have excluded all these women from his final Passover — even his own mother?

We find a further significant detail in Luke which tells us that other disciples were, in fact, together in a group with the remaining eleven apostles, at the time of the resurrection:

> The women who had come with him from Galilee followed, and saw the tomb, and how his body was laid; then they returned, and prepared spices and ointments. On the sabbath they rested according to the commandment. But on the first day of the week, at early dawn, they went to the tomb, taking the spices which they had prepared. And they found the stone rolled away from the tomb, but when they went in they did not find the body . . . and returning from the tomb they told all this to the eleven and to *all the rest* (Luke 23:55-24:9).

"All the rest" doubtless refers to some of those who had been with Jesus and his apostles since their arrival in Jerusalem, and thus include some who would have been present at the Last Supper.

Finally, Luke's account of the afternoon of Easter day gives us another key detail that helps bring the true picture of the Last Supper into focus. A disciple named Cleopas (Clopas?) and another disciple encounter the resurrected Jesus as they walk to the nearby village of Emmaus. As they walk the road with him, Cleopas says:

> "Moreover, some women of our company amazed us. They were at the tomb early in the morning and did not find his body; and they came back saying that they had even seen a vision of angels, who said that he was alive" (Luke 24:22-23).

In other words, Cleopas was one of "all the rest" who heard the first report of the resurrection from the women that morning. This suggests he was part of the continuing group of disciples, including the women, who were still huddled together with the

Eleven since the crucifixion. But then comes an even more revealing point. The two disciples urge Jesus to stay over at Emmaus, and they sit down to supper:

> When he was at table with them, he took the bread and blessed, and broke it, and gave it to them. And their eyes were opened and they recognized him; and he vanished out of their sight (Luke 24:30-31).

". . . he took the bread and blessed, and broke it, and gave it to them. And their eyes were opened." Why is this significant? Because it provides the most convincing evidence yet that others besides the Twelve were present at the Last Supper. It was not Jesus' lengthy teaching or exposition of the scriptures on the road that afternoon that caused them to recognize Jesus: it was that unique action — taking, blessing, breaking, and giving them the bread, just as he had on Thursday evening — that finally made them recognize him. Those unique Eucharistic actions would "open their eyes" only if they had been at the Last Supper three nights before (Luke 22:19). Luke reports both events with nearly identical words; and while it is true that one of the pair at Emmaus is unnamed, it is certain neither were members of the remaining eleven apostles because Luke specifically tells us:

> And they rose that same hour and returned to Jerusalem; and they found *the eleven* gathered together *and those who were with them*, who said, "The Lord has risen indeed, and has appeared to Simon!" Then they told what had happened on the road, and how he was known to them in the breaking of the bread (Luke 24:33-35)

In other words, what we have in Luke is a consistent reference to a larger group of disciples, in addition to the Twelve, who arrived in Jerusalem with Jesus for Passover and who remained together for some time after the resurrection (confirmed further by Acts 1:15). If we are willing to let go of the unnecessary, and unproductive, assumption that *only* the Twelve apostles joined Jesus at the Last Supper, there is little reason to doubt that others besides the Twelve were indeed present at the meal.[3]

The Last Supper In The Fourth Gospel

We know from John's account that the Beloved Disciple was present at the Last Supper and, indeed, plays a "central" role sitting next to Jesus himself. If, as I have suggested, disciples other than the Twelve were at the meal, it opens our investigation to a much broader field of who the Beloved Disciple may have been.

The Fourth Gospel's account of the Last Supper presents a special case. As with the rest of this gospel, its account is so different from the Synoptic gospels that it's hard at times to remember we are reading about the same event. John, for example (as already noted), is the only gospel to include an account of Jesus washing the feet of his disciples, and John's is the only gospel that omits any mention of Jesus giving the bread and sacred cup to his disciples as his "body and blood" during the supper.

The significant differences, however, don't end here. Since John never gives a complete list of the Twelve anywhere in his gospel, and only identifies them as "disciples," never as "apostles," we cannot be at all certain who he includes as present at the Last Supper.[4] He says that "disciples" were there (13:5, 22), but he names only Peter (13:6), Philip (14:8), Thomas (14:5), Judas Iscariot (13:27), the other Judas (14:22), and the Beloved Disciple (13:23). Although he does not mention or name the sons of Zebedee, based on what we know from the Synoptic record, we may safely presume that they were there, too. So, since John only says "disciples" were present, we can include the Twelve, but we cannot exclude anyone else. The man John calls "Judas, not Iscariot" (John 14:22) may be the "Judas, son of James" named in Luke's list of the Twelve (Luke 6:16; Acts 1:13), but we can't be certain of this since John never gives a complete list of the Twelve. If he was not that Judas, this would be further evidence from John that others besides the Twelve were there.

I started down this side-track about the Last Supper simply to demonstrate that if we wish to identify the Beloved Disciple, we must have a clear picture of who was at the Last Supper. Despite the long-held common wisdom that only the Twelve were there, that assumption weakens under close examination of the texts. There is ample evidence to suggest others were present. This, then, opens up the possibility that the Beloved Disciple was a very close friend of Jesus, but not one of the Twelve.

Thus, while we know that Jesus reclined that night at a particular table and was joined by the Twelve, John's account forces us to consider this further reality: if the Beloved Disciple was *not* John bar Zebedee, we know at least one other person, not of the Twelve, was at that table:

> One of his disciples, whom Jesus loved, was lying close to the breast of Jesus; so Simon Peter beckoned to him and said, "Tell us who it is of whom he speaks." So lying thus, close to the breast of Jesus, he said to him, "Lord, who is it?" (John 13:23-25).

First, we notice that while the Beloved Disciple is right next to Jesus, Peter, the leader of the Twelve, is further away. Who was this dear friend and disciple whom Jesus welcomed to "the head table" for this most-important-ever Passover, and gave one of the highest seats of honor, sitting closer to Jesus than even Simon Peter? Early Church tradition suggests that this John, the Beloved Disciple, was a young man, perhaps little more than a boy. I cannot help but wonder if he was given the role of asking that important question traditional at the Passover meal, "Why is this night different from every other night?"

This "disciple whom Jesus loved," of course, is never identified by name, other than the fact that this gospel bears the name John. So, if he was not bar Zebedee, who was this particular John? To seek an answer, we will have to dig in two distinct mines. First, we must dig further into the New Testament itself, and second, we must mine the few records we have from the earliest centuries of Christian history.

Endnotes

1. See Appendix A for a detailed analysis of the focus on Jerusalem in the Fourth Gospel.

2. Despite so much evidence to the contrary, I recognize that some readers will still hold to the "safe," traditional view that John bar Zebedee was the Fourth Evangelist. They are free to believe so, but they may find themselves caught on a thorn from which they can't get free: there is simply *no* evidence in John, or the Synoptic record, to identify these two men as the same man. As I have outlined, the traditional identification of John bar Zebedee as the Beloved Disciple seems to rest solely on the unproven assumption that bar Zebedee wrote all five Johannine books.

There is also this second thorn, noted in Chapter One: the sons of Zebedee are only mentioned once in the entire gospel, and that is in the last chapter (21) which is most likely an addition to the original body of the Fourth Gospel.

Third, the argument that John bar Zebedee simply wanted to keep himself anonymous is weakened by the fact that his own gospel — if it were his — also excludes any significant role for his famous brother James, who is never mentioned by name (though perhaps "assumed" in mention of the Twelve). I have so far never come across any attempt to explain this particular problem. It is true that the Fourth Evangelist keeps himself anonymous (if one excludes the title of the gospel), but that goes no distance toward proving that the anonymous writer is bar Zebedee.

Finally, supporters of the traditional view will snag themselves on this fourth sticking point: why would the writer of chapter 21, who almost certainly was not the Evangelist himself and would therefore have no personal "modesty" motive for keeping the himself anonymous, continue to refuse to identify the gospel's author if he was someone as well-known as John bar Zebedee? This final chapter is the only place where the Fourth Gospel mentions "the sons of Zebedee" at all. They are present that morning by the lake (21:2). Still, even here, the writer of this chapter gives neither man's (well-known) first name. Why? Then, when he refers specifically to the "disciple whom Jesus loved," he does not make any connection — what would have seemed a most obvious and ready-at-hand connection — to the one Zebedee brother standing there. Why? Notice that he doesn't say "Peter turned and saw following them one of the sons of Zebedee . . ." No, Peter sees the Beloved Disciple following. It seems odd in the extreme that having just mentioned the Zebedee brothers' presence the writer would not connect the dots and make that identification, if that connection was so readily at hand.

Once again, the simplest explanation is probably the correct one: the writer doesn't make that identification because he knew "the disciple whom Jesus loved" was *not* John bar Zebedee, but one of the two "unnamed" disciples who were also present that morning (21:2; compare John 1:35, 37). Indeed, since the Beloved Disciple is always *unnamed* in this gospel, but the "sons of Zebedee" *are* mentioned in this passage, that very mention would break the pattern. It is more reasonable — and certainly more consistent — to believe the Beloved Disciple was one of the two disciples left — as usual — unnamed.

3. We find, as we follow Luke's account forward into Acts, that "the Eleven" continued to stay or meet in an "upper room" with a larger group of other disciples, including Jesus' mother Mary and the other women (Acts 1:13-15). Whether this was the same "upper room" where they had all gathered for the Last Supper we cannot be certain, but it is suggestive at least that the group that followed Jesus to Jerusalem before the Crucifixion remained tightly together after the Resurrection and at least until the "birthing" of the Church on the Jewish feast of Pentecost.

4. For those who insist "John the Apostle" (bar Zebedee) was the Fourth Evangelist, it may come as a surprise that the Twelve are never called "apostles" in John.

Three

IF THE BELOVED DISCIPLE was the Fourth Evangelist but not John bar Zebedee, what evidence in the New Testament itself might help us identify this other John? The first step is to look in more detail at what the Fourth Gospel itself tells us about this man.

The Fourth Gospel's Evidence
If the reader is willing to consider what I argued in the previous chapter, the *probability* that disciples other than the Twelve were at the Last Supper, we are free to look beyond their small circle for the identity of the Beloved Disciple. The reference to him as "the disciple whom Jesus loved" makes clear that he was a very dear friend of Jesus; and the fact that this gospel came to be accepted as authentic by some churches very early in the Church's history suggests that its author was a known, respected, and authoritative witness.

Before attempting to identify this disciple, however, let us first consider why even some early commentators believed that this Beloved Disciple was the author of this gospel.

Although the Fourth Gospel mentions this "disciple whom Jesus loved" a number of times, it never directly identifies him as the author. As I noted in the previous chapter, the gospel is indeed anonymous in that sense: the name of the author is never directly given. The same is true of the other three gospels.

In John, however, there are several hints about the Beloved Disciple having been an eyewitness, and thus potentially the author? The most obvious example is his role at the Last Supper. A second significant reference comes during the crucifixion in John 19. Two things stand out there: the Beloved Disciple is present at the foot of the cross with Jesus' mother and several other women. Shortly before his death, Jesus commends his mother to the Beloved Disciple's care (19:25-27). Then we find this, the last sentence of which may well be a note inserted by a later editor:

> But when they came to Jesus and saw that he was already dead, they did not break his legs. But one of the soldiers pierced his side with a spear, and at once there came out blood and water. He who saw it has borne witness — his testimony is true, and he knows that he is telling the truth — that you also may believe (19:33-35 ESV).

Since, according to the Synoptic record, all the members of the Twelve had apparently fled into hiding before the crucifixion, the Beloved Disciple, as far as we have any record, would have been the only male disciple present. Thus, the phrase that "He who saw it has borne witness" to the lancing of Jesus' side is most probably a reference back to the same Beloved Disciple. This is conjecture, but reasonable.

Then, in what were likely the final words of the original body of the gospel, we find this echo:

> Now Jesus did many other signs in the presence of the disciples, which are not written in this book; but these are written *so that you may believe* that Jesus is the Christ, the Son of God, and that by believing you may have life in his name. (20:30-31 ESV, *emphasis added*).

The phrase, "these are written so that you may believe" seems a direct echo of the same words spoken about the man who witnessed the lancing of Jesus. Thus, it may be a further reference to the testimony of the Beloved Disciple as the eyewitness author.

This seems further confirmed in the final (likely additional) chapter of the book. In speaking of a conversation about the

Beloved Disciple between Jesus and Peter (21:20-23), the writer of that chapter says clearly:

> This is the disciple who is bearing witness about these things, and who has written these things, and we know that his testimony is true (21:24).

Now, one can argue that "these things" here refers only to the events narrated in this last chapter; but because it again echoes statements in chapter 19 and 20, it is more likely a reference to the "things" narrated throughout the gospel. The clear implication is that the Beloved Disciple was the author, the eyewitness authority behind this Fourth Gospel.

Who Was The Beloved Disciple?

I mentioned in the previous chapter that the Fourth Gospel could be termed "the Jerusalem Gospel," or the Judea Gospel (see Appendix A). Because this gospel narrates primarily events in and around Jerusalem rather than Galilee, I am persuaded that the author probably lived in or near the Holy City. Since this gospel has always been attributed to a disciple named John, we can assume with reasonable safety that was in fact his name.

The question at this point is, which John? Based on all the objections cited earlier, I rule out John bar Zebedee. Who, then, was he, and what do we know about him for certain? The most factual answer is: not very much. The fragments of evidence both inside and outside the Gospel are scarce. From the Fourth Gospel itself, however, we can surmise these details:

1. He was the "eyewitness author," that is, the evangelist and authority behind this Gospel (John 19:35, 21:24).

2. He was at the Last Supper, sitting directly next to Jesus (John 13:23-26).

3. He was at the foot of the cross with Mary (John 19:25-27).

4. He took Mary into his home immediately after the crucifixion (John 19:27).

5. He heard the news of the resurrection along with Peter from Mary Magdalene early on Easter morning, and ran to the tomb ahead of Peter (John 20:1-8).

6. He was there with Peter and several other disciples (including the sons of Zebedee) when the risen Jesus appeared by the lake of Galilee (John 21).

Consistently, the Beloved Disciple is "unnamed" except for this "nickname"; but we do find two more cryptic references to an "unnamed" disciple that may possibly refer to him:

1. Was he first a disciple of John the Baptist, the unnamed disciple who first followed Jesus with Andrew (John 1:35-42)?

2. Was he the other again unnamed disciple who, alongside Peter, followed Jesus after his arrest to the house of the high priest (John 18:15).

If the second instance here *does* refer to the Beloved Disciple, it is crucial, because, as we will see, this "unnamed" disciple with Peter was personally known to the high priest; and, in fact, was the one who enabled Peter to get into the courtyard that night after Jesus' arrest. This would be further evidence against John bar Zebedee being the Beloved Disciple: if this unnamed disciple known to the high priest was *not* a Galilean fisherman but a different John from Jerusalem or Judea, we can make sense of this detail.

What else can we discern from the gospel itself about its author?

I mentioned in Chapter One that he seems to have been well-educated and literate in Greek. His gospel contains very poetic and artistic use of that language, albeit a Greek that reflects a Jewish thought-world. His use of language and the intentional, well-developed structure of the Fourth Gospel discourses shine through even in translation. Even if, as some have suggested, this gospel was put into its final form by a disciple of John, or a group of several editors (perhaps accounting for the perspective of chapter 21), the main body of composition, whether written or dictated, shows a poetic use of language, a proficient use of Old Testament symbolism, and a very detailed knowledge of Jerusalem and its surroundings, especially the Temple area, where whole parts of the gospel take place.[1]

This gospel bears the voice of a skillful author (or speaker?) who fluently used repetitive phrasing to build its simple yet powerful teachings of Jesus into structured, memorable discourses (very much like 1 John). The prologue in chapter 1 has long been recognized as a masterpiece that weaves Hellenistic words and ideas into an introduction of the Jewish Messiah, come in the flesh.[2]

In other words, it strikes us that the main body of this gospel was the work of one skillful author, not a compilation created by a committee of disciples or a group of editors. Anyone with actual experience in the creation of literature will probably rule out the notion that this gospel was first a creation of a group. It is too orderly, to masterfully structured, and too refined in thought sequence to seem like the work of several writers trying to agree, edit, and adjust. When did a committee ever create anything but literary carnage?

Whoever this John was, he was a deep thinker and an accomplished writer. So we are looking for someone who was:

1. According to early tradition, a fairly young man during the ministry of Jesus, since he lived (as will be shown later) into the 90's A.D.
2. Probably a resident of Judea, or Jerusalem.
3. Well-educated, perhaps trained in one of the rabbinical schools of Jerusalem, a cosmopolitan city where both Hebrew (or, more likely, Aramaic) and Greek were common languages.

4. Skilled in those two languages (three, if we include Aramaic).

5. One who could weave the discourses of Jesus into symphonic-like sentences, expounding the grand themes of light and darkness, spirit and flesh, water and life, God and Man.

6. One who knew Judea and the area around Jerusalem intimately, in particular the temple precincts.

7. One who became a close disciple of Jesus and was held in special affection by Jesus, and by the other disciples.

8. Possibly a friend or acquaintance of members of the High Priest's household.

9. Lastly, since the many details of his gospel reveal the mark of an actual eyewitness, he was someone who could have been "on the scene" during the events of Jesus' ministry in Judea and Jerusalem that are reported in this gospel, many of which that clearly occur before Jesus' period of ministry in Galilee.

As we move on to consider all this, I note again that none of this seems a very likely description of John bar Zebedee, the Galilean fisherman. Whoever this other John was, early Christian records we will examine in later chapters indicate that he eventually settled in Ephesus where the Fourth Gospel was possibly written, or at least finished.

Endnotes

1. We must remember that a driving force that caused some scholars to propose a "Johannine community" of writers behind this gospel was the obvious reality that few believed that the poetry and beauty of the Fourth Gospel was from the hand of a reasonably unlettered fisherman.

2. It has been suggested that the prologue to John (1:1-14) is so finely written that it may have been an Early Christian hymn that the author (or a

later editor) simply tacked on by way of introduction. I find this suggestion uncompelling when the style, symbolism and repetitive phrasing of the prologue matches so perfectly the style and imagery of the discourses in the rest of the Gospel.

Four

IF JOHN BAR ZEBEDEE was not the author of the Fourth Gospel, we recognize the reality that there must have been another well-known disciple named John who was the Evangelist, a man who was a beloved, respected witness to the ministry of Jesus and who, like Matthias and Joseph bar Sabbas (Acts 1:21-23), was not a member of the Twelve. He was one of the first witnesses to the Resurrection (John 20), and was therefore recognized as holding apostolic authority. While not a member of the Twelve, this other John must have held significant teaching authority and respect in many of the early churches.

Our attempt to identify this other John, however, is not as simple a task as we would wish because of the multitude of theories that have been proposed over the centuries as to which "John" wrote 1) the Fourth Gospel, 2) the three Johannine letters, and 3) the Revelation of St. John. Some commentators and scholars, as I have explained, identify all the writers as one man, bar Zebedee: what I have called the "traditional" view. Others postulate a second, or even a third author for various of the books. For example, some argue that John bar Zebedee was John the Evangelist, but suggest a different man, usually called "John the Presbyter" (John the Elder; based on 2 John 1:1 and 3 John 1:1) as the author of the three Johannine letters. The same commentators may, or may not, accept Revelation as being from the hand of the same writer. Others postulate a third author, "John of Patmos" as author of Revelation. If we were to map this out, the possibilities become complex, but are essentially these:

1. John bar Zebedee wrote: the Gospel, 3 letters, and Revelation
2. Or, John bar Zebedee wrote: the Gospel, and 3 letters
3. Or, John bar Zebedee wrote: the Gospel, and Revelation
4. Or, John bar Zebedee wrote: the Gospel only
5. John the Presbyter wrote: the three letters, and possibly Revelation
6. Or, John the Presbyter wrote: the three letters only
7. John of Patmos wrote: Revelation only

Like bunny rabbits, we can multiply the possibilities and quickly get caught in the resulting thickets. What we should remember from this point forward is that nearly all of the confusion grew out of the fact that some early commentators picked bar Zebedee as their choice for John the Evangelist. This forced them to consider some other man as "John of Patmos" to account for the very different Book of Revelation. Others could not see any certain connection between the Gospel and the three letters, so opted to identify the author of those letters as "John the Presbyter," based on the identity the sender uses of himself in two of those letters (2 John, 3 John).[1]

I will examine and try to address this confusion as we move later into the historical evidence we have beyond the New Testament. What I highlight here is simply the fact that once we let go of the assumption that bar Zebedee was John the Evangelist, much of the remaining evidence, otherwise confusing, begins to fall into its proper place and things actually begin to make sense.

Before going on to that external evidence, however, I want to focus further on the New Testament itself to see what it contains that might help us identify the Fourth Evangelist. Did another well-known John exist? Were there in fact *two* men named John, both highly-respected disciples of Jesus, one whom was bar Zebedee and a second, the Beloved Disciple, who wrote the gospel, and perhaps the three letters, and who eventually came to be known as "John the Presbyter" at Ephesus?

There is every reason to believe so. Fragmentary but ancient historical evidence will show that two disciples named John both ended their lives at Ephesus (see Chapter Five). If that evidence is true, and if one of those men was John bar Zebedee, who was the other John?

A Likely Suspect

The first place we should seek an answer is in the pages of the New Testament, for if the Beloved Disciple was, indeed, a man who held apostolic authority in some of the early churches, we might expect to find at least some mention of him in the Bible itself, as is the case with such well-known disciples as Barnabas, Timothy, Titus, Silvanus, Apollos, and Luke.[2]

Interestingly, when we begin such a search beyond the Gospels, we don't have to go far before a possible candidate literally jumps off the pages: the man known in Acts as "John, also called Mark" (Acts 12:12). John (*Johann*) was likely his Hebrew name, and Mark possibly his Greek, secular name (not unlike Saul/Paul). For clarity, I will refer to him hereafter as John-Mark.

Now, I recognize that some readers will immediately cry foul and object that this man named "Mark" in Acts was the author of the Gospel of Mark, not the Gospel of John. That *assumption* has certainly been made often enough, but if I ask, "Based on what?" some objectors will find themselves silent. The pertinent question is, "is it true?"

Yes, many modern commentators pick John-Mark as the Second Evangelist because they *first* make the assumption that John-Mark is the same man identified as a later associate of Peter (1 Peter 5:13), the probable author (as evidence will show) of the Gospel of Mark. As I will show in course, however, the evidence that might equate John-Mark and Peter's "Mark" (his Roman interpreter) is precariously thin: it comes down to the fact that the name of Peter's "son" is the same as the secular, *second* name of

John-Mark. Indeed, that is the only reason I can find that anyone ever equated these two different men, as actual evidence will show (see Chapter Five). On the other hand, we have sound, historical evidence that John-Mark of Acts *could not possibly* have been the Mark who later wrote down Peter's testimony in the Gospel of Mark.[3]

A Look At The Actual Evidence

Is there any evidence in scripture itself to support the suggestion that John-Mark may have been John the Evangelist?

The first and most important point is this: when we meet him in Acts, it is very clear that his "first" name, the name he is regularly known by, is *John.* He is twice referred to simply as John (Acts 13:5, 13:13). Three times he is called "John, who was also called Mark" or "John called Mark" (Acts 12:12, 12:25, 15:37). Only once — the last reference — is he called simply "Mark," but that last *exception* (15:39) follows an instance just two verses prior where he is named "John, also called Mark."

Could this be the other John we are seeking? What do we know about him?

Acts records that this John traveled with Saul (Paul) and Barnabas on an early missionary journey. As they preached in various Jewish synagogues we are told "they had John as their helper" (Acts 13:5 NASB; or "John to assist them" ESV). This in itself is significant. Barnabas was an early, respected disciple, present among the apostles and other disciples since the Resurrection. Saul, of course, becomes a lynch-pin theologian of the early Church. In what way could John-Mark have been a help? Carrying bags is one possibility. If, however, we are willing to consider John-Mark as the Beloved Disciple, we can still see what a tremendous help he would have been in evangelizing fellow Jews.

Indeed, we need to ask why Barnabas and Paul took John-Mark along at all, if he were a mere "helper" in the most basic sense. The Greek word used here of John-Mark is that he was their *hyperestes.* In the New Testament this is variously used for a servant, a helper, an assisting official in the Sanhedrin, or an attendant in a synagogue. In other words, it might be a quasi-official role that carried some authority. What authority or teaching did John-Mark have to offer?

Whatever his role was, it was significant enough that it eventually caused a major falling out between Barnabas and Paul, which led them to part ways and conduct missions separately:

> And after some days Paul said to Barnabas, "Come, let us return and visit the brethren in every city where we proclaimed the word of the Lord, and see how they are." And Barnabas wanted to take with them John called Mark. But Paul thought best not to take with them one who had withdrawn from them in Pamphylia, and had not gone with them to the work. And there arose a sharp contention, so that they separated from each other; Barnabas took Mark with him and sailed away to Cyprus, but Paul chose Silas and departed . . . (Acts 15:36-40).

Despite this separation, there is evidence John-Mark and Paul later reconciled. If, as is likely, John-Mark is the same "Mark" referred to by Paul in Colossians as being his co-worker once again, it means John-Mark was actually a cousin of Barnabas (Colossians 4:10; see also Philemon 24, 2 Timothy 4:11). That could explain why Barnabas felt so strongly in "backing" John-Mark during the earlier dispute with Paul.[4]

If Paul and John-Mark did reconcile at some point, it may help us understand the evidence which will appear in later chapters that John-Mark was the well-respected disciple who became known as "John the Presbyter" in Asia Minor. Since Paul helped found the church in Ephesus (Acts 18-19), if John-Mark was his co-worker in that region during a later period it might explain why John eventually settled in that city.

We can draw a number of inferences from the New Testament references we have looked at so far, but this much, at a minimum, we can establish with certainty from Acts 12-15, and from Paul's letters: from the earliest years of the Church, there was a well-known evangelist and missionary named John ("John, also called Mark") who travelled with Paul and Barnabas and helped spread the gospel in Antioch, Syria, Cyprus and Asia Minor.

Other Intriguing Details
What else do we know about John-Mark that would fit our search for the Fourth Evangelist? We are seeking, recall, someone highly familiar with Jerusalem and the temple, well-educated, and possibly known personally to the high priest at the time of Jesus' crucifixion. Considering our "qualifications" for John the Evangelist, we cannot help being struck by this fact: John-Mark was not from Galilee, but *Jerusalem*, where he apparently lived with his mother (Acts 12:12). Also, when John first joined Paul and Barnabas in missionary work, it was from Jerusalem that they brought him to Antioch (Acts 12:25).[5]

There is something more. If, as I have suggested, John-Mark is "Mark, the cousin of Barnabas" named in Colossians, this provides another intriguing possibility about John-Mark. For Joseph "bar Nabas" ("son of encouragement", a nick-name given him by the Apostles) was from Cyprus but was also a *Levite* (Acts 4:36), the family from which all Jewish priests came. If John-Mark was his cousin, John-Mark himself may have been of the tribe of Levi. He thus might not only have been "known to the high priest" (John 18:15) but could have been a relative or shirt-tail cousin.[6]

Another detail strikes me: in Acts 12, John-Mark is living with his mother. Indeed, the house to which Peter goes is not "John-Mark's house," but "the house of Mary, the mother of John-Mark" (12:12). Why is this noteworthy? Because it suggests John-Mark is still a young man; and, as we know from early tradition, the Beloved Disciple was one of the youngest disciples who was close to Jesus.

Is it then possible that "John, also called Mark" could in fact be John the Beloved Disciple, author of the Fourth Gospel?

Consider this basic question: why is John-Mark mentioned in the New Testament at all? Why is he of such interest? There are literally thousands of unnamed disciples involved in the work of the Gospel in the earliest days of the Church. How many of them are ever named in the New Testament? So, we may justifiably wonder, why does "John, also called Mark" have such an important role — very early on — as a helper of Barnabas and Paul? Yes, in the overall scheme of Acts, written principally to chronicle the work of Peter and Paul, John-Mark plays a relatively minor role; yet he is mentioned by name not once but several times. We should also notice that he is *personally known* to both Peter (Acts 12) and Paul (Acts 12-15), the central figures in Acts. Moreover, if John-Mark is (as I believe) the "Mark" mentioned three times in Paul's letters, we find him named in both early and late books of the New Testament.

The sheer number of references, and his connection with both Peter and Paul (not to mention with Barnabas; and, perhaps, with the high priest in Jerusalem), imply John-Mark was a man of significant stature in the New Testament period. Sadly, we don't know much more about him. A careful look, however, reveals a few interesting details pertinent to our investigation which show that John-Mark does indeed meet some of our qualifications for the Beloved Disciple.

First, as already mentioned, his mother Mary's home was in Jerusalem (Acts 12:12). We can therefore assume with some confidence that John-Mark grew up there. Whether he was still living there full-time at the time of Jesus' ministry, crucifixion, and resurrection, or whether he may have spent time traveling with Jesus and the disciples as far as Galilee, we can't be certain. If he was indeed the Beloved Disciple, he was probably at the wedding in Cana, and perhaps the feeding of the 5000 (John 6; note in particular verse 9).

A natural question arises: was John-Mark's mother Mary one of the other women by that name at the foot of the cross that day? We have no way to know. The name was very common. It is not impossible, so we should not rule this out. The title

Beloved Disciple certainly suggests someone close to Jesus in friendship, if not kinship (see Appendix B). It is possible, then, that this family, Mary and John-Mark, was known to Jesus and his own mother for some time.

There is also this: when John-Mark is first mentioned in Acts, it seems as if readers should already know who he is. When Peter escapes from prison in the middle of the night he goes directly to "the house of Mary, the mother of John, whose other name was Mark, where many were gathered together and were praying. And when he knocked at the door of the gateway, a maid named Rhoda came to answer" (Acts 12:12-13). Neither this Mary, nor her son John, have been mentioned so far in Acts. Yet, it seems the reader may recognize the names. What is also clear is that John-Mark must already be known to Peter. Luke doesn't just say Peter went "to Mary's house," but to the house of "Mary, the mother of John, whose other name was Mark." In short, this Mary and her son John-Mark seem to be well-known among the disciples. Those at her house that night know Peter is in prison. They know what has happened, and they are all praying. In other words, this home is a gathering place for Christians — so much so that Peter feels he can just show up there unexpectedly in the middle of the night. The home is so well-known that we even learn the name of the housemaid who opened the door (a curious detail that echoes similar "odd" details in the Fourth Gospel, such as John 18:11, 18:16, and 18:26). Peter's desperate resort to their house tells us that Mary and her son John-Mark are trusted members of the early Christian community at Jerusalem.

It is noteworthy that Peter can go to this home in safety. Acts does not tell us of anyone else in or around Jerusalem at this point to whom Peter — at the moment an escaped prisoner — could so confidently retreat. We must remember Jerusalem is not his home. Peter is a fisherman from Galilee, but well-known to the Jewish authorities as a follower of Jesus. It was the Crucifixion that brought Peter there, and the Resurrection and Ascension of Jesus that kept him there. We recall that earlier in

Acts, Peter and the other Christians were hiding in locked rooms for fear of arrest. Now, after one of those arrests, Peter feels perfectly safe to go to this particular home. Mary and her son John are trusted by Peter, the apostolic leader. It is natural for us to be curious why.

That curiosity leads to this further question: is there any evidence in the gospels, prior to Acts, to suggest how Peter might have known John-Mark and his mother? Consider this. If my suggestion is correct that John-Mark was the Beloved Disciple, the Fourth Evangelist, we then have *compelling* evidence of a friendship between him and Peter in the Fourth Gospel itself. For John-Mark would then be the disciple who sat next to Jesus at the Last Supper, that disciple to whom Peter beckoned to ask Jesus who the betrayer was (John 13:23-24). If John-Mark was, in fact, that other *unnamed* disciple, a native of Jerusalem and "known to the high priest" who was able to get Peter into the courtyard during Jesus' trial (John 18:15-16), we can understand how completely Peter trusted him. Lastly, of course, if John-Mark was indeed the Beloved Disciple, it was he who outran Peter as they hurried to the tomb on Easter morning (John 20:2-8), and who followed Peter into the tomb "and believed."

The reader will begin to see how the seemingly disparate pieces of evidence actually fit together.

Is all this mere coincidence? Or did Luke include the figure of John-Mark so prominently in the Book of Acts for a more obvious reason: because by the time Luke wrote (around 70-75 AD?), most of the Twelve and Paul were dead, leaving John-Mark as one of the few remaining apostolic eyewitnesses of Jesus' life, death and resurrection, and therefore one of the few remaining authoritative figures of the New Testament Church?

The Anonymous Author
If the author of the Fourth Gospel was some lesser-known figure such as John-Mark, rather than John bar Zebedee, might that help us understand why he kept his name out? In addition, if he were a younger man during the events he recorded, might he have kept

this "lower profile" because he had not reached the age of 30 when, in Jewish tradition, he could be accepted as an authoritative teacher?

We cannot be sure. We only know though that throughout the Fourth Gospel, the author's name remains hidden from us. He is referred to as "the disciple Jesus loved" (13:23-26, 19:26-27, 20:2-9); so also, in 21:20-24, where the future of the Beloved Disciple is discussed by Jesus and Peter. Again, in that chapter, assuming this other John is not bar Zebedee, he is one of two "unnamed" disciples (21:2).

Besides these places, there are two additional instances (one just mentioned) where we find an "unnamed" disciple who plays a role in key events. Is this also "the Beloved Disciple," again remaining hidden?

One such an example is John 1:35-42, where the author mentions two disciples of John the Baptist. One is Andrew but the other, notably, is left unnamed. The second, anonymous disciple is important because, as far as John's record goes, he is one of the first two disciples of Jesus once John the Baptist points to Jesus as being the Messiah, the "lamb of God." The other of these two disciples, Andrew, promptly finds his brother Peter and brings him to meet Jesus. If the second "unnamed" disciple here is the Beloved Disciple, our author, that means Peter met this other disciple very early in their discipleship under Jesus. If the Beloved Disciple is John-Mark, we find a very early potential tie between the two men who will be first among the eyewitnesses to the Resurrection.

Perhaps the most intriguing example of an "unnamed" disciple is the incident mentioned above, where an unnamed disciple gets Peter into the courtyard of the High Priest's house after Jesus' arrest. Is this another typical, cryptic reference to the Evangelist himself, the unnamed Beloved Disciple? The text does not explicitly say so, but the mysterious presence of this unnamed disciple operates in this scene in a way consistent with how the Beloved Disciple appears elsewhere in the gospel. If the anonymous disciple here again is the Evangelist, we have laid hold of *surely* one of the most important pieces of evidence regarding the identity of the author anywhere in the Fourth Gospel:

> Simon Peter followed Jesus, and so did another disciple. As this disciple was known to the high priest, he entered the courtyard of the high priest along with Jesus, while Peter stood outside at the door. So the other disciple, who was known to the high priest, went out and spoke to the maid who kept the door, and brought Peter in (John 18:15-16).

Why is this detail so crucial? For this reason: if the unnamed disciple who got Peter into the courtyard *was* the Evangelist, then this passage would once and for all lay to rest the traditional speculation that John bar Zebedee was the author.

Why? First, because it seems unlikely in the extreme (though, assuredly, not impossible) that a Galilean fisherman would be *personally known* to the high priest in Jerusalem. Second, all three "Galilean" (Synoptic) gospels insist that *only Peter* followed Jesus at this point. None of those other gospels, so long claimed as historical and reliable, place John bar Zebedee with Peter at — or anywhere near — the High Priest's house. All three Synoptics agree that Peter followed the arresting guards alone, and all imply that he just walked into the courtyard on his own, which, considering the political tensions and all attendant circumstances that night, strains our credulity. Peter is recognized almost immediately as a disciple of Jesus — and he is forced to flee. Had John bar Zebedee also been there, another of Jesus' circle of the "inner three," wouldn't the Synoptic writers have included this important detail? And would he not have bolted when Peter did? Realistically, how likely is it that Peter could have just walked into the courtyard of the High Priest's residence unescorted, when they had just arrested his master and had him (Jesus) under close guard; not to mention the fact that some of those guards had just seen Peter attack one of their number with a sword, and cut off his ear? This indeed strains credulity.

John's account seems much more believable, and reliable. In fairness, however, let's pause and at least consider the alternative, that John bar Zebedee was the Beloved Disciples and was with Peter. When we seriously reflect on the resulting picture, our imaginations will be further tortured by these problems:

> 1. If Peter, an unknown fisherman from Galilee, could not get into the courtyard, how could John bar Zebedee, another unknown fisherman from Galilee — another close friend of Jesus — just walk in first?
> 2. Would John bar Zebedee, a Galilean visitor to Jerusalem, be personally known *not only* to the high priest, but also to the servant girl who just happened to be keeping the door of the courtyard that night?
> 3. Even were we to grant those improbabilities, once Peter was recognized and confronted, why wasn't John bar Zebedee also confronted — if he was present? (Jesus had predicted Peter would deny him three times. He did not predict John bar Zebedee would.) If Zebedee was in the courtyard with Peter and did not deny he knew Jesus, how would he have escaped arrest? Or why would that arrest not be reported somewhere in the other gospels?

Exercising our imaginations is a good pastime, but trying to hold onto the belief that John bar Zebedee took part in these events and was the evangelist who reported them, goes far beyond exercise. We are into Alice in Wonderland territory before the queen has had her breakfast.

I recognize that anyone supporting the traditional John bar Zebdee author theory can get around all this by simply arguing that the other "unnamed" disciple in this case (18:15-16) was not "the Beloved Disciple." But that begs the question: if he was not the Beloved Disciple, *who was he*; and why would someone so key, known personally to the high priest and members of his household, not be named?

The reality is this: those supporting the traditional-author view must grapple with, or ignore, the fact that during the whole passion sequence in the Fourth Gospel, beginning with the Last Supper and ending with the resurrection, the *only* disciple closely linked with Peter is the Beloved Disciple. There is also the fact that the whole scene in the courtyard contains the kind of eyewitness detail that we routinely get only from the Evangelist himself throughout the gospel (cf. John 19:35). We recall again that John bar Zebedee is never named in this gospel. If he were the Beloved Disciple, would we not learn that somewhere? Even if the Beloved Disciple was not the disciple who got Peter into that courtyard, nonetheless, "the disciple Jesus loved" is front and center at the Last Supper, the cross, and the tomb. If he were bar Zebedee, why would an editor who likely added chapter 21 after the Beloved Disciple died remain silent on this important fact?

If the unnamed disciple who got Peter into the high priest's courtyard *was* the Beloved Disciple and thus the Evangelist — and the level of detail provided seems to suggest that —the idea that he was John bar Zebedee is simply too farfetched. If, on the other hand, he was John-Mark, a life-long resident of Jerusalem and perhaps even a relative of the high priest's family, our imaginations can begin to relax. Impossible questions are more easily laid to rest. It is easier to understand, for example, how John-Mark would know that the name of the high priest's slave whose ear Peter cut off was Malchus (18:10), and that one of the servants in the courtyard was a relative of the same Malchus (18:26). It is easier to believe that John–Mark might know the servant girl at the gate. It could also explain why in John we have the detail, unknown to the Synoptic writers, that Jesus was actually taken before Annas, the father-in-law of Caiaphas, first before being sent to Caiaphas.

Throughout John's passion narrative, as throughout his entire gospel, we find seemingly insignificant details not known in the Synoptics, many of which reflect the kind of intimate personal knowledge of Jerusalem and its people that only a resident of the city would be likely to know.[7]

Uncomfortable Details

Next, we come to a wonderful detail in the Fourth Gospel which probably causes most supporters of the traditional-author view to squirm. If John bar Zebedee was the "disciple whom Jesus loved," then, after the rest of the Twelve — now including Peter — have *all* abandoned Jesus and fled for fear of arrest (a fact explicit in the Synoptics and implied in John), we find the Beloved Disciple *standing with the mother of Jesus at the foot of the cross.* How can we account for this? In the synoptic accounts, it's clear that John bar Zebedee and his brother fled from the garden with the others at the time of Jesus' arrest. How then would he now be standing, in plain sight, just a few hours later, near the cross with Mary? The scene is poignant, and telling:

> But standing by the cross of Jesus were his mother, and his mother's sister, Mary the wife of Clopas, and Mary Magdalene. When Jesus saw his mother, and the disciple whom he loved standing near, he said to his mother, "Woman, behold, your son!" Then he said to the disciple, "Behold, your mother!" And from that hour the disciple took her to his own home (John 19:25-27).

Despite years of tradition to the contrary, based on the evidence of the gospel itself, and compared to the record of the Synoptics, it seems inconceivable that this could have been John bar Zebedee. As one of the Galilean Twelve, one of the top leaders among Jesus' disciples, he almost certainly would have been arrested the moment he showed his face in public — as Peter nearly was the night before. We are explicitly told that not long after this, in fact, the remaining Eleven and perhaps others *were locked behind closed doors for fear of arrest* (John 20:19). In light of that, it seems almost silly to suggest that one of the Twelve showed up at the scene of the crucifixion.

Even more problematic for the traditional Zebedee theorists is the final sentence about John and Mary: *"And from that hour the disciple took her to his own home"* (in Greek: *kai 'ap ekeines tes horas)*. If the John standing at the foot of the cross was bar Zebedee, how was that possible, since his home was in Galilee? If, however, he was John-Mark, a resident of Jerusalem, this long-standing mystery is instantly solved. There is also the tradition (which we'll explore later) that Jesus' mother Mary lived an extended period of time in Jerusalem with this same John until she moved with him to Ephesus where at least one tradition says she died.[8]

This would mean, of course, that Jesus' mother went to live with John-Mark and his mother Mary, which might, in itself, help explain why their house early-on became a gathering place for the infant Church, and the haven to which Peter turned that night after escaping prison.

We also recall that standing at the cross alongside the Beloved Disciple (in John's account) were Jesus' mother, his mother's sister, Mary the wife of Clopas (possibly the same as the "mother's sister," depending on how one reads the text) and Mary Magdalene.[9] Is "Clopas" the man identified as "Cleopas" in Luke 24? Is this other Mary (his wife) possibly the same Mary identified in Acts as the mother of John-Mark? Mary was a very common name, so we can only speculate. I only note that there is no evidence that would rule this possibility out. If it was the case, then Clopas (Cleopas) would have been John-Mark's father. This detail adds little to our overall picture, except that, if true, it could go a long way in helping us understand why this other Mary, her husband Clopas, and their son John-Mark were such well-known disciples in the infant Church at Jerusalem.[10]

A Link Between John-Mark And Jesus?

If, as I have proposed, "the disciple whom Jesus loved" was not John bar Zebedee but John-Mark, this possibility raises two further questions that we would want to answer: 1) How might John-Mark know Jesus, and, 2) Why were they so close?

We will find no absolute answer to either question because the New Testament contains no direct background information about the relationship between Jesus and this especially beloved disciple; but we can consider possibilities. If my John-Mark suggestion is admitted for consideration, how does the little that we *do* know about John-Mark line up with the overall evidence of John and the other three gospels?

The Synoptics tell us very little of Jesus' ministry in and around Jerusalem, until the week of his passion. In fact, from them we know with certainty of only one trip he made there during his whole public ministry: his last. But the Fourth Gospel reports several visits to Jerusalem — reported in very great detail — including that famous late-night conversation with Nicodemus, a man apparently unknown to the Synoptic writers. If his conversation with Jesus (John 3) was based on a real conversation, and not, as some commentators have suggested, a purely literary creation, then how did the Fourth Evangelist come by such great detail about their discussion? There are two possibilities. Nicodemus (or Jesus?) told John the Evangelist of the conversation, or John was actually present and heard it.

Is the latter possible? It is perfectly possible if my John-Mark theory is correct. Because if John-Mark was known personally to the high priest (perhaps, as I've suggested, even a relative in some degree), he might equally have known Nicodemus, a member of the Sanhedrin, the Jewish High Council at Jerusalem. If John-Mark did know Nicodemus, it could explain why he is the only evangelist who records that Nicodemus helped Joseph of Arimathea bury Jesus. It might also explain why we find in the Fourth Gospel several tidbits of "inside" information about discussions that went on in the Sanhedrin (John 11:47-53; 18:14). Though John himself would not likely have been present, Nicodemus might have shared those details with John later.

There is another possible connection between Jesus and John-Mark which, though admittedly speculative, could explain Jesus' special fondness for his Beloved Disciple. Luke's gospel tells us that Mary, the mother of Jesus, was a relative (in some degree) of Elizabeth, the mother of John the Baptist. Levites customarily married within their tribe to preserve the Aaronic bloodline and the integrity of the priestly office. So Elizabeth, like her husband Zechariah, were both likely descendants of the Levitical tribe (the tribe of Moses and the Aaron). Zechariah was a priest serving in the Temple at the time John the Baptist was conceived. An apocryphal but ancient tradition tells us that Mary was born in Nazareth but raised in Jerusalem, where as a girl she served in the Temple before her betrothal to Joseph, an older widower.[11] As previously mentioned, John-Mark was a cousin of Barnabas (Colossians 4:10), who was also of the tribe of Levi, so John-Mark may conceivably have been of the priestly tribe himself. These details could, if correct, explain how these various "extended" family members might have known each other (see Appendix B).

The same apocryphal tradition about Mary tells us that although her father Joaquin was from Nazareth, her mother Anna (or Anne) was from Bethlehem, and was of the family of David (Judah). Might that be how Mary knew Joseph, who was himself from Bethlehem? This could account for the close relationship recorded by Luke between Mary and her relative Elizabeth who lived near Jerusalem in a small town "in the hill country of Judea" (Luke 1:39). It would also square with the clear implication of the Matthean infancy narrative that Joseph and Mary continued to live in Bethlehem for an extended period of time after the birth of Jesus (Matthew 2:1-6, 2:16-48), fled to Egypt, and only later moved to Galilee to flee possible trouble from Herod the Great's son, Archelaus (Matthew 2:11, 2:22).

Lastly, as noted above, the sister of Jesus' mother was present at the Crucifixion. Had she come from Galilee with the other disciples, or was she herself a resident of Judea? The latter is certainly possible. Depending on the reading of that verse, if there were only three women named Mary at the cross, not four, that is, if the "sister" of Jesus' mother is read as Mary the wife of

Clopas, it becomes nearly certain this Mary was a resident of Judea.[12]

While such connections are speculative, they show the possibility that the family of Jesus and Mary was related to the priestly families in the region of Judea (including Elizabeth and Zechariah). If John-Mark and his mother Mary were part of that larger, extended Levitical family, John-Mark could conceivably have been related to Jesus at some distance (as to his human nature), and thus may have known Jesus before his public ministry began. If, in particular, John-Mark was a younger relative, it might explain the special fondness Jesus had for him.

I have steered through this realm of speculation only to demonstrate possible connections between the family of Jesus and the family of John-Mark. If that connection did, in fact, exist, it would strengthen the view that John-Mark could have been the Beloved Disciple. We might also consider this: if John-Mark was, indeed, a young relative of Jesus, and Jesus held a special fondness for him, we realize why Jesus might have offered him that seat of special honor at the Last Supper. It might also clarify another fact for which we have no certain explanation: why the home of John-Mark and his mother Mary early-on became a well-known gathering place for the young community of Christians in Jerusalem.[13]

Endnotes

1. The first of the Johannie letters does not say it is from "the Presbyter" (Elder) as 2 John and 3 John do. However, the author of 1 John does address his recipients as his "children" in much the same way that 2 John does, so many commentators take for granted that all three letters were from "John the Presbyter." Some identify the Presbyter as bar Zebedee for two reasons: first, they have already assumed bar Zebedee as John the Evangelist; second, they recognize both the linguistic and thematic similarities between the Fourth Gospel and 1 John. Then, connecting 2 John and 3 John to 1 John, they reach the conclusion that bar Zebedee wrote all four. Some will suggest that John the Evangelist was also "John

of Patmos" who wrote Revelation, while others will argue John of Patmos must have been some other John.

2. If this other John was an "apostolic" witness of the first generation of Christians, one who knew Jesus personally and witnessed all (or most) of the events recorded in his gospel, this might account for why some early writers include this John as an "apostle" even though they did not mean John bar Zebedee.

3. See Chapter Five on the likelihood that there were two distinct "Marks", one being John-Mark, the other being the Mark who Peter calls his "son." Peter's one reference to this other Mark (1 Peter 5:13) in no way links him to John-Mark, the former companion of Paul and Barnabas. Indeed, we know from Acts that Peter worked a largely different mission field. So, "Mark, my son" may very well have been a spiritual designation, just as Paul referred to Timothy as his "child" (1 Timothy 1:2); but it may also have been a simple statement of fact: we know Peter was married (Matthew 8:14), so it is conceivable that this other Mark was his actual son who traveled with him to Rome.

4. An interesting question of course is, why did Paul (in his letters) normally refer to this man as "Mark" when Paul's biographer Luke — who likely knew this "Mark" — normally refers to him as "John" in Acts? The explanation might be that Paul, writing to predominantly gentile churches, used John's secular name "Mark," while making it clear he was "of the circumcision," that is, Jewish (Colossians 4:10); whereas, in Acts, Luke may have intentionally used the coupled name, "John, also called Mark," to distinguish him from the other well-known Mark who was friend and interpreter to Peter. What is most interesting is this: Paul's letters were all written before his death around 64-65 AD, while the references to "John" in Acts were probably not written until 5-10 years later. Yet it is the *later* book, Acts, which normally identifies him as *John*, also called Mark. Why? If John-Mark was the man who came to be known as "John the Presbyter" who, like John bar Zebedee, ended his life at Ephesus, it would be sensible for Luke to call him "John," while adding his other name, "Mark," in order to not confuse him with John bar Zebedee.

5. A few translations of Acts, at 12:25, render the Greek preposition *eis* to read that Paul and Barnabas returned "to" Jerusalem, not "from" it. But since 12:12 indicates John-Mark himself was from Jerusalem, and since Acts 11:30 shows that Paul and Barnabas had gone from Antioch to Jerusalem on a relief mission, I think the reading is correct that, having completed that mission, they returned "from" Jerusalem to Antioch, taking John with them. This sequence fits better with the subsequent passage

where Paul and Barnabas next set out from Antioch on a missionary journey, taking John along (Acts 13:1-5).

6. Reinforcing the idea that John-Mark was "Mark, the cousin of Barnabas" mentioned by Paul in Colossians is the fact that when Paul and Barnabas had their dispute about John (Acts 15), Barnabas sided with John, and took John along when he sailed for Cyprus.

7. If the John-Mark theory is correct, we can understand why his account is more accurately detailed than the Synoptics. Yes, the Synoptic writers all know about Peter cutting off the slave's ear (Matthew 26:51; Mark 14:47; Luke 22:50) but they don't know the slave's name (John 18:10). The Synoptics know there were other servants in the courtyard, but not that one of those servants was a kinsman of Malchus, whose ear Peter had cut off (John 18:26). For me, this kind of detail in John supports the view that his gospel has historical integrity and is just as reliable as the Synoptics — if not more so.

8. This tradition is mentioned in a letter, "The Second Epistle of Ignatius to St. John" that, while of doubtful authenticity, may nonetheless preserve an historical fact: "His friend Ignatius, to John the holy presbyter. If you will give me leave, I desire to go up to Jerusalem, and see the faithful saints who are there, especially Mary the mother...". The implication was that Mary was still living with John the presbyter at Jerusalem. This is further confirmed when the letter makes reference to the fact that Ignatius (who was from Antioch) also wants to see "the venerable James, who is surnamed Just," the brother of Jesus, "whom they relate to be very like Christ Jesus in appearance . . . as if he were a twin-brother of the same womb." This of course would be the James who, along with Peter, was a recognized leader of the early Church at Jerusalem (Acts 15, Galatians 2). Even if this letter of Ignatius is spurious, it may embody an early tradition about what happened to Mary between the period described in Acts and her subsequent death in Ephesus. (A translation of this letter can be found in *Christian Classic Ethereal Library*, at www.CCEL.org). See also Chapter Nine, and Appendix E.

9. The Synoptics list various women at the cross. Matthew 27:55-56 places "many women" watching the crucifixion from a distance and names among them "Mary Magdalene, and Mary the mother of James and Joseph, and the mother of the sons of Zebedee." Of course, the *sons* of Zebedee themselves are *notably absent*. Mark says "There were also women looking on from afar, among whom were Mary Magdalene, and Mary the mother of James the younger and of Joses, and Salome who, when he was in Galilee, followed him, and ministered to him; and also many other women who came up with him to Jerusalem (15:40). Luke says only that

"The women who had come with him from Galilee followed, and saw the tomb, and how his body was laid; then they returned, and prepared spices and ointments" (23:55-56). He subsequently tells us that those who went to the tomb with the ointments Easter morning and returned to tell of the Resurrection included "Mary Magdalene and Joanna and Mary the mother of James and the other women with them (24:10). Except for John placing "the Beloved Disciple" at the cross, we have no evidence from any of the gospels that any other male disciple was in sight.

10. A stumbling block to this suggestion may be the fact that in Acts 12, Peter is said to go to the home of Mary which might seem odd if she was married to Clopas (Cleopas?), a man already mentioned by Luke in his gospel. Would Luke not then have said Peter went to the house of Clopas, or Clopas and Mary? (See Note 12.)

11. This apocryphal tradition in "The Gospel of the Birth of Mary," was known among the works of the 4th century Church Father and biblical scholar, Jerome. A recent translation is available in *The Lost Books of the Bible* (see Bibliography). See also Appendix B.

12. The Greek of John 19:35, which has no punctuation to separate the names and phrases, can be read either: 1) "but standing by the cross of Jesus were his mother and his mother's sister, Mary the wife of Clopas, and Mary Magdalene"; or, 2) "but standing by the cross of Jesus were his mother, and his mother's sister Mary the wife of Clopas, and Mary Magdalene." If the second reading is taken, this second Mary named, and her husband Clopas, could be the mother and father of John-Mark. (See Note 10, above.) The second reading would force us to consider that Jesus's mother and her "sister" were both named Mary; but we know that in that culture a "brother" or "sister" did not always mean an immediate sibling.

13. A further point of speculation: could the Beloved Disciple of the Johannine tradition, if a young man at the time of the Crucifixion and Resurrection, but *not* John bar Zebedee, account for the otherwise inexplicable (and seemingly out of place) detail of Mark 14:50-51? "And they all forsook him, and fled. And a young man followed him, with nothing but a linen cloth about his body; and they seized him, but he left the linen cloth and ran away naked."

Five

WE HAVE REVIEWED what little — what precious little — we know or can infer about "the Beloved Disciple" of the Fourth Gospel from the New Testament itself. Based on that evidence, as already indicated, I agree with Raymond Brown that the traditional theory holding John bar Zebedee as the author of this gospel is untenable. I have proposed instead that we consider the figure identified in Acts as "John, also called Mark" as a possible candidate for the author of the "Gospel According To John."

Before I move on to look at the early patristic evidence regarding authorship of the Johannine books, however, I want to consider one further question that may be in some readers' minds: other than John-Mark, is there any other possible candidate known to us in the New Testament period who we should also consider as a possible candidate for John the Evangelist?

The answer is no. Early in the research of this study, I pursued that exact question. The only possible candidate named John is John-Mark. Yes, there are several other "Johns" named in the New Testament, but none remotely meet the qualifications we've identified for the author of "the Jerusalem Gospel."[1]

Further, as I have suggested, the author's age is one important factor in choosing John-Mark. Ancient tradition from as early as the 2nd century identifies the Fourth Evangelist as having been a relatively young man at the time of the Crucifixion and Resurrection. The evidence we have seen regarding John-Mark suggests this was probably true in his case: the most suggestive piece of evidence being that his home is identified as his mother's home, rather than his own (Acts 12, as cited above).

Were John-Mark an older man, in the Jewish culture of the period, he would likely have been named as the head of the household. Luke would have said something like "the house of John, whose other name was Mark, the son of Mary."

Some will ask a further question: is it not possible that there was yet another John who was the Evangelist who is simply never identified by name *anywhere* in the New Testament? That is, of course, certainly possible. My reply, however, would be, is it *likely?* First, would the man responsible for what was early-on accepted in many of the churches as authoritative history of Jesus be entirely unknown to those who possessed the first copies of this gospel? Second, to argue that the author of the Fourth Gospel was otherwise unknown forces us to argue from silence, which is never a safe method. Yes, it is conceivable that John the Evangelist is never named anywhere in the New Testament. My point, however, is that John-Mark *is,* and since he is, and since he appears to be the *only* possible candidate named in scripture (except the John of Revelation; see Note 1 again), he is worth considering.

We should begin by remembering that his primary name was not Mark, but John. He was a cousin of Barnabas who, as we know, was responsible for paving the way for "Saul" to be accepted by the apostles and other Christians in Jerusalem (Acts 9:26-27). Thus, it is quite possible that Barnabas introduced his (likely younger) cousin John of the church in Jerusalem to Paul in the Holy City, since it is from Jerusalem that Barnabas and Paul took John-Mark back to the church in Antioch (Acts 12:25).

These various relationships, like those noted in the previous chapter, should serve to command our notice of John-Mark in asking if he might be John the Evangelist. I want to be clear: the John-Mark proposal is speculative, not definitive. As I have said, the sketchy evidence we have cannot possibly give us an air-tight answer. My goal from this point on is simply to see if the small amount of evidence we have within the New Testament itself will then square with additional details we find in other early Christian records: does that evidence fit reasonably together, and does it support my suggestion that John-Mark was the Evangelist?

From this perspective, then, I will move on to look at further evidence regarding authorship of the Johannine books immediately beyond the New Testament period. Is there evidence outside the New Testament of this "other John" that might support the view that he, not bar Zebedee, was the author of the Fourth Gospel, and perhaps the three letters bearing that name?

The Evidence of Papias

Surprisingly — or perhaps not — without traveling very far down the road of Christian history, we discover some intriguing evidence in the records left by Papias, Bishop of Hierapolis, who lived from about 60-130 AD. Hierapolis, mentioned in Colossians 4:13, was a city in Phrygia in Asia Minor near Colossae, and not far from the major city of Ephesus.

Little is known about Papias, but his writings tell us he was a disciple of "John the Presbyter" (or "John the Elder") in Asia Minor near the end of the 1st century. Papias was a friend of Polycarp, the Bishop of Smyrna, also in Asia Minor, who was martyred about the year 155 AD. (Like Papias, Polycarp apparently also personally knew this particular "John," a disciple of Jesus.)

Papias' writings have survived only in quotations by Irenaeus, Bishop of Lyons (who lived about 130-200 AD), and in the historian Eusebius, Bishop of Caesarea, one of the earliest historians of the Christian Church who wrote in the early 4th century. Here is what we find about Papias in Eusebius:

> Papias has left us five volumes entitled *The Sayings of the Lord Explained*. They are mentioned by Irenaeus as the only works from his pen: "To these things Papias, who had listened to John and was later a companion of Polycarp, and who lived at a very early date, bears written testimony in the fourth of his books; he composed five." That is what Irenaeus says; but Papias himself in the preface to his work makes it clear that *he was never a*

> *hearer or eyewitness of the holy apostles,* and tells us that he learnt the essentials of the Faith from their former pupils: "I shall not hesitate [Papias writes] to furnish you, along with the interpretations, with all that in days gone by I have carefully learnt from the presbyters and have carefully recalled, for I can guarantee its truth. Unlike most people, I felt at home not with those who had a great deal to say, but with those who taught the truth; not with those who appeal to commandments from other sources but with those who appeal to the commandments given by the Lord to faith and coming to us from truth itself. And whenever anyone came who had been a follower of the presbyters, I inquired into the words of the presbyters, what Andrew or Peter had said, or Philip or Thomas or James or John or Matthew, or any other disciple of the Lord, and what Ariston *and the presbyter John, disciples of the Lord, were still saying.* For I did not imagine that things out of books would help me as much as the utterances of a living and abiding voice." Here it should be observed that he twice includes the name of John. The first John he puts in the same list as Peter, James, Matthew, and the rest of the apostles, obviously with the evangelist in mind; the second, with a changed form of expression, he placed in a second group outside the number of the apostles, giving the precedence to Ariston and clearly calling John a presbyter (Eusebius, *History*, pp. 149-50; *emphasis added*).

Here, I note two things. First, by the time Eusebius wrote his history (a ten-volume work published around 324-225 AD), *he already assumes* that John bar Zebedee (in the first list along with his brother James and other members of the Twelve) was, in fact, "the evangelist." As we will see further on, he also says, at least at times, that the same John the Apostle wrote Revelation.

Second, and key to our present inquiry, we must take note of Eusebius' primary point: he provides this citation from Papias to show that *Papias* was distinguishing *two* Johns among the earliest witnesses to the gospel. The reason this detail is so significant is shown by what Eusebius says next:

He thus confirms the truth of the story *that two men in Asia had the same name*, and that there were two tombs in Ephesus, each of which is still called John's. This is highly significant, for it is likely that the second — if we cannot accept the first — saw the Revelation that bears the name of John. Papias, whom we are now discussing, owns that he learnt the words of the apostles from their former followers, but says that he listened to Aristion and *the presbyter John* with his own ears (*History*, p. 150, emphasis added).

This citation raises several very significant issues related to our study. First, we need to be careful to sort out what Eusebius says versus what Papias actually said. Second, we need to notice that in *this* instance, at least, Eusebius expresses doubt that John the Evangelist (whom he believes was bar Zebedee) also wrote Revelation. I concur with the second point, but as I will show further on, it may well be that Eusebius, like other commentators, has the two roles reversed.

Let us take each point in turn. First, what did Papias actually say, and how did Eusebius read it? Eusebius wrote: "That is what Irenaeus says [that Papias "had listened to John"]; but Papias himself, in the preface of his work to which Irenaeus is referring, makes it clear that *he was never a hearer or eyewitness of the holy apostles . . .*." Notice that the term "apostles" here is Eusebius' term, not Papias' word. For in the actual text, Papias refers to members of the Twelve as "presbyters," just as he does to the second, "the presbyter John," who, along with Aristion, were "disciples of the Lord" who Papias *personally knew*.

So, were there, in fact, two Johns? Some readers analyzing that part of the citation where Irenaeus says Papias "had listened to John" may *assume* that both Papias and Irenaeus meant John bar Zebedee. Look carefully, though, at what Eusebius adds, referring to Papias' own work. Papias gives two lists of names: the first group, including one John, are all members of the Twelve; *they are therefore men Papias had never met, or heard, personally*. Then, separately, Papias refers to two more "disciples of the Lord," Aristion, and "the presbyter John," both of whom Papias *had* personally known. That is the *key* distinction in understanding what Papias meant. Papias said he learned about the teaching of the first group of "presbyters" (the Twelve) from "a follower of the presbyters" (the Twelve). In contrast, what Papias learned from Aristion and "the presbyter John" he heard *directly from them*. These last two men Papias knew personally. This means the second "presbyter John" could not have been bar Zebedee (named in the first list). This also tells us that the "John" Papias listened to (according to Irenaeus) was not John bar Zebedee, a member of the Twelve, but the other John. (We will need to remember this when we come to consider Irenaeus later.)

It is significant that *none* of the Twelve, including John bar Zebedee, were available to Papias directly. Either they were then dead, or they lived far enough from Hierapolis that he never saw nor met them.[2] The other John, however, "the presbyter John" listed *after* Aristion, Papias identifies as "disciples of the Lord": that is, both of these men, like the Twelve, had known Jesus personally.

We should next notice that when Papias refers to this other John, he lists him alongside a lesser-known disciple, Aristion. This would seem odd if Papias had been referring to bar Zebedee.

Part of the difficulty in analyzing this passage, as I have already highlighted, is that by the time Eusebius wrote in the 4th century — as we know from other parts of his history — the "common wisdom" that John bar Zebedee was John the Evangelist was already accepted by some. Thus, in this passage we have just looked at, Eusebius puts words into the mouth of Papias: "The first John he puts in the same list as Peter, James, Matthew, and the rest of the apostles [Eusebius' word], *obviously with the Evangelist in mind*." On careful analysis, however, *nothing* in the actual words of Papias' lead to that conclusion.

This brings us to our second point, Eusebius' comment about Revelation. Eusebius begins by reading a 4th century assumption backward into the early 2nd century writings of Papias: that bar Zebedee was John the Evangelist. While elsewhere in his *History* Eusebius suggests that the same John may in fact have written Revelation also, here he expressed doubt, suggesting that perhaps this other John, the man personally known by Papias, may have written Revelation. That doubt probably came about because by the time of Eusebius, other writers had expressed doubt that one man had authored both books.

Regardless of Eusebius' ambivalence here, we must be clear: *Papias himself* does not say that John bar Zebedee was the Fourth Evangelist; and that being the case, we cannot assume *which* John Papias believed may have authored Revelation.[3]

As I have suggested, it may be because of his prior assumption as to which John was the Evangelist that Eusebius had the roles of these two Johns reversed. I have shown why I don't believe bar Zebedee wrote the Fourth Gospel. Further on, however, I will look at evidence that suggests John bar Zebedee could, in fact, have authored Revelation. If we look carefully at the citations of Papias alone, without Eusebius' later interpretations, either might be true. As we go forward, I will present further evidence that can help clarify the roles of John bar Zebedee and the "other" John.

What Papias Actually Tells Us

Despite the possible confusion I have highlighted, this much *is* clear from the record of Papias. The verb tense of Papias' phrase, "and what Aristion and the presbyter John, disciples of the Lord, *were still* saying" suggests that Papias heard the teaching of this other John, and Aristion, from their own lips. Thus, as Eusebius surmised, both men were still alive in Papias' lifetime.

The real significance of the evidence in Papias relative to my John-Mark proposal is that Papias, born around 60 AD, was a second-generation Christian: he was alive when some books of the New Testament were still being written; and his own writings imply that two well-known disciples of Jesus named John were known in Asia Minor toward the end of the 1st century: "He [Papias] thus confirms the truth of the story that two men in Asia had the same name, and that there were two tombs in Ephesus, each of which is still called John's." Since Papias died around 130 AD, his writings come from the late 1st or early 2nd century. Based on their antiquity, I suggest we should put greater stock in the reliability of Papias' personal knowledge — that there were indeed two Johns, both authoritative "presbyters" of the Lord — rather than in 3rd and 4th century traditions, or interpretations, that later confused them as the same man.[4]

We should also notice that when Eusebius refers to the two tombs, "each of which is *still called* John's" (emphasis added), he is telling that two identifiable tombs at Ephesus were still known in his own day, that is, in the 4th century. While the middle east is notoriously full of multiple supposed tombs of the same biblical person, in this case — based on what we have from Papias and Eusebius — there seems to be reasonable grounds for accepting that in the case of the two Johns there may indeed have been two tombs.

When Did The Confusion Begin?

I want to return briefly to an earlier question about the popular tradition. If both John bar Zebedee and a second man known as "the Presbyter John" ended their lives in or near Ephesus toward the end of the 1st century, how did the common wisdom develop which supposed that bar Zebedee was the Fourth Evangelist rather than the other — an assumption already entertained by Eusebius in the 4th century?

We see from Eusebius that there was already debate about whether John the Evangelist also authored Revelation, or whether a different John wrote it. (Revelation, of course, was the only Johannie book that actually contained, internally, the name of its author.) Yet Eusebius apparently had no doubt that John bar Zebedee was the Evangelist. Despite little factual underpinning, this view would certainly be appealing by Eusebius' time, when a large number of heresies — some feeding off the Fourth Gospel — had spread through parts of the Church. The view, which was gaining credence, that John bar Zebedee was the Evangelist would mean this gospel came from the hand of someone who knew a lot about Jesus personally.

Based solely on what Papias wrote, however, it is equally possible this popular view was wrong, and that it was the other John who was the Evangelist, the "Presbyter John" whom Papias knew personally as one of the "disciples of the Lord." His description clearly means that this second John, like the Twelve, was an actual disciple of Jesus. If so, he certainly had the credentials to author a gospel. For Eusebius also records this further information from Papias:

> Papias reproduces other stories communicated to him by word of mouth, together with some otherwise unknown parables and teachings of the Saviour, and other things of a more allegorical nature . . . In his own book Papias gives us accounts of the Lord's sayings obtained from Aristion or learnt direct from the presbyter John (*Eusebius*, p. 151-2).

"By word of mouth": in other words, Papias was taught directly by the "Presbyter John" more of "the Lord's sayings," teaching which this other John heard from Jesus himself. If so, this second John had a level of teaching authority equal to the Twelve, an authority that qualified him to write a gospel, and also meets our qualifications for the Beloved Disciple.

Indeed, if John the Evangelist was not one of "the Twelve", this might help explain why this gospel was sometimes challenged as too different from the Synoptics. Had the Fourth Gospel been, without debate, from the hand (or mouth) of John bar Zebedee, it would most certainly have been accepted without challenge. By contrast, if it was from the hand of this other "John the Presbyter," a less-well-known disciple, we can understand how its authority might have been, initially at least, challenged.

The Two Johns At Ephesus

How might two Johns, both apostolic figures and personal friends of Jesus, have ended up in Ephesus toward the end of the 1st century?

If, as seems likely, the first John in Papias' list was John bar Zebedee (grouped with others of the Twelve), it means that John left Judea at some point — perhaps after the murder of his brother James (Acts 12:1-2) — and eventually ended up in Ephesus, where he later died. (As I will suggest in Chapter Six, however, he may well have come to Ephesus *via* prison on Patmos.) Papias, who lived in that region near Ephesus, might have known of this fact, even if, as a young man, he had never met bar Zebedee. The passage above from Papias suggests that by the time Papias was writing (between 90-120 AD?) John bar Zebedee was dead, while the other Presbyter John was still living. If so, that would push the date at which Papias is writing closer to the 90's date, which would fit if this second John was John-Mark, who was a younger man than bar Zebedee during the ministry of Jesus.

If this was the case, what was the connection of this other John to the region around Ephesus, a connection that would draw him to eventually settle there? Further, where might Papias have had an opportunity to hear the Presbyter John teach in person?

There are several possibilities. First, Papias became Bishop of Hierapolis, a town in Asia Minor about six miles northeast of Laodicea and northwest of Colossae, and about 80 miles west of Ephesus. Hierapolis was part of St. Paul's missionary field, as we learn from his letter to Colossae:

> Aristarchus my fellow prisoner greets you, and Mark the cousin of Barnabas (concerning whom you have received instructions — if he comes to you, receive him), and Jesus who is called Justus. These are the only men of the circumcision among my fellow workers for the kingdom of God, and they have been a comfort to me. Epaphras, who is one of yourselves, a servant of Christ Jesus, greets you, always remembering you earnestly in

his prayers, that you may stand mature and fully assured in all the will of God. For I bear him witness that he has worked hard for you and for those in Laodicea and in Hierapolis (Colossians 4:10-13).

The Mark to whom Paul refers here, as I have argued, is John-Mark, identified as the cousin of Barnabas. We recall that when Paul and Barnabas split up (Acts 15), it was over a dispute about John-Mark's commitment to their mission work. Barnabas defended John-Mark (understandable, if they were cousins) and took him to do missionary work in Cyprus, off the south coast of Asia Minor. Though John-Mark had been at odds with Paul earlier, by the time Paul writes Colossians he and John-Mark are once again working together, and Paul counts John as a fellow-worker in the Gospel who has been a support and comfort.

So, from these facts alone, we can see how the other John, John-Mark, who might visit the Colossian church at Paul's urging, could also have been known to the churches in the region of Ephesus, and nearby Laodicea and Hierapolis, even if John-Mark had not lived in the area before. If John-Mark was to visit Colossae, that could have been the occasion when Papias met him, and heard him teach.

In any case, we can understand why Papias, to avoid confusion with the older John who was, or had been, in Ephesus by this time, might refer to John-Mark as "the Presbyter John" to distinguish him from bar Zebedee, which is exactly what we find in the citation from Eusebius.

Distinguishing Mark The Evangelist

We must not fail to notice another significant detail in this reference to John-Mark in Colossians. Paul tells us that Aristarchus, Mark the cousin of Barnabas (John-Mark), and Jesus called Justus were all "men of the circumcision." That is, they were Jews. However, as C. M. Tuckett has correctly pointed out, it is very unlikely that the author of the Gospel of Mark was a Jew. The author of Mark is sometimes confused about — or perhaps ignorant of — Palestinian geography (see Mark 5:1, 7:31), as well as Jewish customs and laws (Mark 7:3-4, 10:11-12).[5] John-Mark, on the other hand, a Jew raised in Jerusalem, would *not* have been ignorant of Palestinian geography or Jewish custom and law (and, as we know, John the Evangelist certainly was *not*).

In addition to this, as we will see later in this chapter, Papias also recorded that Mark the Evangelist was an "interpreter" for Peter. That would suggest that this other Mark was most likely a *gentile* convert who became a follower of Peter at Rome, and, as a gentile, was familiar with the Latin used in the capital of the empire. Now admittedly, as already noted, if John-Mark is John the Evangelist, he was certainly trained and proficient in Greek, which was still in common use in the eastern part of the empire, and is the single language of the New Testament. It is harder to imagine how he, a Jew raised in Jerusalem, would have been a proficient interpreter in Rome itself, where Latin had been in use for over six centuries.

If, as I propose, the "Mark" Paul names in Colossians, Philemon and 2 Timothy is John-Mark, but *not* Mark the Evangelist, the dilemma is quickly resolved, and the pieces, again, fit.

This other Mark, the Second Evangelist, was the man Peter called his "son" (1 Peter 5:13). In other words, both of these men *were* evangelists: Mark, a gentile and Peter's interpreter, was the author of Mark; and John-Mark, a Jew, the Paul and Barnabas' coworker, was the author of John.

Can we accept this second "Mark" view with safety? Is there other evidence that would distinguish John-Mark from Mark the Evangelist? There is.

We have seen that Papias called the Second Evangelist a "follower of Peter." Then, we find this interesting account: Eusebius (Book 2 of his *History*), records details about a certain well-known heretic named Simon Magus who went to Rome preaching his false version of the Christian gospel. Shortly after, according to this particular tradition, the apostle Peter followed Simon to combat his false teaching:

> Close on his [Simon's] heals, in the same reign of Claudius [41-54 AD], the all-gracious and kindly providence of the universe brought to Rome to deal with this terrible threat to the world, the strong and great apostle . . . Peter himself . . . So brightly shone the light of true religion on the minds of Peter's hearers that, not satisfied with a single hearing or with the oral teaching of the divine message, they resorted to appeals of every kind to induce Mark (whose gospel we have), as he was a follower of Peter, to leave them in writing a summary of the instructions they had received by word of mouth . . . and thus became responsible for the writing of what is known as the Gospel according to Mark . . . Clement quotes the story in *Outlines* Book VI, and his statement is confirmed by Bishop Papias of Hierapolis, who also points out that Mark is mentioned by Peter in his first epistle, which he is said to have composed in Rome itself, as he himself indicates when he speaks of the city figuratively as Babylon:
> The church in Babylon, chosen like yourselves, sends you greeting, and so does my son Mark. (*History,* pp. 88-89).

Eusebius immediately continues in his next chapter with this:

> Mark is said to have been the first man to set out for Egypt and preach there the gospel which he had himself written down, and the first to establish churches in Alexandria itself" (*History*, p. 89).

In other words, this Mark, Peter's "follower" and "interpreter" at Rome, travelled to Egypt where he planted the church, carrying the gospel he had written (the Second) based on Peter's teaching. We notice that Eusebius places the arrival of Peter in Rome sometime around 50 AD. We do not know from Eusebius the year Mark traveled to Egypt, but we can assume it was sometime after 50-55 AD. We do know that he established the church there by about that time, because we learn a very specific date of when Mark turned the Alexandrian church over to the care of the man who would be its next bishop:

> In the eighth year of Nero's reign [62 AD], Annianus was the first after Mark the evangelist to take charge of the see of Alexandria (*History,* p. 103)

Assuming this Mark had led the new church in Egypt for any period of time at all, this means he must have arrived in Alexandria at least in the mid-to-late 50s AD.

We find further confirmation of this in Jerome in his Introduction to the Gospel of Matthew. Jerome concurs with Eusebius' record and confirms that Mark the Evangelist was the first bishop of Alexandria:

> The second [gospel] is Mark, the amanuensis of the Apostle Peter, and first bishop of the Church of Alexandria. He did not himself see our Lord and Saviour, but he related the matter of his Master's preaching with more regard to minute detail than to historical sequence (Schaff, *The Works of Jerome,* p. 1068).

We must pay close attention to several things in what Jerome records. First, he calls the Mark the Evangelist "the amanuensis" (secretary, or scribe) of St. Peter. Again, is this not somewhat odd if Jerome knew he was referring to John-Mark, the man who has such a noted role in Acts? Jerome most certainly knew that John-Mark was one of the earliest members of the Jerusalem church, whose home, with his mother, was a gathering place for the first Christians during their earliest persecution, yet here he does not make the identification of Peter's scribe as John-Mark. Why?

Second, and more importantly, we must not miss this: Jerome says that Mark the Evangelist "did not himself see our Lord and Saviour, but he related the matter of his Master's [Peter] preaching." Now, Jerome may simply be repeating this fact from Papias. We cannot be certain. But the fact remains: if

Mark the Evangelist were indeed John-Mark, who must have seen Jesus at some point — if not before the Crucifixion, certainly after the Resurrection — how do we account for Jerome's statement here? Certainly Jerome, a supreme biblical scholar, would have assumed that John-Mark had seen the Lord after the Resurrection, if not before. Yet Jerome makes no connection here to John-Mark. Quite the opposite: he assures us that Mark *the Evangelist* never saw Jesus personally.

Then, we find in Eusebius this further passage that shines light on the questions about the Second Evangelist like a laser:

> In his own book Papias gives us accounts of the Lord's sayings obtained from Aristion or learnt direct from the presbyter John . . . I must now follow up the statements already quoted from him with a piece of information which he [Papias] sets out regarding Mark, the writer of the gospel: "This, too, the presbyter [John] used to say. "Mark, who had been Peter's interpreter, wrote down carefully, but not in order, all that he remembered of the Lord's sayings and doings. For he had not heard the Lord or been one of his followers, but later, as I said, one of Peter's. Peter used to adapt his teachings to the occasion, without making a systematic arrangement of the Lord's sayings, so that Mark was quite justified in writing down some things just as he [Mark, or Peter?] remembered them. For he had one purpose only — to leave out nothing that he had heard, and to make no misstatement about it." Such is Papias' account of Mark (*History,* p. 152).

Now, since Eusebius knew the tradition that there were two Johns at Ephesus, even though he tends toward the-then common assumption that John bar Zebedee was the Fourth Evangelist, the "Presbyter John" whom Papias refers to in the passage above was clearly the "other" John. If we approach the passage just cited with the assumption that "the Presbyter" John was (as I believe) *John-Mark,* suddenly the lights come on and the picture looks very different: for, if so, it was *John-Mark* who told Papias about Mark the Evangelist writing the Second Gospel.

Is that possible? If Papias learned the origin of the Second Gospel from John-Mark, how and where did John-Mark learn those details? Quite simply: as I will explain below, there is evidence John-Mark was in Rome during Paul's imprisonment there; if so, John-Mark would most likely have spent time with Peter also. We recall from Acts that John-Mark was a friend of both men. Thus, John-Mark could have learned from Peter himself how his helper and "interpreter" — the other Mark — had written the Second Gospel. When John-Mark later returned to the region of Ephesus, mostly probably after the deaths of Paul and Peter, Papias could have learned this history from John-Mark, the Presbyter John. Indeed, this is the most likely period, late in the 1st century, when Papias learned many things directly by Aristion and John "the Presbyter."

If John-Mark was the "the Presbyter" Papias knew and learned from, including Papias' account of the creation of the Second Gospel, then clearly John-Mark and Mark the Evangelist were two different men.

Recall again what Jerome later affirmed: the Presbyter John told Papias that Mark the Evangelist, *"had not heard the Lord or been one of his followers,"* whereas we know, from the earlier citations of Papias, that "the Presbyter John" *was* a "disciple of the Lord."

Looking objectively at this body of evidence in Papias and Eusebius, my proposal that John-Mark might have authored the Fourth Gospel is consistent with the facts; and the common view that John-Mark authored the Second Gospel is much less probable.

Timing

A further point must be mentioned here that relates to whether or not John-Mark and the Mark Peter called his "son," were one man, or two. It has to do with timeframes and dates.

To review: in the passages already cited (above), Eusebius tells us the Peter's "son" Mark, armed with the gospel he had written (almost certainly at Rome), was the first to evangelize

Egypt (*History,* p 89). This is confirmed by other early writers including Epiphanius, Jerome, Nicephorus, and the document Acta Barnabae.[6] Eusebius reports that this same Mark later appointed Annianus as first bishop of Alexandria to succeed himself (Mark) "in the eighth year of Nero's reign," that is, 62 A.D. (*History,* p. 103). While Eusebius does not provide the year that Mark first *arrived* in Egypt, we can safely assume that it must have been, at the very least, several years prior to the time he turned the work over to his disciple Annianus. Thus, *this* Mark must have arrived in Egypt carrying the Second Gospel by about 60 AD or, more likely, some years prior.[7]

Here, then, is the puzzle: this means that *Mark the Evangelist* (Peter's "son") was already in Egypt some few years *before* St. Paul mentions John-Mark being still alongside him, most likely in Rome, during his imprisonment there. Paul mentions John-Mark not only in Colossians, but likewise in Paul's letter to Philemon, who lived at Colossae. Both letters were almost certainly written at the same time, *around 62-63 AD,* and sent to Colossae together. Further, in Colossians Paul says that John-Mark may travel to (or through?) Colossae, that the church there has received instructions about him, and that they are to welcome him.[8]

Now, without marshaling all the relevant arguments and evidence here, which is far beyond my scope (but see endnote 9), I fall in with those who believe the preponderance of evidence indicates that Colossians and several other of the "prison letters" were, in fact, written from Rome after Paul arrived there as described in Acts 28. (Other letters likely written from Rome include Ephesians, the Pastorals, and perhaps Philippians).[9] Colossians would therefore have been written sometime *after* Paul's arrival at Rome about 61-62 AD.

There lies the problem for those who argue John-Mark was the Second Evangelist: by that time, Peter's "son" Mark had already spent some years planting the gospel in Egypt and building up the church there. Since Mark appointed Annianus as his replacement in 62 AD, and assuming even a conservative leave-date from Rome (allowing time to for the journey to Egypt), that Mark (the Second Evangelist) must have left Rome around 55-58 AD. Yet *John-Mark* was in Rome, with Paul, some years after that.

One final, important detail must be noted. We have the unassailed tradition within the Coptic Church that Mark the Evangelist died in Alexandria, and was originally buried there. Relics of St. Mark (including, reportedly, his head) are venerated in the St. Mark's Coptic Cathedral in Cairo to this day. Mark's body (or most of it) was moved, through a somewhat scandalous arrangement, to Venice in about 828 AD, where it now resides in St. Mark's Basilica.

When we assemble all these facts into a whole, the supposition that John-Mark was Mark the Evangelist becomes very weak. The popular tradition that John-Mark and Peter's "son" Mark were the same man is thin indeed, and is hard to maintain when closely scrutinized. We know Mark the Evangelist was buried in Egypt. By contract, based on the several late references to John-Mark in Rome, including 2 Timothy 4:11, it is probable that John-Mark remained in Europe and Asia Minor to the end of his life. We also have the report, still current in Eusebius's own day, that there were two tombs in Ephesus of Christian leaders named John.

Moreover, we have no evidence indicating that one "Mark" — as the popular tradition would require us to believe — traveled back and forth between Rome, Alexandria, Rome, Colossae, and other places unknown, yet died in Alexandria apparently not long after he appointed his replacement, Annianus, in 62 AD.

So, when we try to overlay Mark, Peter's "son," and John-Mark, we stumble over several hurdles. If John-Mark, however, was John the Beloved Disciple, the Fourth Evangelist, who died not in Egypt in the 60s AD but at Ephesus near the year 100 AD, all our evidence once again fits together.

Contrary Evidence

There is a point of contrary evidence I will point out about the origin of the gospels. In his later Book V, Eusebius includes a citation from Irenaeus (late 2nd century) which suggests that the Second Gospel was not written until after Peter's death. Eusebius cites Irenaeus thus:

> Matthew published a written gospel for the Hebrews in their own tongue, while Peter and Paul were preaching the gospel in Rome and founding the church there. *After their passing,* Mark, also, the disciple and interpreter of Peter, transmitted to us in writing the things preached by Peter. Luke, the follower of Paul, set down in a book the gospel preached by him. Lastly, John, the disciple of the Lord, who had leant back on His breast, once more set forth the gospel, while residing at Ephesus in Asia (*History*, pp. 210-11, *emphasis added;* see Also *Early Christian Fathers, Vol. 1*, p. 370).

There are several interesting points here that I will deal with in more detail further on, including that the Gospel of Matthew was first written in Hebrew (or possibly Aramaic). Here, though, I want to focus on these points:

1. Irenaeus believed Matthew was the first of the gospels written. That, in itself, would provoke wide debate today, since for many decades the broad scholarly consensus has been that Mark was the first of the four, and that both Matthew (at least in its present form) and Luke used Mark as one of their written sources.

2. "After their passing" clearly means that Irenaeus believed the Second Gospel was not written while Peter was still alive — as we are assured by Eusebius in his Book 2 that it was. (Students of Eusebius will know that such periodic contradictions are not uncommon in his *History*. We know he was working with not only a large volume of written sources but had received oral traditions as well, so he will sometimes

include a detail knowing full-well that it contradicts some other evidence he had.) If Irenaeus himself believed *John-Mark* was the Second Evangelist, but knew he was still alive after the death of Peter and Paul (which is certainly correct), Irenaeus would have had to assume that Mark's gospel came after the death of the two Apostles.

3. Irenaeus may not have known of the tradition, later reported by Eusebius, that Mark wrote the Second Gospel while Peter was still preaching in Rome, and carried it to Egypt while Peter was still alive. Since Irenaeus suggests that Mark was not written until after Peter's death, we have a clear conflict. A possible solution would be that both accounts hold some truth: that an early, original version of Mark is what this Mark carried to Egypt in the late 50s, but that there existed an expanded or later edition known in Rome from after Peter's death.[10]

4. Notice that Irenaeus calls Mark the "disciple and interpreter" of Peter. It is quite like what Papias had said. Irenaeus' statement may, indeed, be based on his reading of Papias. It is significant for this reason: knowing Acts and Paul's epistles, we would expect that someone writing in the time of Irenaeus would refer to John-Mark as a "disciple" or "co-worker" of Paul," not a "disciple" or "interpreter" of Peter. This, again, points to some Mark who was not John-Mark.

5. We should also note that a few words later Irenaeus calls John the Evangelist "the disciple of the Lord" who wrote his gospel from Ephesus. Since, as we have seen, there were likely two Christian leaders named John who lived in Ephesus in that time period, we could argue for either as the man to whom Irenaeus refers in this passage. As I will show in a later chapter, however, this particular name-designation for John the Evangelist is *consistent* in Irenaeus, and does not seem accidental.

Even when we accept conflicting records about *when* the Second Gospel was written, we have, nevertheless, a fairly strong case that there was not one Mark, but two. So, although it is still the common wisdom (with some commentators today) that John-Mark was Mark the Evangelist, I view this as very unlikely.[11]

Sorting Out The Few Facts

The partial records of Papias preserved by Eusebius suggest that in addition to the apostle John bar Zebedee, there was a second well-known John whom Papias referred to by the interesting title "the Presbyter," (the "elder"). Papias never met bar Zebedee, but had known this second John personally.

The further tradition of the two tombs at Ephesus reinforces the "two-John" theory. The tombs tradition has been challenged, written off by some as mere confusion on the part of Eusebius. But the two-tombs "tradition" has this weight behind it: although it dated from the late 1st or early 2nd century, the tradition was still "well-known" when Eusebius wrote in the early 4th century.

In addition, the fact that this figure Papias knew as "the Presbyter John" was an eyewitness "disciple of the Lord" is extremely important. If this second John was "the disciple whom Jesus loved" (notice again how Irenaeus refers to John the Evangelist) and was, in fact, author of the Fourth Gospel, it would instantly explain why his word and teaching would have been so valuable and cherished, on a level of authority equal with the Twelve. If this other John was, as I suggest, the well-known John "also called Mark" of the early Jerusalem church, it would further explain why his witness would have been as valuable as that of the Twelve.

I have spent this considerable space considering the identity of Mark the Evangelist in order to show that he was someone other than John-Mark, because that then frees us to consider John-Mark as our candidate for the Fourth Evangelist. From that perspective, and from this juncture forward, my working proposition will be:

1. Mark, Peter's "son" (1 Peter 5) was not John-Mark, but was possibly a gentile convert who became a disciple of Peter in Rome, and acted as his interpreter there, where Latin, not Greek, was the more common vernacular. Where and when they first met, we do not know. Eusebius places Peter's arrival at Rome — at least his first arrival — around 50-54 AD. If his "son" Mark worked with him in that time period, it fits that this Mark could have learned the gospel from Peter, written the Second Gospel, and left for Egypt about 55-58 AD.[12]

2. John-Mark of Jerusalem arrived in Rome sometime around 62-63 AD, after the other Mark had left. John-Mark must have reached Rome after Paul, since he is not mentioned by Luke as being a companion during the journey from Jerusalem to Rome. Later, as Paul referenced, John-Mark probably traveled back to the region of Ephesus and Colossae, where he became known as "the Presbyter John" to distinguish him from John bar Zebedee who was also well-known in that region.

3. During this time, John-Mark had contact with the church in Colossae, and possibly Hierapolis where Papias was then (or later) bishop. Papias called John-Mark "the Presbyter John" to distinguish him from John bar Zebedee.

4. It was thus John "also called Mark" whom Papias referred to as "John, the disciple of the Lord" who authored the Fourth Gospel that bears his name, which he wrote from Ephesus. (See Chapter Six regarding Irenaeus' use of this phrase.)

Based on these suppositions, let us move on to examine the evidence of other early Christian records that may support the John-Mark theory.

Endnotes

1. The only other men named John identified in the New Testament are:
   a. John the Baptist: obviously ruled out.
   b. John bar Zebedee, whom we have ruled out on scriptural evidence.
   c. John, the father of Simon Peter (John 1:42; 21:15-17): ruled out by age. Peter, as an accepted "elder" and teacher would have been around 30, or older. That would preclude Peter's father being able to survive into the 90's AD, as the record will show.
   d. John, frequent companion of Peter in the early chapters of Acts: this is most likely John bar Zebedee, though Luke never explicitly says so. The Synoptics, in referring to "the three" usually list them "Peter, James, and John." In Acts 1:13, however, Luke lists the Eleven as "Peter, John, James . . ." From this association, the subsequent references in early Acts to "Peter and John" (Acts 3:1 ff; 4:1 ff; 8:14 ff; and 12:2) John bar Zebedee is most likely meant.
   e. John, of the Sanhedrin (Acts 4:5-6): We know only that he was one of the Council who interrogated Peter and John. It is impossible to identify him further.
   f. John (Galatians 2:9): "James, Peter, and John . . .": one of the "pillars" of The Jerusalem church. Again, as in early Acts, most likely John bar Zebedee.
   g. John (Revelation 1 & 22): The author of Revelation, whose identity is also disputed. His identity, versus the Fourth Evangelist, will be discussed in due course.
2. Or, in the case of John bar Zebedee, if he was (as we will discuss later) the author of Revelation, he was still confined on Patmos.
3. As to John bar Zebedee being the Evangelist, not only does Papias never say this, his words actually argue against it. From the beginning of the passage, it seems clear that Papias is claiming *not* to have learned directly from the first group of "presbyters," the Twelve. Thus, Papias never heard John bar Zebedee teach.
4. Whether Papias was speaking of two Johns or just one continues to be debated. Commentator Bruce Vawter, for example, writes: "Whether there was ever a John the Presbyter distinct from the Apostle [bar Zebedee] and resident at Ephesus at the same time is still the subject of scholarly debate" (Jerome Biblical Commentary, 1968 edition, p. 415). Of course, scholars today also debate whether or not Jesus rose from the dead, and whether or not he ever lived. In any case, apart from Eusebius' confusion about Papias' words, or what we might *like* those words to mean, we have to

stand on what Papias actually said: he was discussing those he considered authoritative teachers who relied not on books (that, is, second hand information), but on the *eyewitness testimony* of those who had actually heard Jesus. He learned some things from "followers" of the Twelve, but what he learned from "John the Presbyter" he apparently learned directly.

5. C. M. Tuckett, Introduction to the Gospel of Mark, *Oxford Bible Commentary*, p. 886 (see Bibliography).

6. Schaff, *Eusebius,* p. 203, footnote 394: "That Mark labored in Egypt is stated also by Epiphanius (Hær. LI. 6), by Jerome (de vir. ill. 8), by Nicephorus (H. E. II. 43), and by the Acta Barnabæ, p. 26 (Tischendorf's Acta Apost. Apocr. p. 74), which were written probably in the third century."

7. There is a tradition among the Coptic Christians that Mark the Evangelist arrived in Egypt as early as 49-50 AD, and served as its leader for 19 years until he appointed Annianus to replace him.

8. We know nothing further about this planned travel by John-Mark in terms of the date, whether he went directly from Rome to Colossae, or traveled anywhere else. Mark is mentioned in a late letter, 2 Timothy, but was not with Paul at that moment.

9. Scholars differ on the dates, and origins, of Paul's letters, and even which he wrote. But there seems to be a present consensus that at least Colossians, Philemon, and Ephesians were written from Rome during his time of imprisonment there, roughly between 62-66 AD. The Pastorals, if accepted as genuinely from Paul (which I personally accept) would also have been written from Rome at a somewhat later date, closer to his martyrdom. Some believe Philiipains may also date from Rome around the same time.

Part of the dilemma in dating the letters from Rome is that some commentators postulate *two different periods* of imprisonment for Paul there: the first from his arrival in Acts, around 60-62 AD and ending at some undocumented year; and a second period of around 64-65 AD, just prior to his death around 66-67 AD. These two separate periods of imprisonment (or detention?), while referred to by some early commentators, are based on no solid evidence, but are *inferred* principally on Paul's comments in Romans (15:24, 15:28) that he hoped one day to travel to Spain to carry the gospel to the western reaches of the empire.

The further complication is that we are also unsure where and when the Letter *to* the Romans was written. A possibility is that he wrote from Corinth around 57 AD (based on the reference to his host, Gaius (Romans 16:23), who may have been the Gaius who lived in Corinth (1 Corinthians 1:14). In Romans, Paul expressed his hope to visit Rome directly, then travel on to Spain; and it seems his letter to Rome was in part intended to build support in the church there that would eventually help him on his way west.

Of course, that did not happen. His subsequent return to Jerusalem, his arrest there, his various trials, and his lengthy trip to Rome (Acts 21-28) derailed his original plan. When he arrived at Rome, Luke tells us Paul was under "home detention" for at least two years (Acts 28:30-31). Beyond that, however, we have no reliable evidence that Paul ever left Rome or traveled further. Some early commentators assert he did later travel to Spain, but this, again, may have been speculation based on his stated plans in Romans.

Obviously, Acts ends around the end of that first two years in Rome, where Luke tells us Paul was able to preach and have visitors. We have no record of why Luke did not continue, or conclude, Acts after Paul's death. A reasonable and simple assumption why Luke could not continue might be this. Paul was executed by Nero (66-67). Eusebius tells us that Peter was executed in the same time frame, and both apostles were both buried at Rome, although we do not know the precise date of either death (*History*, Book 2, Ch.25, pp 104-05). Since Nero falsely accused the Christians of starting the great fire that devasted 70 percent of the capital (July, 64 AD), it is possible that Peter and Paul were executed as punishment, along with many other Christians. The reason Acts has no real "end" could simply be that Luke was one of those.

10. Philiip Schaff in his commentary on Eusebius argues against Eusebius' record and believes Peter did not arrive in Rome "until late in the reign of Nero," that is, until shortly before his death. As his principle evidence, Schaff points out that Peter was in Jerusalem at the time of James bar Zebedee's murder in about 44 AD; that he was again known to be there for the Council of Acts 15, about 51 AD; and that he traveled "a little later" to Antioch. I would only point out that these dates certainly do not preclude Peter from having traveled to Rome to combat Simon Magus' heresies sometime in the early-to-mid 50s, which would still fit with the timeframe Eusebius reports, and with my supposition that Peter's gentile "interpreter" at Rome could have written the Second Gospel around that same time. Indeed, if heresy had already infected the Church at Rome, we can understand the urgency and need for Mark's gospel, to set down and preserve Peter's orthodox teaching.

Schaff further argues that "at some time during his life he [Peter] labored in various provinces in Asia Minor, as we learn from his first epistle . . ." I would point out that nothing in 1 Peter actually indicates that Peter had "labored" among the "elect exiles of the Dispersion" to whom this letter was addressed. It is conceivable that Peter may have passed through or near a number of the areas named in the letter on his journey to Rome in the early 50s, but that, again, would not preclude his arrival there within the timeframe reported by Eusebius. See: Schaff, Eusebius, Footnote 385, CCEL edition, p. 199.

11. Despite the consistent witness in several early fathers that the Mark who wrote the Second Gospel was a disciple of Peter, some modern critical scholars don't believe this gospel came from anyone connected with Peter, or, for that matter, with any member of the apostolic generation. Personally, I believe that the consistent reports across the early centuries of the Church should be given more weight than hypothetical modern analyses that hope to determine authorship based on such things as vocabulary quirks, varying syntax, seemingly misplaced verses, and so forth. I hold to the same view regarding the Fourth Gospel.

12. Regarding the whole question of "who" the Second Evangelist was, I must in fairness note that there are various ancient traditions, some maintained in Eastern churches to this day, which suggest there were not only two Marks, but *three,* based on supposed lists of the Seventy (variously Seventy-Two) disciples mentioned in Luke 10. In this regard, Eusebius tells us:

> The names of our Saviour's apostles are in the gospels for all to read: of the seventy disciples no list has ever been found. It is stated that one of them was Barnabas, who is mentioned several times in the Acts of the Apostles, and notably by Paul in writing to the Galatians. (*History,* Book 1 Ch 12, p. 64;).

Nevertheless, various lists of "The Seventy Apostles" did develop over time, one attributed (unreliably) to Hippolytus of Rome. All are questionable, and the earliest solid evidence we have for them comes from the early Middle Ages. Some were undoubtedly developed (we know not by whom) under the influence of oral traditions or written fragments preserved differently in different parts of the Church. At least three of these lists show three separate men named Mark:

    a.   14. Mark the Evangelist
    b.   56. Mark the cousin of Barnabas
    c.   65. Mark, who is also John

A second list shows among "the Seventy":

    a.   36. Mark, who is also John, of Biblopolis, or Biblus.
    b.   37 Mark the Evangelist, bishop of Alexandria.
    c.   38. Mark, the nephew of Barnabas, bishop of Apollonia.

Notice that Mark the cousin of Barnabas is here designated his "nephew." A third list shows this:

a. II. Mark the Evangelist
b. LXI. Mark, the Apostle, whose shadow healed the sick, Bishop of Byblos in Phoenicia.
c. LXVI. Mark, cousin to Barnabas, Bishop of Apolliana, Barnabas' nephew

The lists cited here, last accessed March, 2024, can be found at:
https://en.wikipedia.org/wiki/Seventy_disciples
https://www.biblicalcyclopedia.com/S/seventy-disciples-of-our-lord.html
https://orthodoxwiki.org/Seventy_Apostles

Six

OUR NEXT IMPORTANT SOURCE of information about John the Evangelist, writing just a few decades after Papias, is Irenaeus, Bishop of Lyons in Gaul, who lived from about 130-200 AD. We have already had noted a reference to him in Eusebius.

Irenaeus was one of the most significant theologians of the early church and authored the classic defense of the Christian Faith, *Against Heresies*. He was close to the second generation of early Christians. As we saw in Chapter Five, it was, in part, through the works of Irenaeus that the records of Papias have survived. The quotations of Papias which Eusebius eventually preserved in his own history of the church were culled from the writings of Irenaeus. So Irenaeus was, and remains, one of the most important early Christian authorities just beyond of the New Testament period.

Important to this present study is the fact that Irenaeus frequently referred to a well-known John as the Fourth Evangelist who lived at Ephesus toward the end of the 1st century. If there were, as some traditions suggest, two Johns who lived at Ephesus, which was the Evangelist? Irenaeus, of course, certainly knew of the report of "two Johns" because it was Irenaeus himself who preserved Papias' records that seem to differentiate between John the apostle who Papias had never met, and "the Presbyter John" who Papias had heard teach. We must ask, then, when Irenaeus refers to John the Evangelist, which John did he mean? Is it even possible to tell? Some later (and present-day) commentators would simply reply that he always meant John the Apostle, the son of Zebedee. As we will see in what follows, however, a closer look at Irenaeus' own words brings that easy assumption into doubt.

In his *Against Heresies,* Irenaeus refers to the Fourth Evangelist with this unique designation: "John, the disciple of the Lord." John is the only person Irenaeus refers to this way. At first notice, this may seem insignificant; but as we read, we find this unusual designation over, and over. We find the following example where Irenaeus is clearly referring to the Fourth Gospel. We learn from Irenaeus and others that the "spiritual gospel" of John was feeding ground for some of the early Gnostic heretics, and Irenaeus sought to combat this. Attacking one early Gnostic group known as the Valentinians, Irenaeus writes:

> Further, they teach that John, the disciple of the Lord, indicated the first Ogdoad, expressing themselves in these words: John, the disciple of the Lord, wishing to set forth the origin of all things, so as to explain how the Father produced the whole, lays down a certain principle, —that, namely, which was first-begotten by God, which Being he has termed both the only-begotten Son and God, in whom the Father, after a seminal manner, brought forth all things (*Against Heresies,* I.8.5).[1]

In this passage, referring to John 1, Irenaeus twice uses his unique identifier for John the Evangelist: "John, the disciple of the Lord."[2] As we read on through the work, he will use this phrase often. The important point, for purposes of the present study, is that in such passage Irenaeus never connects this John to the "Apostle John," and never specifically identifies "John, the disciple of the Lord" as John bar Zebedee.

By contrast, as we will see, when Irenaeus refer to the author of Revelation, he calls him simply "John"; but we do find this one important exception:

> When these things, therefore, pass away above the earth, John, the Lord's disciple, says that the new Jerusalem above shall [then] descend, as a bride adorned for her husband; and that this is the tabernacle of God . . . (*Ag. Her.* V.35.2).

So, as further quotations will show, it seems likely from this that whoever Irenaeus believed "John, the disciple of the Lord" to be, he believed without question that he authored the Fourth Gospel, Revelation, and, likely, the three letters.

The confusion about who Irenaeus is speaking about arose because he simply never identifies *this* John as John bar Zebedee. There are only two passages in *Against Heresies* where Irenaeus clearly refers to bar Zebedee. He once refers to him among those present at the Transfiguration: "namely, Peter, and James, and John, and Moses, and Elias" (*Ag. Her.*, II.24.4). Then, one other time, he refers to these three of the inner circle, who he identifies among the "apostles" of Jesus:

> Thus did the apostles, whom the Lord made witnesses of every action and of every doctrine— for upon all occasions do we find Peter, and James, and John present with Him— scrupulously act according to the dispensation of the Mosaic law, showing that it was from one and the same God . . . (*Ag. Her.* III.12.15).

What leaps out in these two instances, and is important for this study, is that when he is clearly referring to John bar Zebedee, Irenaeus does *not* call him "the disciple of the Lord," either directly, or in the wider context. He simply calls him "John."

The question, of course, is, why? Did Irenaeus consistently use the unique title "John, the disciple of the Lord" to differentiate the Evangelist? In other words, did he believe, or did he know, that this John was *not* bar Zebedee, and so used a different way to refer to him? The answer is crucial to the present study, so let us examine the question in more detail.

Connections, Or Accidents

We have an interesting connection here: it was Irenaeus who preserved portions of the writings of Papias, and Papias who spoke about this "other" John: Aristion and the Presbyter John, "disciples of the Lord." It is almost as if Irenaeus is echoing that phrase, the phrase he will use so prevalently throughout *Against Heresies*. We recall, also, that just as Irenaeus seems to refer differently to John bar Zebedee, Papias too listed the members of the Twelve separately from Aristion and the other John.

If we hear a further echo of the Fourth Gospel phrase, "the disciple whom Jesus loved," it may well not be an accident.

Now someone may object that Irenaeus must have *meant* John the Apostle, but just expressed it differently at different times. Is that objection credible? Why does he use this unique phrase of John the Evangelist, but *never* of the John who was a member of the Twelve? When we look at the many instances where Irenaeus refers to John, the disciple of the Lord, we find no justification in the actual text to connect that John with John bar Zebedee, unless we have *brought to* the text our preconception that John bar Zebedee was the Fourth Evangelist.

Let us, however, for argument's sake, go along for a moment and examine the *assumption* that "John, the disciple of the Lord" was indeed bar Zebedee. Did Irenaeus routinely mean the Apostle (bar Zebedee), but chose instead the generic term "disciple"? We must look at further examples before trying to answer this fairly. We find one such reference further in the same chapter:

> But as many as separate from the Church, and give heed to such old wives' fables as these [of the Valentinians] are truly self-condemned; and these men Paul commands us, "after a first and second admonition, to avoid." And John, the disciple of the Lord, has intensified their condemnation, when he desires us not even to address to them the salutation of "good-speed" (*Ag. Her.* I.16.3)

The reference here is to 2 John 10-11, so Irenaeus believed this same John authored that letter, and perhaps the other two. We should notice, however, that just after mentioning the great Apostle, Paul (referencing 1 Corinthians 9:1), Irenaeus again calls this John "the disciple of the Lord." Why not call him —

here, at least — "John, the apostle of the Lord," which would have set him on equal footing with Paul? This seems curious, unless it was intentional.

We should notice this especially: Irenaeus is thus identifying "John, the disciple of the Lord" as the author of the letter which bears the greeting, *"The elder [presbyter] to the elect lady and her children . . .* (2 John 1). Again, if we hear an echo of Papias' references to *"the Presbyter* John," we are not imagining it. Is this, too, another mere coincidence?

We must not miss that by referring to the author of 2 John with his unique title for this John, Irenaeus is connecting that letter (and, for the same reason, 3 John) directly to the Fourth Evangelist. This is important because in the early centuries of the Church, some questioned the authenticity and authority of 2 John and 3 John. That doubt arose, in part, because if those two short letters were from John bar Zebedee, it seemed odd that he would refer to himself by the title "presbyter."[3] In their greetings, Peter and Paul had generally titled themselves "an apostle" of Jesus Christ (1 Peter 1:1; Romans 1:1, 1 Corinthians 1:1, and others; but see Endnote 3). This is significant: Irenaeus quotes 2 John as authoritative, and attributes to the same John he believes was the Fourth Evangelist, "John, the disciple of the Lord." Is this a further indication that Irenaeus believed, or knew, that the Fourth Evangelist was not John bar Zebedee?

Further on, addressing the Nicolaitan heresy, Irenaeus writes:

> The Nicolaitans are the followers of that Nicolas who was one of the seven first ordained to the diaconate by the apostles. They lead lives of unrestrained indulgence. The character of these men is very plainly pointed out in the Apocalypse of John (*Ag. Her.* I.26.3).

With the reference to Acts 6, "apostles" certainly means the Twelve (including Matthias). Here, Irenaeus does not call the author of Revelation "John, the Lord's disciple," as he did in the one instance already cited. What is so interesting is that with his reference to the Twelve conveniently at hand, Irenaeus does *not* connect John of the Apocalypse as one of their members. He simply calls him "John." Is he, again, thinking of a second John? This passage alone is ambiguous so it cannot settle the question.

Next, In Book II of the same work, Irenaeus makes this reference to John the Evangelist:

> His own Word is both suitable and sufficient for the formation of all things, even as John, the disciple of the Lord, declares regarding Him: "All things were made by Him, and without Him was nothing made" (*Ag. Her.* II.2.5).

Once again, if we are expecting a reference to bar Zebedee, we find instead the Fourth Evangelist called simply "John, the disciple of the Lord" (See again Endnote 2). The same thing occurs In Book II.22.3, with no identification to John bar Zebedee. Then, however, we come to a more ambiguous passage:

> He [Jesus] still fulfilled the office of a Teacher, even as the Gospel and all the elders ["presbyters"] testify; those who were conversant in Asia with John, the disciple of the Lord, [affirming] that John conveyed to them that information. And he remained among them up to the times of Trajan. Some of them, moreover, saw not only John, but the other apostles also, and heard the very same account from them, and bear testimony as to the [validity of] the statement. Whom then should we rather believe? Whether such men as these, or Ptolemaeus, who never saw the apostles, and who never even in his dreams attained to the slightest trace of an apostle? (*Ag. Her.* II.22.5).

The passage first refers to "John, the disciple of the Lord," but then mentions those who "saw not only John, but the other apostles" in Asia. Now, we could certainly infer from this that Irenaeus is referring here to the "Twelve Apostles," but he does not make that clear connection. It is equally possible, referring to those who taught in the same time period in Asia, that Irenaeus has in mind apostles such as Paul, Barnabas, Timothy, Titus, and others. There is simply no way to be certain. What is certain is that if Irenaeus *meant* the Twelve and *meant* to connect "John, the disciple of the Lord" as one of their number, he does not make such a connection explicit, as he easily could have. We must remember that many of the early missionaries were routinely called "apostles" in this time period: those just named, along with the various lists of "The Seventy Apostles" which sometimes included John-Mark. Since John-Mark was a co-evangelist with Paul and Barnabas, he certainly might have been called an "apostle" in the broader New Testament sense.[4]

Irenaeus does not make any specific reference in this passage — as he does elsewhere — to members of the Twelve. Had he, he would have resolved this dilemma. What we should notice, however, is that whoever these other authoritative "apostles" were, he groups "John, the disciple of the Lord" on an authoritative par with them. We notice, also, that this John lived in Asia (Ephesus) until the reign of the Emperor Trajan (98-117 AD). This suggests that if there were, indeed, two Johns who lived their later years in Ephesus, this John was no doubt the older.

Since Irenaeus makes clear that "John, the disciple of the Lord" was John the Evangelist, he has placed this John alongside all other "apostles" as those who were eye-witnesses to the ministry of Jesus (cf. Acts 1:21-22), as I believe the Fourth Evangelist was. Irenaeus preserved the books of Papias, a man who lived only one or two generations before Irenaeus himself, and Papias was quite clear that *this John* (the Evangelist) had known Jesus personally. If Irenaeus believed this John to be bar Zebedee, he never tells us so — though having ample opportunities — but we can have no doubt that Irenaeus believed him to have been an actual, reliable eye-witness to the ministry of the Christ.

Can we argue that this last citation suggests that Irenaeus believed "John, the disciple of the Lord" was one of *the* Apostles (that is, the Twelve), in other words, John bar Zebedee? My answer is that we can read that meaning *into* the passage, if we choose, but the passage does not actually say this, nor even imply this. It is more likely that Irenaeus was simply showing why "John, the disciple of the Lord" (the Evangelist) held apostolic authority equal to all the other apostles.

We can say this much with certainty: up to this point, Irenaeus has always called the Evangelist "John, the disciple of the Lord," and has nowhere specifically identified him as John bar Zebedee. Moving forward, then, we should keep this key point in mind: when Irenaeus or any early Christian writer refers to John *the Evangelist* either directly or indirectly as an "apostle," this does not necessarily mean the writer was speaking of John bar Zebedee. It simply means the Evangelist held recognized apostolic authority in the first generation of the Church. In that regard, John-Mark qualifies in every respect.

Putting Weights On The Balance Scale

I have focused in on Irenaeus because he is one of our earliest authorities just outside the New Testament period. Though not a second-generation Christian, he is certainly of the third. If, then, we reflect on the similarity between his consistent use of the phrase "John, the disciple of the Lord" and the Johannine phrase, "the disciple whom Jesus loved," we cannot easily avoid the magnitude of the oddity we are facing: if the Fourth Evangelist was John bar Zebedee, one of the Twelve, *why don't any of these early writers — including the New Testament writers — ever say so?* Why does Irenaeus, who knew the "two Johns" tradition through Papias, consistently call the Evangelist "John, the disciple of the Lord" rather than "John, the son of Zebedee"? When we recall that John the Evangelist never even gives us the names of all of the Twelve in his gospel, including John bar Zebedee, we are justified in asking: is this unique identifying phrase for John the Evangelist in Irenaeus merely an accident of history, or carelessness on the part of Irenaeus, or is it, as I think more likely, quite intentional?

While we will not find a perfect answer, at least in this life, we can weigh the pieces of evidence we have for, and against, my "John-Mark" theory; and as we add them one by one onto the scale, we find that the identity of the Beloved Disciple, author of the Fourth Gospel, begins to become less elusive.

To that purpose, I want to return to a passage from Eusebius that I cited in the previous chapter, where he quoted Irenaeus. Because that citation holds several important clues about "John, the disciple of the Lord," It will be helpful to consider it again here:

> Matthew also issued a written Gospel among the Hebrews in their own dialect, while Peter and Paul were preaching at Rome, and laying the foundations of the Church. After their departure, Mark, the disciple and interpreter of Peter, did also hand down to us in writing what had been preached by Peter. Luke also, the companion of Paul, recorded in a book the Gospel preached by him. Afterwards, John, the disciple of the Lord, who also had leaned upon His breast, did himself publish a Gospel during his residence at Ephesus in Asia (*Ag. Her.* III.1.1)

If we analyze this passage carefully, we can point out several intriguing facts:

1. Matthew and Peter, who both knew Jesus and were members of "the Twelve", are not called "disciples of the Lord."

2. Mark, Peter's interpreter, is designated his (Peter's) "disciple."

3. Paul, a recognized "apostle," is also not referred to as a "disciple of the Lord."

4. Yet *John the Evangelist,* identified clearly as the Beloved Disciple who "had leaned upon His breast" at the last supper, Irenaeus specifically calls — again — "John, the disciple of the Lord."

What should we make of this consistent, and different, designation for this John? Is it, in fact, a linguistic carryover from the Fourth Gospel's phrase, "the disciple whom Jesus loved"? Moreover, if by "disciple of the Lord" Irenaeus meant "one of the Twelve," why then are Matthew and Peter never so designated? Why is it only the Fourth Evangelist who is called by this "title"?

We could multiply such questions like Spring hares, but they are questions, not answers, and must remain such. So, I will move on in Irenaeus to Book III where we find this:

> But Polycarp also was not only instructed by apostles, and conversed with many who had seen Christ, but was also, by apostles in Asia, appointed bishop of the Church in Smyrna, whom I also saw in my early youth . . . having always taught the things which he had learned from the apostles, and which the Church has handed down, and which alone are true. To these things all the Asiatic Churches testify, as do also those men who have succeeded Polycarp down to the present time . . . There are also those who heard from him that John, the disciple of the Lord, going to bathe at Ephesus, and perceiving Cerinthus within, rushed out of the bath-house without bathing, exclaiming, "Let us fly, lest even the bath-house fall down, because Cerinthus, the enemy of the truth, is within" . . . Such was the horror which *the apostles and their disciples* had against holding even verbal communication with any corrupters of the truth . . . Then, again, the Church in Ephesus, founded by Paul, and having John remaining among them permanently until the times of Trajan, is a true witness of the tradition of the apostles (*Ag. Her.* III.3.4, emphasis added).

Once again, having just spoken about how Polycarp had been instructed by "apostles," Irenaeus identifies this particular John as "John, the disciple of the Lord" as though this is a special title reserved only for him. Of course, the phrase "the apostles and their disciples" may include this John under either or both categories since, as noted earlier, many disciples other than the

Twelve were called apostles. The point is this: even with all these references to apostles and disciples running headlong through this passage, the one unambiguous identification is that of "John, *the disciple of the Lord.*"

We should also notice that Irenaeus' reference to "the apostles" unquestionably includes Paul and this John, "the disciple of the Lord": "Then, again, the Church in Ephesus, founded by Paul, and having John remaining among them permanently until the times of Trajan, is a true witness of *the tradition of the apostles.*"

Square Pegs and Round Holes

The reader may begin to see why some who have tackled this whole issue have given up in despair and run off to greener academic pastures. Discovering the actual identity of the Fourth Evangelist is a little like trying to put square pegs into round holes. We have so many pegs, but it seems next to impossible to place them all in the right spot. In the midst of such frustration, however, I remind myself that it is possible to put a square peg into a round hole, if the hole is big enough.

So, let us see what further help Irenaeus provides that might enlarge the hole sufficiently to hold my John-Mark proposal. Further in Book III, Irenaeus writes:

> John, the disciple of the Lord, preaches this faith, and seeks, by the proclamation of the Gospel, to remove that error which by Cerinthus had been disseminated among men (*Ag. Her*. III.11.1).

Further in this same chapter he refers again to "the disciple of the Lord" without the name John attached, but the context makes clear he is speaking of John the Evangelist. One chapter later, however, Irenaeus calls Peter not "a disciple of the Lord" but "Apostle":

> The Apostle Peter, therefore, after the resurrection of the Lord . . . (*Ag. Her*. III.12.1).

"Curiouser, and curiouser." If the Fourth Evangelist and Peter were both of the Twelve, why would Irenaeus not call them both "Apostle"? Why does he *never* use that term of the Fourth Evangelist?

What I consider the most likely explanation is this: that Irenaeus knew "John, the disciple of the Lord" was *not* John bar Zebedee. Like Papias, who knew of the two Johns at Ephesus, Irenaeus is careful not to confuse them. If there were in fact two Johns, both disciples of Jesus but only one of whom was of "the Twelve," these earliest writers would be careful to identify the second by some special title; and that is exactly what we find in both Papias and Irenaeus, our earliest authorities on this matter outside the New Testament.

This view is reinforced by another interesting — and very telling — fact: when Irenaeus speaks of the events recorded in Acts 3 and 4 involving Peter and John bar Zebedee, he *never* calls that John "John, the disciple of the Lord," the phrase he consistently uses for the Fourth Evangelist. Referring to those events in Acts, Irenaeus simply calls him "John" (*Ag. Her.* III.12.3). We must be willing to ask: if they were the same man, why would Irenaeus not use his consistent designation? The simplest and most probable answer, again, is that Irenaeus knew they were not the same man, and is being careful to differentiate them.

Similarly, in a passage referring to the three pillars of the early Jerusalem Church, Irenaeus writes this:

> Thus did the apostles, whom the Lord made witnesses of every action and of every doctrine — for upon all occasions do we find Peter, and James, and John present with him . . . (*Ag. Her.* III.12.15).

The same question arises: if this John (bar Zebedee) was the Fourth Evangelist, Irenaeus here has the perfect opportunity to reveal that fact, simply by adding his consistent title "the disciple of the Lord" to "John." He does not do so.

We add more weights on the scale: is all this just coincidence, or do we have here a careful, consistent differentiation being made by Irenaeus between the two different Johns?

Further in Book III, Irenaeus debates with the heretics about the relative "apostolic" authority of Peter and Paul as described by Luke in Acts:

> Thus the statement of Paul harmonizes with, and is, as it were, identical with, the testimony of Luke regarding the apostles . . . But that this Luke was inseparable from Paul, and his fellow-labourer in the Gospel, he himself clearly evinces, not as a matter of boasting, but as bound to do so by the truth itself. For he says that when Barnabas, and John who was called Mark, had parted company from Paul, and sailed to Cyprus . . . (*Ag. Her.* III.13.3—III.14.1).

Here we have the only direct mention of John-Mark in this particular work. Irenaeus might have ended our inquiry right here by simply adding that *this* John was "John, the disciple of the Lord." Helpful as that might have been, he doesn't. Instead, he uses the identification of John-Mark as it occurs in Acts: "John who was called Mark." While this passage doesn't directly solve our problem by identifying John-Mark as "John, the disciple of the Lord," neither does it rule this out. We are left to wonder. Did Irenaeus know John-Mark was "John, the disciple of the Lord," but failed to say so?

Now, in this context, I want to point out two other things: Irenaeus uses a number of quotations from the Gospel of Mark; but beyond the reference to Mark already cited in Eusebius (in the previous chapter), the only other place Irenaeus gives us a clear "identification" of the Second Evangelist is this:

> Wherefore also Mark, the interpreter and follower of Peter, does thus commence his Gospel narrative: . . . (*Ag. Her.* III.10.5).

I point this out because in the same Book III he will refer to John-Mark (just cited above) but does not identify him as the Second Evangelist; then here, in this passage, he calls the Second Evangelist "the interpreter and follower of Peter." Is this just one more "oddity" or is Irenaeus again differentiating two men? It is a valid question, for we also find this:

> The opinion of the apostles, therefore, and of those (Mark and Luke) who learned from their words, concerning God, has been made manifest (Ag. Her. III.15.3).

Irenaeus is again implying that Mark, the Second Evangelist learned the gospel from Peter, as Luke did from Paul; yet Irenaeus *does not link* this Mark with John-Mark, who he has referred to in this same book.

There remains the possibility that "John, the disciple of the Lord" and "John who was called Mark" were indeed the same man, but that Irenaeus himself never made that connection. We will not find an absolute answer, but as bizarre as this suggestion may at first seem, we cannot exclude it. Irenaeus knew and accepted the tradition of the two different Johns at Ephesus, and certainly believed that "John, the disciple of the Lord" was the Fourth Evangelist. Nevertheless, it is possible that Irenaeus simply never connected "John, the disciple of the Lord," and Papias' "Presbyter John," with the "John, who was called Mark" of Acts. Irenaeus depends on Papias and other earlier writers like Polycarp for his information, but he is writing many years later. That being the case, it is possible that he failed to make what now, in retrospect, might look like an obvious possible connection.

We are left again to dangle from a rope of speculation on this particular point; but what we need not speculate about is the fact the Irenaeus considered "John, the disciple of the Lord" to be not only the Evangelist and author of 2 John, but also author of 1 John:

> The Gospel [of John], therefore, knew no other son of man but Him who was of Mary, who also suffered; and no Christ who flew away from Jesus before the passion; but Him who was born it knew as Jesus Christ the Son of God, and that this same suffered and rose again, as John, the disciple of the Lord, verifies, saying: "But these are written, that ye might believe that Jesus is the Christ, the Son of God, and that believing ye might have eternal life in His name . . . For this reason also he has thus testified to us in his Epistle: "Little children, it is the last time; and as ye have heard that Antichrist doth come, now have many antichrists appeared . . . Who is a liar, but he that denieth that Jesus is the Christ? This is Antichrist (*Ag. Her.* III.16.5).

Unmistakably, Irenaeus, one of our earliest authorities, believes the same John who wrote the Fourth Gospel also wrote 1 & 2 John, even though some critics hotly debate this today.[5]

Another piece of evidence regarding John the Evangelist appears in Book III of *Against Heresies*. Speaking about the reality that our Lord's physical body required rest, Irenaeus quotes John's gospel:

> . . . nor, again, would John His disciple have said, when writing of Him, "But Jesus, being wearied with the journey, was sitting [to rest] (*Ag. Her.* III.22.2, citing John 4:6).

Here again, why does he use "John His disciple" rather than "John His apostle"? The phrase used here seems to be a variant of "John, the disciple of the Lord." Is Irenaeus again making an intentional distinction?

Links In A Chain

It is important to remember that these earliest records from Papias and others, passed along by Irenaeus, are like links in a chain: bits of tradition and written records handed down directly — person to person — from the apostolic age, which came into Irenaeus hands. In that chain of apostolic teachers, we should understand, these were some of the key links:

1. Papias was a disciple of "the Presbyter John," a "disciple of the Lord," in Asia Minor toward the end of the 1st century.

2. Papias was also an acquaintance and friend of Polycarp, Bishop of Smyrna in Asia Minor, near Ephesus where "the Presbyter" lived.

3. Like Papias, Polycarp tells us that he had been instructed by "apostles," many of whom had seen Jesus, but he also, like Papias, knew the other "John, the Presbyter" at Ephesus.

4. Lastly, Irenaeus as a young boy knew Polycarp.[6] So, we can rightly ask, is the man Irenaeus often calls "John, the disciple of the Lord" the same man Papias calls the Presbyter John, "a disciple of the Lord"?

Because these records about a second John at Ephesus toward the end of the 1st century are very early records, we can have reasonable confidence that what they tell us is true. This other John had known Jesus: he was a first-generation Christian, one among the apostles, presbyters, and other disciples who saw Jesus after the Resurrection (1 Corinthians 15:6). These records represent a direct chain of witnesses from the beginning through the apostolic age. Thus, this Presbyter John could certainly be the Beloved Disciple, the Fourth Evangelist. He was known personally by Papias and Polycarp, men of the second generation; and Irenaeus is of the third. If their evidence is not considered reliable, then reliable evidence will not be found.

It is at least plausible, therefore, that John-Mark could have been the Beloved Disciple who leaned against Jesus' breast at the important Passover supper, who became a co-worker with Paul and Barnabas in Asia Minor, and who came to be known as "John the Presbyter," "the disciple of the Lord" at Ephesus.

So far, we have seen a significant number of pieces of evidence that would support this possibility, and none that would rule it out.[7]

An Important Piece Of The Puzzle: Revelation

Before leaving Irenaeus, I want to return briefly to the question about the authorship of Revelation mentioned in Chapter Five, which I will examine in more detail in Chapter Eight. I do so because despite Eusebius' later speculation regarding the two Johns (that one authored the Gospel and the other Revelation), Irenaeus seemed persuaded that the same man wrote both. I have given one citation already (V.35.2) where Irenaeus refers to the author of Revelation simply as "John." Similarly, in Book IV, he writes:

> Now John, in the Apocalypse, declares that the "incense" is "the prayers of the saints" (*Ag. Her.* IV.12.6).

We also find this in Book IV:

> The altar, then, is in heaven (for towards that place are our prayers and oblations directed); the temple likewise is there, as John says in the Apocalypse (*Ag. Her.* IV.18.6).

However, as we read on in Book IV, Irenaeus becomes clear who he is talking about:

> John also, the Lord's disciple, when beholding the sacerdotal and glorious advent of His kingdom, says in the Apocalypse: "I turned to see the voice that spake with me" (*Ag. Her.* IV.20.11).

Then, in Book V, we have this, which may or may not refer directly to The Apocalypse:

> The predicted blessing, therefore, belongs unquestionably to the times of the kingdom, when the righteous shall bear rule upon their rising from the dead; when also the creation, having been renovated and set free, shall fructify with an abundance of all kinds of food, from the dew of heaven, and from the fertility of the earth: as the elders who saw John, the disciple of the Lord,

related that they had heard from him how the Lord used to teach in regard to these times (*Ag. Her.* V.33.3).

This certainly seems a reference to John of the Apocalypse, although the passage does not say that explicitly. (It could be argued, here, that "John, the disciple of the Lord" who heard these things related directly from the Lord's lips was simply confirming what a different John wrote about in detail in Revelation. In that respect, this passage is still ambiguous.) If Irenaeus here means that the author of the Apocalypse was "John, the Lord's disciple," it tells us he believed the same man also wrote the Fourth Gospel. Indeed, here in Book V, we find references to John "the disciple of the Lord" both when he speaks of the Gospel (*Ag. Her.* V.18.2) and the Apocalypse (*Ag. Her.* V.26.1). His reference to "the elders who saw John, the disciple of the Lord" may well refer to Papias and Polycarp, and perhaps others. The important thing is that we see again how close in date to Jesus these records fall. The "information chain" is very short.

Nonetheless, even with all these references, Irenaeus still never identifies this "John" with John bar Zebedee. It is fair to wonder why. Irenaeus knew the tradition of the two Johns at Ephesus (from Papias), yet seems to believe that only one of them wrote both Revelation and the Fourth Gospel. From that assumption, as we have seen, Eusebius inferred that Irenaeus meant bar Zebedee. As we see from Irenaeus himself, though, that identification is not made. Why does Irenaeus use the unique title "the disciple of the Lord" so commonly, yet never refers to this John as one of the Twelve? That is the dilemma. The fact that he never connects the two leaves us with a large question mark.

Summing Up

How might we sum up the various evidence found in Irenaeus? We can say only this for sure:

1. Irenaeus received from Papias and Polycarp, and perhaps others, the apostolic teaching of a man who lived at Ephesus traditionally known as "John, the disciple of the Lord" (sometimes translated "John, the Lord's disciple".)

2. This man may have been the one also called "the Presbyter John."

3. Irenaeus believed this man wrote the Fourth Gospel, at least the first and second letters bearing the name John (thus, likely, also the third), and was also the author of Revelation.

4. Despite his many references to other first-generation apostolic figures, including members of the Twelve, Irenaeus *never* identifies this John as John bar Zebedee.

5. While Irenaeus once refers to John-Mark, he does not specifically connect him with "John, the disciple of the Lord," but neither does he rule this connection out.

Our understanding and interpretation of these facts becomes more complicated as we move forward because some later writers (Eusebius among them) assumed that every time Irenaeus spoke of "John, the disciple of the Lord" he meant John bar Zebedee. That assumption grew as time progressed and partly explains how the common wisdom eventually became so widespread: the view that bar Zebedee, and he alone, authored all five Johannine books.

As to the present study, while the evidence from Irenaeus does not directly support, let alone prove, the John-Mark proposal, neither does it disprove it. Nothing that we have looked at in Irenaeus would rule out the possibility that John-Mark *may* have been this other John, "the disciple of the Lord," the Beloved Disciple and author of the Fourth Gospel.[8,9,10]

Endnotes

1. All citations from Irenaeus' Against Heresies (*Ag. Her.*), are from the translation by Philip Schaff found in his Anti-Nicene Fathers, Volume 1, accessed at CCEL.org: https://ccel.org/ccel/schaff/anf01/anf01
The edition contains no page numbers, only Book, chapter, and paragraphs numbers as given.
2. Irenaeus refers to "John, the disciple of the Lord" many times in the five books of Against Heresies:

    a. Referring specifically to the Fourth Gospel, or its author: *Ag. Her.* I.8.5; II.2.5; II.22.3; III.1.1; II.16.5.; IV.18.2.

    b. Referring to the gospel generically: ". . . as the Gospel and all the elders testify; those who were conversant in Asia with John, the disciple of the Lord, [affirming] that John conveyed to them that information. And he remained among them up to the times of Trajan." *Ag. Her.* II.22.5.

    c. He often refers to him simply as "John," but in most cases in the same section where he has used the "disciple of the Lord" title: *Ag. Her.*IV.17.6; IV.18.6., IV.20.11; IV.21.3; V.26.1; V.28.2; V.34.2; V.35.2; V.35 5; V.36.2.

    d. In one place, referring to Jesus (John 4), he speaks of "John His disciple": *Ag. Her.*III.22.2.

    e. Referring to the author of Revelation (the Apocalypse), Irenaeus sometimes calls the author "John, the disciple of the Lord": *Ag. Her.* IV.20.11; IV.30.4; V.33.3; but other times he refers to the author of Revelation simply as "John": *Ag. Her.* IV.14.2; V.26.1.

    f. Referring to the author of 2 John 10: I.16.3.

    g. Referring to the story of a visit to the public bathe in Ephesus where he encountered the heretic Cerinthus: III.3.4.

    h. He also refers to teachings on the new creation V.33.3 (cited) where he refers to "the elders who saw John"; and then refers again to the same "John" in V.33.4: "And these things are borne witness to in writing by Papias, the hearer of John, and a companion of Polycarp, in his fourth book; for there were five books compiled (συντεταγμένα) by him."

    i. Apart from simple citations of the gospel text, and references to John the Baptist, Irenaeus refers to John by his first name only: I.8.5; I.9.1; I.9.2; I.9.3; I.26.3; III.3.4; III.8.3; III.11.2; III.11.8; III.16.2, IV.2.3; IV.10.1; but seems to be referring to "John, the disciple of the Lord."

    j. In III.21.3, he writes that "Peter, and John, and Matthew, and Paul, and the rest successively, as well as their followers, did set forth all prophetical [announcements], just as the interpretation of the elders contains them." This reference could be to bar Zebedee, or the one Irenaeus calls "the disciple of the Lord."

3. We must remember, though, that Papias and other early writers sometimes called members of the Twelve "presbyters"; and Peter uses the title of himself once (1 Peter 5:1).

4. It is important to remember that many of the early evangelists were called "apostles" though they were not members of "the Twelve." As already noted, both Paul and Barnabas bore that title (Acts 14:1-4; 14:14; Romans 1:1, 11:13, 16:7; 1 Corinthians 1:1, 4:9, 9:1, 9:9, 15:9; et. al.). We could also note Paul's statement, "I saw none of the other apostles except James the Lord's brother" (Gal 1:19). This James was not James bar Zebedee, but a "brother" in Jesus' own household and (likely) the first "bishop" at Jerusalem, although he was not one of the Twelve. Paul calls him an apostle, placing him on a level of apostolic authority on par with Peter (Galatians 1:18). And Paul refers not only to himself but also to Silas and Timothy as "apostles" (1 Thessalonians 2:6). See Chapter Five, Note 12.

5. In his Book III, Irenaeus gives this statement about the Scriptures:

> Since, therefore, the Scriptures have been interpreted with such fidelity . . . truly these men [the heretics] are proved to be impudent and presumptuous, who would now show a desire to make different translations, when we refute them out of these Scriptures . . . *For the apostles,* since they are of more ancient date than all these [the heretics], agree with this aforesaid translation; and the translation harmonizes with the tradition of the apostles. For Peter, and John, and Matthew, and Paul, and the rest successively, as well as their followers, did set forth all prophetical [announcements], just as the interpretation of the elders contains them. For the one and the same Spirit of God, who proclaimed by the prophets what and of what sort the advent of the Lord should be, did by these elders give a just interpretation of what had been truly prophesied; and He did Himself, *by the apostles,* announce that the fulness of the times of the adoption had arrived, that the kingdom of heaven had drawn nigh (*Ag. Her.* III.21.3-4, *emphasis added*).

We might infer that since he "cites" Peter, John, Matthew and Paul" in a group, Irenaeus may be referring to John the Evangelist since all these men authored books of the New Testament, and he is speaking here about interpretation of scripture; but he does not use his usual designation for John, but rather lumps him together with others who held apostolic teaching authority. On the other hand, since he is speaking of the "apostles" as authoritative sources of scripture, so we could equally infer that he is speaking of John bar Zebedee here, which would account for the absence of "the disciple of the Lord" title.

6. A fragment of a letter possibly composed by Irenaeus to a certain Florinus regarding the latter's heretical views contains this:

> These opinions, Florinus, that I may speak in mild terms, are not of sound doctrine; these opinions are not consonant to the Church . . . these opinions, those presbyters who preceded us, and who were conversant with the apostles, did not hand down to thee. For, while I was yet a boy, I saw thee in Lower Asia with Polycarp . . . so that I can even describe the place where the blessed Polycarp used to sit and discourse — his going out, too, and his coming in — his general mode of life and personal appearance, together with the discourses which he delivered to the people; also how he would speak of his familiar intercourse with John, and with the rest of those who had seen the Lord . . . Whatsoever things he had heard from them respecting the Lord, both with regard to His miracles and His teaching, Polycarp having thus received from the eye-witnesses of the Word of life, would recount them all in harmony with the Scriptures (Irenaeus, *Fragments II* found at CCEL).

Irenaeus refers to Polycarp as "that blessed and apostolical presbyter" because he had been taught by John of Ephesus. Also significant for our purpose, he emphasizes that this John was one "who had seen the Lord," one of the "eye-witnesses of the Word of life." While this demonstrates this John was known as an "apostle" who walked with the Lord, this passage offers no specific help in resolving our question of whether or not *this* John was John bar Zebedee.

7. In another letter fragment we find this:

> For neither could Anicetus persuade Polycarp to forego the observance [in his own way], inasmuch as these things had been always [so] observed by John the disciple of our Lord, and by other apostles with whom he had been conversant (Irenaeus, *Fragments,* found in CCEL).

What makes this snippet notable is that it groups "John the disciple of our Lord" with "other apostles" Polycarp had personally seen or heard. There is no record (that I know of) that would indicate any other of the Twelve (beside John bar Zebedee) settled around Ephesus. The reference may of course be to Paul and Barnabas, or other "apostles." What it makes plain is that Irenaeus did not limit his usage of "apostle" to mean only one of the Twelve.

8. *Against Heresies*, Book II Irenaeus frequently refers to "the apostles," and consistently calls Paul "the apostle," but he never refers directly to John the Evangelist, "the disciple of the Lord," in those contexts. The

exception is the reference already cited from II.22.5, but there it seems that "other apostles" included Paul, who had been frequently cited by Irenaeus in these chapters, and thus does not link "John, the disciple of the Lord" to the Twelve. It is a significant fact that each time he refers to the Twelve Apostles in Book II, he *never mentions* John the Evangelist.

9. Referring to the gospels, Irenaeus refers to "Matthew the apostle (*Ag. Her.* III.9.1) and "Peter the apostle" (*Ag. Her.* III.12.1), but never "John the apostle." And though he writes, "Thus has Matthew set it down, and Luke in like manner, and Mark the very same; for John omits this passage. They, however, who would be wiser than the apostles . . ." (*Ag. Her.* IV.6.1), mentioned the John the Evangelist alongside Matthew, an "apostle." It need only be pointed out, however, that he also here puts Luke and Mark in his list, neither of whom were "apostles" in the narrow sense (meaning the Twelve).

10. In one intriguing but cryptic passage, Irenaeus refers to "a presbyter, a disciple of the apostles," but it is not clear that he means John the Evangelist, or "John, the disciple of the Lord":

> After this fashion also did *a presbyter, a disciple of the apostles,* reason with respect to the two testaments, proving that both were truly from one and the same God. For [he maintained] that there was no other God besides Him who made and fashioned us . . . But if any one believes in [only] one God, who also made all things by the Word, as Moses likewise says, "God said, Let there be light: and there was light;" and as we read in the [Fourth] Gospel, "All things were made by Him; and without Him was nothing made;" and the Apostle Paul [says] in like manner, "There is one Lord, one faith, one baptism, one God and Father, who is above all, and through all, and in us all" . . . And then shall every word also seem consistent to him, if he for his part diligently read the Scriptures in company *with those who are presbyters* in the Church, among whom is the apostolic doctrine, as I have pointed out (*Ag. Her.* IV.32.1, emphasis added).

Who is the "presbyter, a disciple of the apostles"? This passage quotes the Fourth Gospel, and the reference to God making all things by "the word" may be another reference to John 1, but the "presbyter" here might be someone entirely different, who used the Fourth Gospel and Paul to support the reasoning. If Irenaeus meant John the Evangelist, it is very interesting that he calls him "a presbyter, a disciple of the apostles." We recall how Papias spoke of learning the teaching of the Twelve not from them directly but from those who were their "disciples."

Seven

OUR NEXT STRETCH OF road is to return to the man who was our source regarding Papias, Eusebius Pamphilius (c. 260-340 AD) whose invaluable work *The History of the Church from Christ to Constantine* is our first comprehensive history of the Christian Faith and Church. His painstaking research preserved many of the earliest records of the Church, such as the writings of Papias and others, that might otherwise have been lost forever (as many early records, no doubt, were).

As I suggested in Chapter Five, an examination of his entire *History* shows that Eusebius was, at times, of a mixed mind about who authored the various "Johannine" books. His mixed opinions appear to be based on apparent conflicts in the records of earlier writers to which he had access. As we also saw in Chapter Five, he seemed convinced that John bar Zebedee was John the Evangelist, yet was ambivalent about which John wrote Revelation. Because of that ambivalence, it will be wise here to look at a few further bits of evidence in his *History*.

Regarding the Fourth Gospel, we find an example of his general opinion about authorship. Referring of the Twelve apostles, he writes, "Yet of them all Matthew and John alone have left us memoirs of the Lord's doings" (*History*, p. 132).[1] We cannot know for certain if this conclusion, which seems at variance with what we found in Irenaeus, was the result of direct evidence Eusebius had from other sources, or evidence he possessed but we no longer have. It may simply have been the case that by Eusebius' day, the "climate of opinion" had accepted the simple and "safe" conclusion that John bar Zebedee was the presumed author of all five Johannine books.

We find clear evidence that this was Eusebius' judgment on the question of who John the Evangelist was. Commenting on the discrepancies between the Gospel of John to the Synoptics, Eusebius writes:

> . . . for this reason the apostle John was urged to record in his gospel the period which the earlier evangelists had passed over . . . Once this is grasped, there no longer appears to be a discrepancy between the gospels" (*History*, pp. 132-33).

While his judgment here about there being "no discrepancy" between the four gospel accounts may be over-simplified (an issue I have already addressed in some detail), this quotation shows that he was certain "the apostle John," by whom he consistently means bar Zebedee, was the Fourth Evangelist. This reality is very important to our present study because *Eusebius'* opinion on this "fact" was largely followed by later writers, many of whom relied on his authority as the first systematic historian of the Church. Over the succeeding centuries, this helped form the "traditional" opinion that was gradually accepted as the standard position of many Christian historians and commentators. It remains so today.

On closer examination, however, we discover that Eusebius based this assumption in part — perhaps in *large* part — on the writings of Irenaeus, which we have just looked at. Without giving the source of his information on this, other than the living tradition of the Church, Eusebius begins Book III of his *History* with this statement:

> Meanwhile the holy apostles and disciples of our Saviour were scattered over the whole world. Thomas, tradition tells us, was chosen for Parthia, Andrew for Scythia, John for Asia, where he remained till his death at Ephesus. Peter seems to have preached in Pontus, Galatia and Bithynia, Cappadocia and Asia, to the Jews of the Dispersion. Finally, he came to Rome where he was crucified, head downwards at his own request (*History,* p.107).

Since all those named here were members of the Twelve (who he here also terms "disciples"), this John must mean bar Zebedee. Further in Book III, Eusebius writes:

> Many were the victims of Domitian's cruelty . . . There is ample evidence that at that time the apostle and evangelist John was still alive, and because of his testimony to the word of God was sentenced to confinement on the island of Patmos (*History*, p. 125).

We can have no doubt, therefore, that Eusebius was convinced bar Zebedee was John the Evangelist. More importantly, the last sentence tells us he was also certain, at least here, this same John wrote Revelation. We should pause, however, and recall that Eusebius, in reflecting on words of Papias, had himself raised the question of whether perhaps some other John had written Revelation. In this present citation, he either avoids or ignores that doubt (*History*, p. 150).

Eusebius also appears to believe this John wrote Revelation after Domitian's rule ended (95 AD) and that John survived into the reign of Nerva (Roman emperor from 96-98 AD):

> . . . the apostle John, after his exile on the island, resumed residence at Ephesus, as early Christian tradition records" (*History,* p. 127).

"Resumed residence" confirms that Eusebius believed this John had been living in Ephesus *prior to* his exile to the island. I will, further on, suggest a different possibility.

I would pose this question: other than what the early "tradition records," upon what did Eusebius base his assumptions about which John authored Revelation? As just noted, at a different point, Eusebius seemed uncertain, suggesting that perhaps "the other John" had authored the Apocalypse. Here, he seems quite confident it was bar Zebedee. Did he have actual records on this point, or was he, perhaps, conflating different traditions that originally may have referred to two different Johns, both of whom had been living at about the same time in Ephesus?

We cannot be certain. We know at times Eusebius mentions "what they are saying" or "what they say," suggesting that some of what he writes down was still living, oral tradition in his own time. We know he worked in part from written records at his disposal. He no doubt did his best to collect and reconcile a mass of sometimes conflicting details. He summarizes and writes about people and events from over two hundred years before his time. So, it is perfectly possible that he held, at times, a mixed opinion about the authorship of the Johannine books. His one "supposition" was that if we dare not attribute Revelation to John bar Zebedee, perhaps this "other" John wrote it. I will suggest an alternate solution later in this chapter.

Put simply, Eusebius, authoritative historian though he was, was no doubt at times speculating, trying diligently to make sense of conflicting — or perhaps absent — details. Some of those details in Irenaeus, for example, conflicted with Eusebius' general view that the Apostle John bar Zebedee authored the Fourth Gospel. So, when reading Irenaeus — the citations we examined carefully in the last chapter — Eusebius may have *brought to* that material the preconception that whenever Irenaeus spoke of "John, the disciple of the Lord" he must have meant John bar Zebedee. As I have shown, Irenaeus himself never made such an identification explicit.

If that was Eusebius' assumption (and I think it was), we can understand why he "interprets" Irenaeus as he does when he writes the following passage:

> In Asia, moreover, there still remained alive the one whom Jesus loved, apostle and evangelist alike, John, who had directed the church there since his return from exile on the island, following Domitian's death. That he survived so long is proved by the evidence of two witnesses who could hardly be doubted,

ambassadors as they were of the orthodoxy of the Church — Irenaeus and Clement of Alexandria. In Book II of his *Heresies Answered*, Irenaeus writes:

> All the clergy who in Asia came in contact with *John, the Lord's disciple,* testify that John taught the truth to them; for he remained with them till Trajan's time [*emphasis* added].

In Book III of the same work he [Irenaeus] says the same thing:

> The church at Ephesus was founded by Paul, and John remained there till Trajan's time; so she is a true witness of what the apostles taught (*History*, p. 128).

We looked at those two citations previously. The question, of course, is: was Irenaeus, as Eusebius *presumes,* speaking of John bar Zebedee when he referred to John "the disciple of the Lord"? As I have shown, that is not necessarily the case. If we look back again carefully at Irenaeus' actual words (as cited just above) we realize:

1. In the first quotation, Irenaeus does not call this John "apostle" or "evangelist."

2. To the contrary, Irenaeus (as he consistently did) called this John "the Lord's disciple" (or "the disciple of the Lord").

3. In the second quotation, Irenaeus says this John who was alive in Trajan's time was part of the church at Ephesus, and that this *church* was "a witness" of what the apostles taught.

In other words, neither quotation in Irenaeus actually identifies *this John* as John bar Zebedee.

This reality is consistent with what I pointed out in Chapter Six: although Irenaeus seemed to believe one man was both the Evangelist and the author of Revelation, he never identifies that John as John bar Zebedee, even when that opportunity was right at hand. The one quotation emphasizes that the church at

Ephesus was a true witness to the teaching of the apostles; it does not say this John was the "Apostle John," as Eusebius infers.

When Eusebius, therefore, links the quotations from Irenaeus with one cited below from Clement, he may simply have done so because that was his preconceived idea: John bar Zebedee was the Fourth Evangelist. Immediately after these citations from Irenaeus, Eusebius quotes a lengthy tale in the writings of Clement of Alexandria (c.150-215 AD) about how "John the apostle" placed a young man in the care of one of the bishops in the region around Ephesus:

> Listen to a tale that is not just a tale but a true account of John the apostle, handed down and carefully remembered. When the tyrant [Domitian] was dead, and John had moved from the island of Patmos to Ephesus, he used to go when asked to the neighboring districts of the Gentile peoples . . . (*History*, pp. 128-29).

Now, there is little question that Clement in speaking of "John the apostle," he most likely means bar Zebedee. The ambiguity, however, remains, because Clement does not identify this John as the Fourth Evangelist. If Clement's "John the apostle" does refer to John bar Zebedee, then, if anything, we may be assured that Clement is telling us that John bar Zebedee was the author *of Revelation*. Further, I would call attention to another detail in Clement: he does not say that bar Zebedee "resumed" residence in Ephesus, as Eusebius reports. He says John "moved from the island of Patmos to Ephesus . . ." only after Domitian had died. That is, the apostle John moved "to Ephesus," not "back to Ephesus." This may seem like a minor detail, here at least. As I will show below, however, it may be more important than it seems at first glance.

Eusebius quite clearly has put these citations from Irenaeus and Clement back-to-back because he obviously assumed both writers, years apart, were talking about the same John. But were they? Irenaeus speaks of "John, the Lord's disciple," the phrase he routinely used to identify the Evangelist. But Clement speaks simply of "John the apostle," at the same time making it clear he is speaking of the author of Revelation. As Eusebius himself has made us aware, even at this early date some Christians doubted that the same man authored both the Gospel and Revelation. So I ask: is it not possible that Irenaeus and Clement were talking about the two different Johns, but Eusebius didn't grasp this fact? We have seen that Eusebius himself, at some points, wrestled with this question about these two books; and we know Irenaeus was aware of the "two Johns" tradition from Papias.

We need to consider this possibility that Clement and Irenaeus were speaking of two different men; and one particular factor should be part of that consideration. So, I want to slow here and run along another side track briefly.

The Age Question

The quotations from both Irenaeus and Clement just cited hit squarely on what has been a long-standing problem regarding "John" in terms of whether we accept that there was only one John, or two, who ended their lives at Ephesus. A key question — and its answer — relates to the probable ages of this man, or, more likely, these men.

The citation from Clement (just above) suggests that "John the apostle," the author of Revelation, lived at least until the death of the Emperor Domitian in 96 AD. Domitian had carried out a bitter persecution against the church, and many believe it was during that persecution that John (or one of them) was exiled to the island of Patmos, not far off the coast of Ephesus.

On the other hand, Irenaeus, speaking specifically of John the Evangelist, the man he called "John, the disciple of the Lord," says this John lived into the reign of the Emperor Trajan, who did not come to power until 98 AD. (His predecessor, Nerva, ruled only from 96-98 AD.)

If both of the writers were speaking of one and the same man, John bar Zebedee, it means that by the time Trajan came to power (98 AD) he would have been nearly 100 years of age. Is that a realistic assumption? Let's look at alternatives.

If, as we glean from Papias, there actually were two Johns who lived during this approximate time at Ephesus, how old might these two men have been by the time they died? To answer this, we have to speculate how old they were at the time of Jesus' ministry.

St. Luke tells us that Jesus was about 30 years old when he began his ministry (Luke 3:23), as was John the Baptist, about six months his senior. It is likely, then, that John bar Zebedee was also around 30 at the time of the Jesus' ministry, Crucifixion, and Resurrection. Why? Because Peter and both Zebedee brothers, the "inner three" of Jesus' disciples, were the leading elders (presbyters) of his apostolic band, and it is unlikely Jesus would have selected men much younger than 30. Long Jewish custom recognized age 30 as the time a man was considered fully mature, so men under 30 were less likely to be put into authoritative roles as religious leaders or teachers, which the Twelve were almost from the beginning (see Luke 9; cf. Genesis 41:46, 2 Samuel 5:4, 1 Chronicles 23:3).

By contrast, we have a long-held, competing tradition that "the Beloved Disciple" was a much younger man, perhaps not much older than a teenager. This tradition in itself can be seen as one more strike against the belief that John bar Zebedee was the Evangelist. If John-Mark was the Evangelist, of course, this still fits.

If, then, we estimate that John bar Zebedee was about 30 plus around the year 32-33, the latest year in which the Resurrection could have fallen,[2] this John would have been about 94 years old when Domitian died, when Clement says he moved "to Ephesus." He would have been around 96 when Trajan's reign began. Is that likely? We know that Polycarp was reputedly 86 when he was martyred, but 96 seems a stretch, considering typical longevity in those days, not to mention that this man may have just spent time as a prisoner on Patmos.

What happens when we consider instead the other John, whom I have suggested may have been John-Mark? If the early tradition of the Church was accurate, this John, the Beloved Disciple, was a fairly young man at the time of Jesus' ministry, perhaps (as I hinted in our discussion of the Last Supper) little more than a boy. That could explain two things. First, it could be the reason he did not originally hold an authoritative position among the apostles, and thus would not have been one of the Twelve even though he was personally so close to Jesus. Second, it would explain why, when it came time to replace Judas Iscariot (Acts 1), John the Beloved Disciple would still not have been among those considered.

If we conjecture that this much younger John was about 20 years old at the time of the Resurrection (about 32 AD), and possibly younger, he would have been about 84-85 when Domitian died, and about 86 when Trajan came to power. Could this John have survived "into the reign of Trajan." This is certainly more plausible.

If we work from these age suppositions, it is perfectly possible that Irenaeus and Clement, in the passages coupled by Eusebius, were talking about the two different Johns. Irenaeus referring to John the Presbyter, the "disciple of the Lord," records that this man lived until 98 AD, and perhaps some years beyond. Clement, speaking more likely of John bar Zebedee, tells us that he lived until the death of Domitian in 96 AD, at which point he was released from Patmos and moved to Ephesus. (Was his release related to advanced age?)

If these suppositions are correct, they remain consistent with the proposal I have put forth, granting that John bar Zebedee would still have reached perhaps his early 90s before release from Patmos, and the younger John-Mark, too, would have been quite elderly when he died.

We should consider the possibility that the reports regarding the very aged John at Ephesus who lived into the reign of Trajan originally referred to the Presbyter John, and that Clement mistakenly connected that report to John bar Zebedee.

We must also keep in mind that when Eusebius writes about these traditions, he also may have mixed up two men, since he sometimes suggested that a *single* John wrote both the Fourth Gospel and Revelation, yet at other times considered the possibility of two Johns.

Did Clement know of the tradition found in Papias, that two different men named John lived at Ephesus toward the end of the century? We can't be sure. If he believed there was only one, we then understand why he would record that "John the apostle" lived until at least 96 AD.

A Further Supposition

Regardless of the age questions, if Clement was indeed talking about John bar Zebedee living to the death of Domitian, then his detail that this John "moved from the island of Patmos *to* Ephesus" is particularly intriguing. For that supports, as I will suggest below, the belief that John bar Zebedee could indeed have been the author of Revelation (either on Patmos, or once in Ephesus). The question that arises is, *How and when did bar Zebedee get to Patmos?*

As we saw earlier, Eusebius assumed that John the author of Revelation had been living in Ephesus before he was exiled to Patmos, and "resumed residence" in Ephesus upon his release (around 96 AD). Although he says there is "ample" evidence, he does not give us any specifics, other than Clement's statement that this John moved *to* Ephesus upon release from detainment on the island.

Let me suggest an alternate possibility. It has been long held that Patmos was a formal penal colony of the Roman Empire. Some modern commentators still hold this view. Whether it was an organized prison island or not, we know from Revelation itself that John was on the island "on account of the word of God and the testimony of Jesus" (Revelation 1:9 ESV). There was certainly a persecution under Domitian, so John may have been sent to Patmos as punishment for preaching, or he may simply have fled there to avoid arrest in Ephesus — if that is where he was living just beforehand.

On the other hand, the island could also have been more a place of political exile (the end result being much the same). How, and when, might John bar Zebedee have ended up there? Was it under Domitian, or much earlier?

We know from the New Testament that John bar Zebedee's brother James was executed in Judea during an earlier persecution under Herod Agrippa I around 42-44 AD (Acts 12:1-2). Curiously, though, Acts never tells us what became of John himself. From the scant set of facts that exists — and based largely on Eusebius — many commentators have inferred that John bar Zebedee first moved to Ephesus, and was only later arrested and exiled to Patmos. We have, however, no actual evidence of this in Scripture, or in the historical record before Eusebius (at least that I can find).

An alternative is this: what if John bar Zebedee was arrested during the same persecution in which his brother James died? We know for a fact that Peter was. Indeed, it was that arrest which preceded Peter's miraculous escape from prison on the night he ended up at the house of Mary — and her son John-Mark (Acts 12:3-17).

Further, we know that John bar Zebedee had been arrested before, with Peter, and warned to stop preaching about Jesus (Acts 4). Is it possible he was arrested again during that same persecution along with his brother and Peter, and was then, or sometime not long after, sent to exile on Patmos? Someone might object that this would seem to be a long journey, from Jerusalem to Patmos, just to imprison John. I would only reply that Paul was shipped from Jerusalem all the way to Rome, in custody, for his appeal before Caesar.

Is this alternative possible? Here is what little we have of the account of the persecution under Herod Agrippa I:

> About that time Herod the king laid violent hands upon some who belonged to the church. He killed James the brother of John

with the sword; and when he saw that it pleased the Jews, he proceeded to arrest Peter also. This was during the days of Unleavened Bread. And when he had seized him, he put him in prison, and delivered him to four squads of soldiers to guard him, intending after the Passover to bring him out to the people. So Peter was kept in prison; but earnest prayer for him was made to God by the church (Acts 12:1-5).

James bar Zebedee was executed. Peter was thrown in prison (again). But what happened to John? John is mentioned here, but we are not told what became of him. Was he perhaps arrested with James before Peter's arrest? Was he arrested along with Peter, as before? Or, equally possible, was he arrested *after* Peter's escape, as a punishment when Peter was not recaptured? Acts does not tell us, but that is what is so odd: after this verse *we never hear another word about John bar Zebedee in Acts*. Could it be that this was when he was sent to Patmos?

This is admittedly speculative, but it would fit uniquely with the statement from Clement, not many years later, that John bar Zebedee moved *from* Patmos *to* Ephesus after Domitian's death. Nowhere, that I have found, does Clement or any other 1st or early-2nd century authority say that John bar Zebedee lived in Ephesus *before* he was imprisoned on Patmos. Many writers, like Eusebius, made that assumption, but there seems to be no hard evidence.[3]

Is it, then, possible that "the other John" (John-Mark) was the one already living in Ephesus when John bar Zebedee moved there upon his release from Patmos about 96 AD? This would accord with the "two Johns" tradition recorded by Papias. If, as Paul's letters suggest, John-Mark resumed work with Paul at some point, it would be perfectly natural that after being with Paul in Rome, and perhaps witnessing his death, John-Mark might have settled in Ephesus, a church Paul had founded, and a place he would have been known and welcomed (see again Colossians 4).[4]

The ancient tradition was that two Johns both lived their last years in or near Ephesus, both respected disciples of Jesus and eyewitnesses to his ministry. One, who had lived for a time on Patmos, wrote Revelation. Was the second, "the Presbyter John" also John the Evangelist, the one Irenaeus called "John, the disciple of the Lord"? Was he, in fact, the Beloved Disciple? Were these two men simply mixed up by later writers? (Recall again the tradition of the two tombs in Ephesus, both of which were still known in Eusebius' time in the 4th century).

Further Details In Eusebius

Near the end of his Book III, Eusebius relates further details about the Johannine works as he understood them. Believing he was speaking of John bar Zebedee, although his sources may actually have meant "the other John", Eusebius writes:

> And when Mark, and Luke had now published their gospels, John, we are told, who hitherto had relied entirely on the spoken word, finally took to writing for the following reason. The three gospels already written were in general circulation and copies had come into John's hands. He welcomed them, we are told, and confirmed their accuracy, but remarked that the narrative only lacked the story of what Christ had done first of all at the beginning of His mission. This tradition is undoubtedly true. Anyone can see that the three evangelists have recorded the doings of the Saviour for only one year following the consignment of John the Baptist to prison . . . We are told, then, that for this reason the apostle John was urged to record in his gospel the period which the earlier evangelists had passed over in silence and the things done during that period by the Saviour, i.e., all that happened before the Baptist's imprisonment; that this is indicated by his words "Thus did Jesus begin His miracles" . . . once this is grasped, there no longer appears to be a discrepancy between the gospels (*History*, pp. 132-3).

As I noted before, we may easily disagree with Eusebius that this tradition erases all discrepancies between the gospels. As I demonstrated in Chapter One, the differences are much more than the fact that John covers a longer (and earlier) time period. There are major differences related to geography — the whole focus in John being on Judea rather than Galilee — and the fact that John contains a great deal of eyewitness testimony to particular events that the synoptic authors apparently lacked.

Of the other Johannine books Eusebius says this:

> Of John's writings, besides the gospel, the first of the epistles has been accepted as unquestionably his by scholars both of the present and of a much earlier period: the other two are disputed. As to the Revelation, the views of most people to this day are evenly divided (*History*, p. 134).

Of course, as I've already discussed, one reason scholars questioned the authenticity of 2 John and 3 John was because they were from "the presbyter," whereas Eusebius and others who followed him held the view that John "the apostle" (bar Zebedee) was the Evangelist, and therefore author of 1 John. As I showed in Chapter Six, however, Irenaeus accepted both 1 John and 2 John as being from the same hand as the Fourth Gospel, meaning that "the presbyter" who authored 3 John was almost certainly the same man: John the Evangelist.

It is my view, and consistent with Irenaeus, that literary comparison between the three letters themselves, and between the letters and the gospel, can support a strong argument that all four books came from the same hand. If this was *not* the hand of John bar Zebedee, but rather of "the Presbyter John" known to Papias, many of the traditional objections, and much of the traditional confusion, quickly fades away.

As to Eusebius' point about people being evenly divided about Revelation, we face the same issue, and similar confusion. As I have suggested, it seems likely to me that the "common wisdom" that John bar Zebedee authored the Fourth Gospel (and perhaps 1 John) has been held for so long simply because that would seem to give that gospel unquestioned "apostolic" authority. On the other hand, based on the actual text, language, content, and style of Revelation, I, like many others, seriously question whether or not the same man could have authored both the Fourth Gospel and Revelation.

That fact, I believe, was (and is) the primary reason some rejected Revelation as being of doubtful authority: since they believed John bar Zebedee authored the Fourth Gospel, they went on to assume that he did *not* write Revelation, because it was so obviously different. On that assumption alone, the latter book lost strength of authority, apart from its strange and unusual contents.

If, however, we approach this whole question from my "other John" supposition, that John-Mark was John the Evangelist, a major objection to Revelation falls away. If Revelation was, in fact, written by John the Apostle — as both Clement and Justin Martyr tell us — then the puzzle is easily solved and the supposed conflicts created by the "traditional" view dissolve (see Chapter Eight).

Returning now to Eusebius, we find in the very next section (following the last cited) that he lists those books considered sacred and authoritative in his time, including the "holy quartet of gospels," Acts, and Paul's letters. Then he writes:

> . . . after them we must recognize the epistle called 1 John; likewise 1 Peter. To these may be added, if it is thought proper, the Revelation of John . . . These are classed as Recognized Books. Those that are disputed, yet familiar to most, include the epistles known as James, Jude, and 2 Peter, and those called 2 and 3 John, the work either of the evangelist *or of someone else with the same name* (*History*, p. 143, *emphasis* added).

Here, again, Eusebius seems almost forced back to the suggestion that there was some other well-known John who was the source of some of these books. His final suggestion no doubt related to the fact, as I have pointed out, that 2 and 3 John are from "The Presbyter."[5] That he here again acknowledges almost the necessity of there being "another" John behind some of the Johannine works supports the argument I have been making. We saw that Eusebius was familiar with the tradition about "the Presbyter John" known to Papias, who also lived at Ephesus, so Eusebius may have had that particular John in mind when he suggests "someone else with the same name" as being "the Presbyter" who lay behind 2 and 3 John. Again, if my John-Mark theory is correct, the odd pieces not only fit, it would completely resolve this difficulty as well.

Eusebius also provides some thought-provoking details about the death of one "John" at Ephesus. While he probably assumes his source is speaking of John bar Zebedee — because Eusebius believed him to be the Evangelist — the source may well have been speaking of "the other John," since the man is not identified as bar Zebedee:

> The date of John's death has also been roughly fixed: the place where his mortal remains lie can be gathered from a letter of Polycrates, Bishop of Ephesus, to Victor, Bishop of Rome [died c. 198 AD]. In it he refers not only to John but to Philip the apostle and Philip's daughters as well: "In Asia great luminaries sleep who shall rise again on the last day, the day of the Lord's advent, when He is coming with glory from heaven and shall search out all His saints — such as Philip, one of the twelve apostles, who sleeps in Hierapolis with two of his daughters . . . Again there is John, who leant back on the Lord's breast, and who became a sacrificing priest wearing the mitre, a martyr and a teacher; he too sleeps in Ephesus" (*History*, p. 140-141).

I want to go slow here and look very carefully at several fascinating details in Polycrates' letter.

First, even though Eusebius assumes Polycrates means John bar Zebedee, Polycrates does not say that. What does he say? He calls Philip "one of the Twelve apostles" but then, only a few words later, he does *not* identify this John as one of the

Twelve. He simply identifies him as that John who leaned on the Lord's breast at the Last Supper, the Beloved Disciple.

Second, there is a very intriguing detail which is of unique significance to my John-Mark proposal: this John "became a sacrificing priest wearing the mitre, a martyr [witness] and a teacher." Why is this noteworthy? Because, as I suggested in Chapters Three and Four, John-Mark was a cousin of Barnabas, who was a *Levite*. This raises at least the possibility that John-Mark himself may have been of the priestly tribe as well. If so, that could explain this otherwise inexplicable and cryptic comment from Polycrates that *this* John became "a sacrificing priest wearing the mitre." In those earliest years of the Church, when so many of the leaders were converted Jews, it might be natural for someone like John-Mark — if he was indeed of the priestly tribe — to be vested as a "sacrificing priest wearing the mitre," the turban-like traditional headdress of the earlier Jewish priesthood. This is an intriguing possibility, on several levels. It would suggest that some, at least, of the earliest Jewish-Christian disciples carried over into the Church some of the liturgical customs of the Temple. Moreover, if the Beloved Disciple was indeed of the priestly family (see again John 18:15), this might bear on why he bore a special place in Jesus' heart, who himself was at least indirectly related to the tribe of Levi (Luke 1:36). It might explain why, being now a Christian "priest" (presbyter), he might continue to wear the traditional mitre in common with the Jewish priesthood. (See Appendix B.)

We leave Eusebius considering one further point. Despite his general opinion that John bar Zebedee was the Fourth Evangelist, we should recall here that he concluded his account of the apostolic period (Book III of the *History*) with the opinion (previously cited)[6] that there probably *were* "two Johns" revered in the late 1st century who both died at Ephesus, each of whom left New Testament books that bear the name "John." With that conclusion I agree, the difference being that I believe Eusebius got the two Johns reversed.

I in no way mean to belittle Eusebius' incredible work, a labor of devotion and many years. He clearly strove for thoroughness and accuracy. Nevertheless, he was of two minds about the two Johns, and about who wrote what books. It is easy to understand how, as he worked through the mass of information he had as the basis of his Book III, he may have stumbled — as many researchers and commentators have since — because he (and they) began from the *preconception* that John bar Zebedee was the Beloved Disciple, and therefore the Fourth Evangelist. If we simply turn that around, and begin from my supposition, that the Beloved Disciple was in fact a different John, many of the seemingly intractable conflicts that have beset Johannine scholars can be resolved.

Connecting The Dots

It will be helpful, once again, to review what I have proposed up to this point, and what evidence we have found so far:

1. I suggest that another "John," not John bar Zebedee, was the Beloved Disciple, author of the Fourth Gospel and the three Johannine letters.

2. I have suggested that this other John may in fact have been John, also called Mark who we know from Acts and Paul's letters.

3. If the "two Johns" information from Papias is accurate, as I believe it is, both John "the disciple of the Lord" and John bar Zebedee lived their last days in Ephesus, though John-Mark was a good number of years younger than Zebedee, and lived longer. Both were buried there, and both of their tombs were still distinguishable in the time of Eusebius (early 4th century).

4. John "the disciple of the Lord" in Irenaeus, while sometimes referred to as an "apostle" is *never* identified as John bar Zebedee, nor as one of the Twelve.

5. The other John, John-Mark, came to be known as the Presbyter John (or John the Presbyter, or just the Presbyter)

at Ephesus perhaps to distinguish him from John bar Zebedee who also lived there after release from Patmos.

6. "The Presbyter" title would explain the greeting at the opening of both 2 and 3 John.

7. It was indeed John bar Zebedee who was exiled to Patmos (we are not sure when), perhaps sent directly from Jerusalem after his brother James' martyrdom, who wrote Revelation, as some of the earliest witnesses record (see Chapter Eight, following).

Based on all the evidence I have examined so far, this set of facts is consistent with that evidence, whereas the traditional theory that John bar Zebedee wrote all five Johannine books cannot, in my view, be reconciled with all the scriptural, literary, and historical evidence we have.

Endnotes

1. Citations from Eusebius here are from the Williamson edition (see Bibliography).

2. Scholars generally agree that Jesus was born about 6-4 BC, and scripture tells us he was about 30 years old when he began his three-year public ministry (Luke 3:23, plus the longer chronology of John). This would place the crucifixion and resurrection around 28-32 AD.

3. This assumption may be partially based on the further assumption that the author of Revelation must have been a leader of the church at Ephesus before he wrote Revelation. However, he addresses not only Ephesus but *six other* regional churches in chapter 2-3. John speaks with apostolic authority over all of them, not simply as a leader of one. Further, we must remember it is not really John who addresses the seven churches, but Jesus himself. John bar Zebedee, if he had been confined on Patmos for many years, could certainly have learned much about these seven churches through other leaders, even if he had never visited them. Moreover, he identifies himself to those churches only as their "brother," never as their leader, presbyter, bishop, or apostle. If he had lived in Ephesus first and was then exiled to Patmos, those seven churches certainly would have known this fact. Why then would he have to inform them of his

whereabouts (Revelation 1:9)? One interpretation of the phrase "To the angel of the church . . ." is that it refers to each local church's *leader*. If so, John could not himself have been that leader, but would have been speaking as a respected Apostle, one of the Twelve, one of the Three.

4. ". . . and Mark the cousin of Barnabas (concerning whom you have received instructions—if he comes to you, welcome him) . . ." (Colossians 4:10).

5. It is ironic that one of his most reliable sources, Irenaeus, seemed to accept that both were from the hand of John the Evangelist.

6. Eusebius, *History,* p. 150, cited in Chapter Five.

Eight

WE HAVE EXAMINED some of the early historical data we have regarding the Fourth Evangelist up to the time of Eusebius.[1] It is my view that there is not much to be gained by pursuing documentary evidence beyond Eusebius, for several reasons. The first and most important is that by the time of Eusebius we are nearly three centuries beyond the original sources who knew the people and events around the writing of the New Testament books. To find pristine and unbiased evidence beyond the time of Eusebius becomes very precarious. As is usually the case, in any investigation, that the earliest evidence is the least biased and most reliable. The few scraps of evidence we have regarding the origin of the Fourth Gospel and the other Johannine works that survived into Eusebius' time had been written 100-150 years earlier. So, to seek useful, authoritative evidence beyond his time would be to rely on third-and-fourth-hand reports that, as we've seen, were already subject to misunderstanding and misinterprettation.

Second, because Eusebius developed such a detailed history, albeit one with occasional errors or misunderstandings, many later biblical commentators seem to have followed his general opinion that John bar Zebedee was the author of the Fourth Gospel (and likely 1 John).

As I have shown, however, we ought not accept that assumption uncritically. As we saw, Eusebius himself was of mixed mind about who wrote certain Johannine books. He may have thought the Evangelist wrote 1 John, but doubted the same man wrote 2 and 3 John. In addition, his sometimes unsteady interpretation of earlier sources should be cautionary; yet the same unsteady interpretations seem to have had out-sized impact on what developed into the "traditional" view still common in much of the Church today, that all five Johannine books came from the hand of John bar Zebedee. So, the further beyond Eusebius we move, the more we tend to find other authorities of the Church merely upholding that over-simplified view.

Third, as the canon of the New Testament began to be hammered out in the 3rd and 4th centuries, there was, as I have explained, great pressure to insure that the holy books of Christian scripture rested on apostolic authority. This desire, coupled with the uncertainty about who wrote the Johannine books (2 and 3 John and Revelation were often contested), may have reinforced the acceptance of the shaky but popular solution that John bar Zebedee authored them all. Though unproven, this solution gained all five books stronger authority and encouraged wider acceptance. Revelation and 2 and 3 John were ultimately accepted into the canon and were never seriously challenged until the 19th century, with the advent of the historical-critical approach to scriptural study.

From the 4th century forward, therefore, those preferring the traditional view held sway. I have already made my opinion clear, that simply accepting the "John bar Zebedee wrote everything" theory can only be done by ignoring major literary differences between the Fourth Gospel and Revelation, not to mention much of the historical record that I have already discussed.

Upheaval

This traditional view, that John bar Zebedee was the Beloved Disciple and wrote all five Johannine books, began to be vigorously challenged by 19th and 20th century commentators who attacked the problems anew in the name of critical scholarship. Unfortunately, since a good many of them still began from the traditional "base line" that John bar Zebedee must have been the Fourth Evangelist (or at least the authority behind that gospel), they began with their feet in a trap which severely limited scholarly movement in other directions. That is, they ran right into the same thorny maze that Eusebius faced, and some resulting theories became unnecessarily convoluted, trying to explain how such a fine literary work came from the hand of a Galilean fisherman. Coupled with related theories as to why or why not that the same man also wrote Revelation, or the three letters, the theories multiplied and were often contradictory.[2] Indeed, the more one reads recent scholarship, the blurrier the picture turns, and the more tortured the theories become.

The problem, of course, is that when you begin to build on the foundation of a faulty assumption, every new brick you lay atop it will cause further trouble. As you progress, nothing fits the way you hoped it would. This led to what I call the tossed salad approach to the historical details surrounding the Johannine books, which generally includes an outright refusal to give weight to the significant literary differences in content, character and style of the five books — all in name of cementing their apostolic authority. This was never a good path to set out on. The whole process from the 19th century forward, in my opinion, created far more problems than it ever solved.

As I explained in my introduction, I sought to follow a different approach, starting, as it were, with an entirely clean slate, free of any assumption that John bar Zebedee wrote even one of the books. Only with that approach did I believe I could follow where the actual evidence might lead.

As I have begun to lay out, I believe there is an alternative and much simpler explanation that plows through the confusion, sets facts in their proper light, and ends in a solution regarding authorship of all five books that accounts for — and squares with — the earliest historical data we have about them.

The Key: Revelation

I have hinted in previous chapters that in trying to settle the authorship of the Fourth Gospel we must be able to settle the question of who wrote Revelation, primarily because so many commentators past and present (and a good many ordinary readers) cannot believe they came from the same hand. The traditional approach was to assume John bar Zebedee was the Fourth Evangelist, and then try to sort out who may have written Revelation.

So, let us instead pretend it's the end of the first quarter of football and reverse the ends of the field completely. Let us work toward the authorship of the Fourth Gospel from the opposing point of view first: who wrote Revelation?

The place to start is with the obvious and most frequent objection to common authorship: it is very difficult to believe that the same man wrote the beautiful, highly-organized, flowing, poetic Greek of the Gospel but also the patched together, almost piece-meal language and images of Revelation written in almost stumbling Greek. It is a formidable problem debated by students of Scripture for centuries: why would two such books by the same man be so radically different in style, vocabulary and content, not to mention essential theology and viewpoint? Is it simply that the same man sought to create this outright, almost bizarre disparity intentionally? Or, do we have instead two very different books from two very different men?

So, let us consider only a partial reverse of the traditional theory (bar Zebedee wrote everything): that John bar Zebedee did *not* write the Fourth Gospel but *did* write Revelation. If we will risk this, we discover that a possible solution, and the resolution of several difficulties, lay quickly at hand.

As to Revelation: John bar Zebedee was a fisherman from Galilee who Jesus nicknamed one of the "sons of thunder." He was not likely well-lettered or proficient in written Greek. As I said in an earlier chapter, having grown up in Galilee under Roman rule, he would certainly have known basic "*koine*" Greek (the "street" Greek of the empire) that would have been used in daily commerce. He might also have learned, especially if he was imprisoned on Patmos for any length of time, how to write this Greek in an effective if not always lovely form. That is what we find when we look at the language and style of Revelation.

G. B. Caird, a well-respected biblical scholar, in his excellent commentary on Revelation, points out one of the curious things about the Greek found in Revelation. For all its idiosyncrasies, Caird says, John's Greek is not really ungrammatical, rather it is unique: it has a grammar of its own, "unparalleled in any other ancient writing, but none the less real and consistent." Referring to the opinion of R. H. Charles, Caird suggests that John's style in Revelation represents "the hybrid grammar of a man *thinking in Hebrew while he wrote in Greek*" (Caird, p. 5, *emphasis* added).[3]

In other words, John's highly unusual Greek vocabulary and style in Revelation is the product of a man whose first and primary language was Hebrew (or, at that time, Aramaic). He is not completely incompetent in Greek, but simply adopted the language for his particular literary purpose: to record and convey staggering spiritual visions that would be extremely difficult to set down in any language.

Now, if the author of this work was, as I believe, John bar Zebedee, we can easily understand, 1) how he might be somewhat limited in his command of written Greek, but also, 2) why he might take great (and perhaps careless) liberties with this second language which he was essentially forced to use in order to communicate to the churches of Asia Minor to which his seven letters, and his overall book, were specifically addressed. In that case, Charles' central insight is right on the mark and is significant in our attempt to pin down the identity of the author: while writing in Greek, the author was *thinking in Hebrew*. This could certainly describe John bar Zebedee, the Galilean fisherman who knew enough Greek for daily use but was certainly not fluent in Greek literature. This insight lends strong support to my suggestion that John bar Zebedee could certainly have been the author of Revelation, but, with almost equal certainly, could *not* have written the Fourth Gospel.

If we follow this conjecture, the long-standing grammatical and stylistic objections related to "common" authorship of the Fourth Gospel and Revelation simply disappear. There was no common author. We can easily understand how a reasonably unlettered Jewish fisherman from Galilee living in a Roman penal colony might try to communicate his visions to a largely gentile Christian audience in stumbling Greek, while still thinking mainly in his native Hebrew. This "mental translation" process shows up when it is reduced to writing. That is what Charles and Caird point out.

In his general introduction to the commentary, Caird includes these additional insights about the controversy regarding the authorship of Revelation:

> In the second century Justin Martyr (*Tryph. 81*), Melito of Sardis (Eusebius, *H.E.* iv.26.2), the author of the Muratorian Canon, Irenaeus (*Haer.* Iii.11.1; iv.20.11; v.35.2) and Tertullian (*Marc* iii.14.24) all accepted Revelation as scripture and attributed it to the apostle John [that is, bar Zebedee] . . . The recipients of the Revelation knew the identity of the author, and we do not. But there are three distinct points involved here. As we have seen, there was a strong tradition from the time of Justin Martyr, whose debate with the Jew Trypho is located in Ephesus c. AD 135, that the author was John the Apostle, though some vigorously denied this. The evidence of a man who lived in Ephesus only forty years after the probable date of the writing of Revelation might seem to be unassailable. But in fact second-century traditions about the apostles are demonstrably unreliable . . . Moreover, the John who wrote Revelation does not give the impression of being an apostle; he does not appeal to apostolic authority, and he speaks of the twelve apostles in a way hard to understand if he were one of them (Caird, pp. 2-4).

Caird was obviously trying to steer away from the long-established assumption that John bar Zebedee authored Revelation, even though he admits that Justin Martyr, who debated Trypho right there in Ephesus 40 years after John would have written the book in question, is strong evidence indeed. If Caird held to the view that bar Zebedee wrote the Fourth Gospel (I am uncertain on this), his excellent commentary on Revelation makes very clear that it was not written by John the Evangelist; in other words, Caird was building the case that Revelation came from a different man. (There I agree.) I simply ask, did Caird, like Eusebius, have the basic case correct but have the two men reversed?

Caird does make one absolutely key point: "The recipients of the Revelation knew the identity of the author, and we do not." This fact alone should cause us to hesitate in attributing Revelation to someone other than bar Zebedee. If the book was from a relatively unknown disciple, the original recipients in those seven churches would have suspected a fraud. While others later raised doubts about the author, the members of these churches apparently did not. How do we know this? For the simple reason that they carefully preserved the book — a book which by its very nature would have been difficult to preserve, intact and copied without errors, especially considering the stark exhortation of Revelation 22:18-19.

Caird argues that Irenaeus "wrongly supposed that Papias had been a disciple of the apostle John."[4] On the one hand, I agree that Papias was, in fact, a disciple of the "other" John, the Presbyter. On the other hand, I disagree with Caird on his criticism of Irenaeus, for the reasons laid out in Chapter Seven. It is my view that Irenaeus carefully distinguished "John, the disciple of the Lord" from John "the Apostle" (bar Zebedee) knowing that he meant two different men.

To Caird's further objection that this John, the author of Revelation, did not give the impression of being an apostle himself, I would reply thus: we must remember that throughout Revelation John is not recording personal thoughts or opinions but is recording heavenly visions and other voices. Those visions often emanate from an other-worldly perspective (things of earth seen from heaven) in which "the Twelve" have a lesser overall significance. In short, John had no need (and likely no desire) to appeal to his own "apostolic authority" for the very reason that he makes plain in Revelation 1: the visions were given to him directly by the Lord Jesus Christ and his angels, and John,

Apostle or otherwise, personally pales into insignificance by comparison. On this specific point, we must also take into consideration the reality that John was probably in prison or political exile when he began to write; the entire book seems written in a kind of theological code that his readers would understand (better than we) but Roman authorities probably would not. So, John would have nothing to gain — and perhaps a great deal to lose — by reminding his Roman captors (who might see the book) of his position as one of the leaders of the Christian movement, and the surviving brother of James who had already been executed by the Jewish authorities in Jerusalem, and surviving friend of Peter who had probably already been put to death at Rome.

There is also this: although it has been debated whether Revelation was written during the Domitian persecution (as some argue) or the earlier Neronian persecution in the early 60s AD (as others claim), we should not be surprised by the fact that one of the Twelve (indeed one of "the Three") might downplay his identity as a leading apostle in the hope that his prophetic "letters" to the seven churches might actually be allowed to reach them. (If the book was written during the Neronian persecution, it would certainly help solve the age question about the author that I outlined above.)

I have made clear that I agree Revelation came from a different man than the Gospel of John. Based on what I have suggested so far, though, and despite Caird's apparent skepticism, I am inclined to accept what Justin Martyr recorded (for the reasons laid out above) that Revelation *was in fact* written by the Apostle, John bar Zebedee. Short of some obvious evidence which I have yet to come across, this John stands as the author, consistent with the claims of Justin and the several ancient authorities Caird listed in the citation.

Putting Revelation Into Its Time

If we look at the authorship dilemma in its historical context, we must remember that the early doubts about Revelation's authenticity and value rested in large part on the fact that if John bar Zebedee had been the Fourth Evangelist, this other book was simply too far afield to accept as his work also. This is part of the reason Revelation struggled to be accepted into the canon of the New Testament. Not only was there disagreement over the author, but over its contents. St. Jerome said "The Apocalypse of John has as many secrets as words . . . It is beyond all praise," but Martin Luther centuries later condemned it as vindictive and unchristian in spirit.[5]

If we are willing to let go of the idea John bar Zebedee wrote the Fourth Gospel, we will find no compelling reason to doubt that he could have written Revelation — just as our earliest authorities assert. Then, once we accept that bar Zebedee indeed wrote Revelation — and I have found no reason to utterly rule this out — we are free to pursue the reality that some other John wrote the Fourth Gospel. We are freed from the historic objections about common authorship and can continue our consideration of the "other John" who was the Fourth Evangelist.[6] In the next chapter we will look for other early evidence that might be helpful in deciding if my John-Mark proposal holds any water.

Endnotes

1. See Appendices B & C for additional references.
2. See Raymond Brown's *An Introduction To The Gospel Of John,* for an outstanding summary of some of the major arguments. As I have shown, if we begin from a view that bar Zebedee was not the author of the Fourth Gospel, some of the intricate theories regarding its composition and authorship become superfluous.
3. Caird, *Revelation.* Caird, as noted, was quoting the opinion of R. H. Charles. We should know also that when scholars refer to the disciples

speaking "Hebrew," it is likely they spoke the Aramaic language common in 1st century Palestine.

4. See Caird, *Revelation.* When Caird argues that Irenaeus "wrongly supposed that Papias had been a disciple of the apostle John . . .", it is uncertain to what specific passage in Irenaeus he is referring. Does he mean that Papias was not a disciple of *anyone* named John; or does he (more likely) mean that Papias was a disciple of a different John, not "the apostle" bar Zebedee? If so, I of course agree. For as we've seen, the record of Papias quoted by Irenaeus (cited in Chapter Five) does imply there were two well-known "Johns" in the apostolic generation and that Papias himself was a pupil of "John, the presbyter." Yet we must remember that Irenaeus refers to the author of Revelation *with the same title* he used of the Fourth Evangelist.

5. Caird, p. 2.

6. We saw in a previous chapter that Irenaeus accepted the common authorship view, by referring to the author of both the Fourth Gospel and Revelation simply as "John" (for example, *Ag. Her.,* V.36.2) but also as "John, the Lord's disciple" (V.35.2). As I explained, however, Irenaeus differentiated this John ("the disciple") from bar Zebedee. In the same Book V, we find this interesting reference to the author of the Apocalypse:

> Such, then, being the state of the case, and this number [the name of the "beast"] being found in all the most approved and ancient copies [of the Apocalypse], *and those men who saw John face to face* bearing their testimony [to it] . . ." (V.30.1).

He gives us no help in knowing who "those men" were who saw the author of Revelation themselves, and likely heard him talk about the book. The possibilities are simply too wide to even attempt speculation. Since Irenaeus personally knew Polycarp when he (Irenaeus) was a boy, however, and Polycarp was a friend of Papias, they certainly may be meant here.

Nine

I FOCUSED IN PREVIOUS CHAPTERS on two important historical sources, Irenaeus and Eusebius, because they both contain multiple references to the Fourth Evangelist and to the author of Revelation. As we have seen, they both tend to accept the common authorship viewpoint, although Eusebius waivered at times by thinking perhaps a different John wrote Revelation. They do not agree on which John may have been the common author. Irenaeus calls him "John, the disciple of the Lord," and seems to differentiate him from bar Zebedee, whereas Eusebius seems convinced John bar Zebedee wrote the Fourth Gospel, and perhaps Revelation.

In other words, in two of our earliest, primary sources, we find a difference of opinion, and, in one case (Eusebius) a wavering of opinion. This is not surprising, of course, since from the outset we have acknowledged that the authorship of the five Johannine books has been a point of contention and uncertainty from the earliest years of the Church.

I would like now to move on to several other early sources which though lesser known are equally important. They date from before the time of Eusebius, so we must not neglect sources of such antiquity.

Other Significant Evidence

The first of these sources, and the most fruitful for our study is an ancient historical document known as the Muratorian Canon which details bits of history about various New Testament books. The presently existing text of this document is a Latin fragment that dates from the 8th century, but it seems to be a translation of a Greek original that dated from the end of the 2nd century, around 170 AD. If it is authentic, it thus predates Eusebius, and originated around the time of Irenaeus. Although we do not know its author, scholars over the centuries have considered it a reliable source regarding the bits of information it contains regarding the New Testament books generally known and read in the churches of that time.[1]

The Canon contains the following details that are pertinent to this present study:

> The Fourth Gospel is that of John, one of the disciples. When his fellow-disciples and bishops exhorted him he said, "Fast with me for three days from today, and then let us relate to each other whatever may be revealed to each of us." On the same night it was revealed to Andrew, one of the Apostles, that John should narrate all things in his own name as they remembered them . . . The Epistle of Jude indeed, and two bearing the name of John, are accepted in the Catholic Church . . . We receive also the Apocalypse of John and that of Peter (Bettenson, *Documents*, p.40-41).[2]

The 2nd century origin of this document cannot be established with certainty, but is generally accepted by scholars today. If we are willing to accept it as genuine, we find several of the same kind of intriguing oddities about "John" that we saw in other early sources:

    1. The fourth Gospel was authored by "John, one of the *disciples*".
    2. This John, one of the "disciples" was exhorted to write by his "fellow-disciples and bishops."
    3. Yet only a few words later, we have a reference to "Andrew, one of the *Apostles*."

Now, "Andrew, one of the Apostles" almost certainly means the brother of Simon Peter, one of the Twelve. Why did the writer of the Canon make this distinction between a "disciple" and one of "the Apostles" unless he is meaning to differentiate this John from the John who *was* one of the Apostles (bar Zebedee)? Is this, as in Irenaeus, an intentional differentiation, or is it merely a quirk of usage? We have to be careful because even if genuine, this document may be a Latin translation of an earlier Greek text; and we cannot be certain these two terms were in this arrangement in the original, because we don't have it.

Nevertheless, the distinction of John the Evangelist as "John, one of the *disciples*" stands out by contrast with the reference to Andrew, and echoes the familiar phrase that Irenaeus consistently used for the John the Evangelist. We notice, though, that John is named not only among "fellow disciples" but his fellow "bishops."

I would point out something else that we should not ignore, which if not *intended* by the writer of the Canon is certainly a very striking coincidence. In Chapter Three, I suggested that the "unnamed" Beloved Disciple in the later chapters of the Fourth Gospel might also be the "unnamed" disciple of the two mentioned in John 1:35, who were originally disciples of John the Baptist. The other, of course, was *Andrew*. If that suggestion was right and Andrew and the Beloved Disciple were friends from the time they were disciples of the Baptist, we should not miss the significance when the writer of the Canon says it was Andrew who personally urged John to write his gospel.

Is this merely coincidence, a curious detail we should just ignore? Coincidences do occur, but this one seems just a little more than unusual.[3]

To return to the main issue, the Latin of this text of the Canon[4] is very specific. In verse 10, referencing John, the Latin is *Iohannis ex discipulis* (John of the disciples); whereas in verse 14, referencing Andrew, we have *Andreae ex apostolis.* (Andrew of the apostles). This seems to me to be an intentional distinction, in such close proximity. Further on, when the Canon refers to the two known letters of "John," we have the name singly, as we also find in two references to the Apocalypse of John. Does the reference to "John" here mean the same John earlier called "one of the disciples," or a different John? Is the different designation carelessness, or intentional? Or, does the writer simply meant the same John?⁵ We cannot be certain; but we also cannot fail to notice *the echo* of Irenaeus who — writing at about this same time — routinely called the Fourth Evangelist "John, the disciple of the Lord."

Besides the reference to the Apocalypses of John and Peter, the Canon contains two other oblique references to John:

> 31 But it is necessary that we have a discussion singly concerning these, [32] since the blessed Apostle Paul himself, imitating the example of his predecessor, John, wrote to seven churches only by name [and] in this order: [33] The first [Epistle] to the Corinthians, the second to the Ephesians, the third to the Philippians, the fourth to the Colossians, the fifth to the Galatians, the sixth to the Thessalonians, and the seventh to the Romans. 34 But, although he wrote twice to the Corinthians and to the Thessalonians, for reproof (?), [35] nevertheless [it is evident that] one Church is made known to be diffused throughout the whole globe of the earth. [36] For John also, though he wrote in the Apocalypse to seven churches, nevertheless he speaks to them all.⁶

It is fascinating that this passage mentions "the blessed Apostle Paul himself, *imitating the example of his predecessor, John* . . ." (referring to the author of Revelation); but the passage leaves a number of questions dangling. Is the Canon author suggesting that, 1) John wrote Revelation (containing the letters to the seven churches) before Paul wrote *his* seven named letters; or 2) that John wrote other letters also to the wider church (the Canon mentions two of the Johannine letters and quotes one); or, 3) is the writer of the Canon harking back to his mention of "John, one of the disciples," who was the Fourth Evangelist? I cannot tell. What I am sure of is that he refers at least to the author of Revelation as the "predecessor" of Paul. If that is a reference to

John bar Zebedee, he was certainly a "predecessor" apostle, if not a predecessor writer. Because of badly broken wording in places, some scholars believe there are gaps in the text as we have it. So, we must not make too much of these last details.

As to the Evangelist, one might argue that "disciple" and "apostle" (John, and Andrew) are merely equivalent terms in this document; but if so, why use the distinct terms at all? If he meant two members of the Twelve, why not call both apostles? It seems more likely to me that this writer, like Irenaeus, was trying to distinguish between Andrew, of the Twelve, and those other "disciples" who were later *bishops* of the Church.[7]

It could be argued that if our text is indeed a Latin translation of a Greek 2nd century original, the inept 8th century scribe, whose Latin is rather "barbarous,"[8] may simply have confused the terms in translating. Perhaps in the original all were called disciples, or apostles. Apart from making an argument not only from silence but from deafening silence, the problem with this suggestion is that the terms "apostle" and "disciple" are just as distinct in Greek as they are in Latin. One would need to postulate some reason as to why that clear distinction would not have been carried over in translation.

In whatever way we wish to sort out the other references to John and his "fellow disciples and bishops," the important fact I want to highlight is that the Canon tells us this "John of the disciples" personally knew "Andrew of the apostles." In other words, John the Evangelist was a member of the *first generation* of disciples. That would fit bar Zebedee, but it also fits John-Mark.

Another intriguing detail of the Canon is that the "disciples" and "bishops" are fasting and praying about how to best preserve the record of the gospel entrusted to them. Then "Andrew, one of the Apostles" directs "John, one of the disciples" to write down everything he recalls *"in his own name."* That is interesting because it suggests perhaps that "John's own name" might not carry the weight of, say, an Andrew or a Peter. That leads to another question: why did John need Andrew's direction, or encouragement? Was it because the authority of this particular John might have been challenged, apart from Andrew's support? That would certainly not have been true of John bar Zebedee. It might certainly have been true of John-Mark. If bar Zebedee were to write a gospel, he would not need Andrew's approval, or backing, or even encouragement. If, on the other hand, John the Evangelist was the "other John," a younger man not yet as highly respected as the Twelve, the importance of Andrew's "backing" might have been critical to that gospel being received in the Church. We know some questioned the Fourth Gospel because it was so different from the Synoptics. Andrew, however, held a unique position among the Twelve that is not always credited. First a follower of the Baptist (perhaps with John-Mark?), it was Andrew who first brought his brother Peter to meet Jesus. In other words, Andrew would have known that earlier part of Jesus' ministry that happened in Judea — as is only reported in the *Fourth* Gospel. He was a follower of Jesus long before the Galilean ministry reported in the Synoptics began. Was that why Andrew specifically encouraged this John to write another gospel, and said it was to be "in his own name"? That could explain this otherwise mysterious phrase in the Canon.

One last detail of the Muratorian Canon should be noted. The fragment first cited (see Note 2.) mentions two letters "bearing the name of John" besides the "Apocalypse of John." A break in the text means we cannot be certain if the writer means the same John in all three references. If he was *not* speaking of bar Zebedee in regard to the Gospel, he *may* have meant bar Zebedee in regard to the letters (less likely, since they tie to the Gospel), or to Revelation. We simply cannot say for sure; but we can exclude either possibility.[8,9]

Dionysius Of Alexandria

Eusebius' *History of the Church* preserves another piece of information pertinent to this study from Dionysius of Alexandria, who died about 264 A.D. Dionysius was known for his independence as a biblical commentator, and set forth strong arguments for denying the common authorship of the Fourth Gospel and Revelation.[10]

Dionysius, as quoted in Eusebius, argues that some earlier commentators had rejected Revelation altogether and "pulled it entirely to pieces" as not being the work of John the Apostle (bar Zebedee). Dionysius responds with this about who the author might have been. Because of the complexity of his argument, I quote him at length:

> That he was called John, and that this work is John's, I shall therefore not deny, for I agree that it is from the pen of a holy and inspired writer. But I am not prepared to admit that he was the apostle, the son of Zebedee and brother of James, who wrote the gospel entitled According to John and the general epistle. On the character of each, on the linguistic style, and on the general tone, as it is called, of Revelation, I base my opinion that the author was not the same. The evangelist nowhere includes his name or announces himself in either the gospel or the epistle . . . whereas the writer of the Revelation puts himself forward at the very beginning: "The Revelation of Jesus Christ, which He gave Him to show to His servants at once; and He sent and signified it by His angel to His servant John" . . . Next he writes a letter: "John to the seven churches in Asia" . . . Nor again in the second and third extant epistles of John, though they are so short, is John named: he is mentioned anonymously as "the presbyter." But this writer [of Revelation] did not even think it enough, after naming himself once for all, to go on with his story, but goes back to it again: "I John, your brother and partner in the oppression and kingdom and in the patience of Jesus" . . . That the writer was John he himself states, and we must believe him. *But which John?* . . . Many, I imagine, have had the same name as John the apostle...We find too, *another John in the Acts of the Apostles, John surnamed Mark* . . . Was he the writer? I should say not, for he did not go as far as Asia with them as the record shows: "Setting sail from Paphos, Paul and his companions came to Perga in Pamphylia; but John left them and went back to Jerusalem." I think there was another John among the Christians

in Asia, as there are said to have been two tombs at Ephesus, each reputed to be John's . . . we shall readily conclude that this writer was different from the other [the Evangelist]. There is complete harmony between the gospel and the epistle [1 John], and they begin alike . . . But there is no resemblance or similarity whatever between them and the Revelation . . . By the phraseology also we can measure the difference between the Gospel and Epistle and the Revelation. The first two are written not only without any blunders in the use of Greek, but with remarkable skill as regards diction, logical thought, and orderly expression. It is impossible to find in them one barbarous word or solecism, or any kind of vulgarism . . . That the other [the author of Revelation] saw revelations and received knowledge and prophecy I will not deny; but I observe that his language and style *are not really Greek*: he uses barbarous idioms, and is sometimes guilty of solecisms . . . I have not said these things in order to pour scorn on him—do not imagine it—but solely to prove the dissimilarity between these books (Eusebius, *History*, pp. 310-13, emphasis added).

We can sense Dionysius' frustration, to the point that he postulates a *third* John who must have lived in Asia and written Revelation. Before we delve into the various difficulties he found himself facing, however, let us begin by noticing his fundamental viewpoint that *underlies* all those difficulties: he starts from *the assumption* that John bar Zebedee was the Fourth Evangelist. His whole dilemma arises — as it has for so many others — from that assumption: since he believes John bar Zebedee was the Evangelist, and he cannot believe the same man wrote Revelation, he is forced to find a different author for the Apocalypse. Of course, I think he is correct on this last point, although I disagree with his ultimate resolution.

Notice this also. Dionysius does not really reject the authorship by John the Apostle based on the character or content of Revelation, but simply on the fact that he is certain bar Zebedee wrote the Fourth Gospel and rejects the notion that the same hand could have written both: "But I am not prepared to admit that he was the apostle, the son of Zebedee and brother of James, *who wrote the gospel* entitled According to John and the general epistle" (*emphasis* added).

He goes on to make the strong case that others have made about the differences not only between Revelation and the Gospel, but between Revelation and the letters. The language, style, and careful structure of the Gospel and the letters he contrasts with the almost reckless use of Greek in Revelation. (This harks back to Caird's point about a writer thinking in Hebrew but writing in Greek.)

That there is genuine harmony between the Fourth Gospel and the letters I fully agree, which is why I believe one John, "The Presbyter," wrote all four.

What I find most intriguing (perhaps ironic?) is that after wading through these troubles, struggling to identify who this "other John" might be, Dionysius lands *first* on John-Mark. He quickly dismisses the thought almost out of hand without giving John-Mark serious consideration based on the fact that John-Mark abandoned Paul and Barnabas during their first missionary journey. In analyzing Dionysius' overall argument here, I have yet to find why he jumps to that particular conclusion. He seems to have missed, or forgotten John's later history with Paul. As we have seen from Paul's own letters, the earlier falling out with John-Mark (it was really a falling-out with Barnabas) does not override the fact that John-Mark later rejoined Paul in the missionary field, nor the fact that John-Mark may have ultimately settled in the region of Ephesus, one of the churches that preserved Revelation for Dionysius and the rest of us to stew over. (It is possible, of course, that Dionysius did not connect John-Mark of Acts with Mark in Colossians 4. Since John-Mark is identified there as the cousin of Barnabas, and so clearly connected with Barnabas in Acts, I'm not sure why Dionysius would miss this.)[11]

In any case, it is because Dionysius began from the assumption that John bar Zebedee authored the Fourth Gospel that he finds himself entangled in the same thicket that so many other commentators have been caught in over the centuries: if bar Zebedee authored the gospel, then he almost certainly did not author Revelation — despite early evidence that he did, such as that from Justyn Martyr, to the contrary.

If we simply reverse Dionysius' lengthy argument, we can solve the puzzle. If Dionysius had *not* begun from the belief that John bar Zebedee was the Fourth Evangelist, might Dionysius all those centuries ago, in momentarily considering John-Mark as the "other John," have held the solution to the problem in his hand — on the very tip of his pen? If I am correct with my John-Mark proposal, Dionysius had the solution, only backward, and failed to recognize it.

The Supposed Letters of Ignatius

I want to return briefly to consider further the four letters attributed of Ignatius of Antioch that I mentioned in Chapter Four.[12] As I said there, we do not know if these four letters are authentic or pseudonymous forgeries, and we cannot be sure of their dates of origin.

Let me say immediately that I am not trying to vouch for the authenticity of these letters. As I will suggest, though, even if they are of dubious origin they may nonetheless provide some evidence related to "the other John" for whom we are looking. How? In this respect: "pseudepigraphal" works, works falsely attributed to some famous and authoritative person, only gain any notice at all because they typically refer to known historical persons, events, or traditions. Most commonly, they are titled in a way that suggests they are from a respected, authoritative person, in order to give the body of the document the support of the named person's authority. If such works referred to individuals or events that were completely unknown, they would garner little attention, and no traction, among the readers who received them.

For example, if I planned to forge a religious document for which I sought authority and recognition, I would not title it "Baltazar of Galatia to the Irena, the blessed sister of Jesus." Such names would be unrecognizable. Instead, I would choose names or information or events that readers would instantly recognize and likely accept as authentic.

That is precisely what we find, of course, with four of the letters supposedly from Ignatius of Antioch mentioned in Chapter Four. Two of the letters claim to be from Ignatius (Bishop of Antioch who lived from approximately 35-107 AD) and "John the holy Presbyter." The other two claim to be exchanges between Ignatius and Jesus' mother Mary. These letters imply that the recipient "John" was living with, or near Mary, and were undoubtedly based on the scriptural record that John the Beloved Disciple took charge of Mary's welfare and took her into his home after the crucifixion (John 19:26-27).

The interesting thing, for this study, is that the two letters addressed to the Beloved Disciple are to "John, the holy Presbyter." Why? If they are indeed forgeries (they may well-be), why would the forger not make them to "John, the holy Apostle," or "John, son of Zebedee," if that was what the historic tradition around this particular John was? If a forger were trying to garner interest in, or authority for, his letter, wouldn't he choose the John who would be best known to the various churches? Yet he does not identify this John as John bar Zebedee. Why not? The most reasonable answer must be that the forger, in his time, knew that "John the holy presbyter" was also well-known and well-respected, and would possess authority for those who would receive these letters.

Part of our problem is that we have no real idea when these four specific letters, whether authentic or forgeries, were written. Seven of fifteen known (supposed) letters of Ignatius to various churches and to his friend Polycarp were written before his death around 107 AD (some argue for a later date around 140 AD). We know, also, that the tradition about "John the Presbyter" at Ephesus comes from toward the end of the 1st century. If these four letters were forged in Ignatius' name, they most reasonably would have come into circulation not long after that, perhaps in the 2nd century, and no later than the 3rd. Of course, as we know from Eusebius, that by the 4th century many commentators had already begun to confuse, or identify, John the Presbyter with John bar Zebedee.

I have to wonder if part of the reason for the rejection of these letters by some 18th-19th century scholars was precisely because those scholars presumed the "John" meant here was John bar Zebedee, the man so many already *assumed* was the Beloved Disciple. Indeed, even the editorial titling of one of the letters says it is from "Ignatius to *St. John the Apostle,"* even though the text reads that it is to "John, the holy presbyter" (see Appendix E).

Even if these four letters are forgeries, "John the Presbyter" may have been chosen, in part, based on the identification of the author of 2 and 3 John. The problem with that suggestion is that this might simply create a further credibility problem for the forger, since 2 and 3 John were both "contested" books in the early Church — in large part because commentators and early scholars were not certain *who* John the Presbyter was.

The other possibility, which we must not dismiss out of hand, is that these four letters (two to John the Presbyter, and two between himself and Mary) were genuinely from Ignatius, who like his contemporaries Papias and Polycarp would have known "the Presbyter John" well, a man who was not John bar Zebedee but lived in Asia Minor toward the end of that first Christian century. Ignatius was a well-beloved Bishop of Antioch in the 1st century, the 2nd successor to Peter as bishop there.[13] More importantly, for our interest, he was a contemporary of Papias of Hierapolis who was a disciple of this "John the Presbyter." As noted, Ignatius was also a contemporary with Polycarp of Smyrna, who also likely knew this particular John, the Presbyter. Indeed, one of his last letters was to Polycarp. Because Ignatius' wrote several of his other (believed to be authentic) letters during his journey toward martyrdom in Rome around 107-108 AD, any additional letters supposedly from his hand would have gained immediate notice as the words of a beloved bishop and martyr, but only if they sounded authentic.

The most we can say on this matter is this: if the four letters I have referred to were in fact genuine, and were in circulation fairly early in the church, they give support to the view that "John the Presbyter" was a well-known leader. If, on the other hand, we land with the majority of scholars today who believe these four letters to be pseudonymous forgeries, they tell us, at least, that the forger had used the tradition about John the Beloved Disciple also being known as John the Presbyter.

We also find in one of these letters another intriguing detail: the letter is addressed (supposedly) from Ignatius to "the Christ-bearing Mary." The writer ("Ignatius") refers to himself as "a disciple of your [beloved] John." It implies, as does one of the letters of Ignatius to John the Presbyter that Ignatius first came to know this John, the caretaker of Mary, while she was still living with him *in Jerusalem*. This is interesting, of course, because, 1) John-Mark was originally from Jerusalem, but more-so because, 2) John-Mark spent time in Antioch with Paul and Barnabas before their first missionary journey, at a time when Ignatius would have been a young man in the church there.

The fourth letter, supposedly a reply from Mary to Ignatius, is also interesting for this detail:

> The things which you have heard and learned from John concerning Jesus are true . . . Now I will come in company with John to visit you).[14]

Did Mary, in fact, ever visit Ignatius at Antioch? Is this pure legend, or based on an historical event? It is not out of the realm of possibility, if the visit occurred while she and this John were still living at his home in Jerusalem. Travel between the Christian communities at Jerusalem and Antioch was common, as we know from the Book of Acts. Exactly how long John and our Lord's mother remained in Jerusalem we don't know. If, as one later tradition suggests, this John and Mary both left Jerusalem, perhaps during one of the violent persecutions of the

Church, that may be when "John the Presbyter" went and settled in Ephesus.[15]

The point is that if these are indeed forgeries, the forger knew of these early traditions and believed they would lend credibility to what he wrote. Seemingly innocuous letters like these about visits, however, do not seem like something a forger would make up out of whole cloth. What purpose would they actually serve? They tell us nothing, as some of the other pseudo-Ignatian letters do, about later theological controversies. If these details were simply fabrications of a writer's mind, it would not seem to help purchase much credibility for his "letters."

We will find no certainty here, but it is worth considering these short letters because they provide one more small piece of evidence for the existence of our elusive "John the Presbyter" by identifying him as John, the Beloved Disciple. If they reflected genuine early tradition, it is helpful to our overall understanding.

Summary

Based on all the evidence considered so far, I concur with those who believe that the "other John," the Fourth Evangelist, was the Beloved Disciple to whom Jesus commended his mother Mary at the foot of his cross, and that this John was later known as the Presbyter John who died at Ephesus near the end of the 1st century.

I would suggest this rough chronology: After the Crucifixion, Mary went to live immediately at this John's house in (or near) Jerusalem; she remained there after the Ascension and Resurrection of Jesus. She may have traveled with John to churches in that region, perhaps Antioch, which was the other early center of the Faith (Acts 11:26). Eventually, she and John left Jerusalem permanently and traveled to their new home in Ephesus. There, John the Presbyter became a leader of the regional churches, along with John bar Zebedee, who arrived at Ephesus either before, or after, his time on the island of Patmos.

John the Beloved Disciple, no doubt with the assistance of Mary, likely wrote down many parts of what later became the

Fourth Gospel. Sometime during those later years, with the possible encouragement of his close friend Andrew, John wrote the original body of the Fourth Gospel. During the Ephesus period, he also wrote the three epistles to regional churches to encourage them to stand fast against false teachers who were already raiding the Church. Also (as I will develop in the next chapter), it may have been during those years in Ephesus that Luke, the co-worker of Paul, had the opportunity to talk not only with John-Mark but with Mary herself, in researching his own gospel.[16]

Endnotes:
1. A full English translation of the text of the Canon can be found online at https://www.earlychristianwritings.com/muratorian.html An English translation accompanied by the original Latin text is found at https://www.earlychristianwritings.com/text/muratorian-latin.html
2. Bettenson, *Documents of the Christian Church,* following Wescott's translation. A possible reading of the last phrase cited, according to Bettenson, would be "the Apocalypse of John and one epistle only of Peter." There was, however, a known "Apocalypse of Peter" that dated from around 100-150 AD that may have been meant here. It is said to have been nearly as popular as John's Apocalypse (Revelation), although it was never accepted into the New Testament canon.

> In a different translation found at www.earlychristianwritings.com, we find these further details about the man called simply "John":
>> [20] What marvel, therefore, if John so constantly brings forward particular [matters] also in his Epistles, saying of himself: [21] "What we have seen with our eyes and have heard with [our] ears and our hands have handled, these things we have written to you." [22] For thus he declares that he was not only an eyewitness and hearer, but also a writer of all the wonderful things of the Lord in order.

We should note that although the quotation is from 1 John 1:1, the writer speaks of John's "epistles" in the plural.
3. John 1:35-41: "Again the next day John was standing with two of his disciples, 36 and he looked at Jesus as He walked, and *said, "Behold, the Lamb of God!" 37 The two disciples heard him speak, and they followed Jesus . . . 40 One of the two who heard John speak and followed Him, was

Andrew, Simon Peter's brother. 41 He found first his own brother Simon and *said to him, "We have found the Messiah" (which translated means Christ)" (NASB).

4. The Latin text is included at
https://www.earlychristianwritings.com/text/muratorian-latin.html
(see note 1.).

5. In the translation of the Canon cited from www.earlychristianwritings.com (Note 1.), we find this at verses 41-43:

> The Epistle of Jude indeed and the two with the superscription "Of John," are accepted in the General [Church] . . . We accept only the Apocalypses of John and of Peter, although some of us do not want it to be read in the Church.

We cannot be certain here which two of the Johannine epistles are meant, although the Canon does quote 1 John 1:1 (Note 2).

6. Citation from:
https://www.earlychristianwritings.com/text/muratorian-latin.html

7. Some may argue that "bishops" were equivalent with "presbyters," so either could be applied to Andrew, or some other disciple. That can be argued within the bounds of the New Testament itself, but here we are dealing with someone writing probably one hundred years after the New Testament books themselves, when bishops had emerged as supervisors of the body of local presbyters.

8. Bettenson, p. 40.

9. In his Preface to the Gospel of Matthew, Jerome (342?-420 AD) gives this catalogue of the four gospels. Although Jerome falls beyond the date of Eusebius, I provide this additional source here because it seems Jerome has used at least some material from the Muratorian Canon as one source for this listing, perhaps along with Irenaeus and Eusebius:

> The first evangelist is Matthew, the publican, who was surnamed Levi. He published his Gospel in Judæa in the Hebrew language, chiefly for the sake of Jewish believers in Christ, who adhered in vain to the shadow of the law, although the substance of the Gospel had come. The second is Mark, the amanuensis of the Apostle Peter, and first bishop of the Church of Alexandria. He did not himself see our Lord and Saviour, but he related the matter of his Master's preaching with more regard to minute detail than to historical sequence. The third is Luke, the physician, by birth a native of Antioch, in Syria, whose praise is in the Gospel. He was himself a disciple of the Apostle Paul, and composed his book in Achaia and Boeotia. He thoroughly investigates certain particulars and, as he himself confesses in the preface, describes what he had heard rather than what he had seen. The

last is John, the Apostle and Evangelist, whom Jesus loved most, who, reclining on the Lord's bosom, drank the purest streams of doctrine, and was the only one thought worthy of the words from the cross, "Behold! thy mother." When he was in Asia, at the time when the seeds of heresy were springing up (I refer to Cerinthus, Ebion, and the rest who say that Christ has not come in the flesh, whom he in his own epistle calls Antichrists, and whom the Apostle Paul frequently assails), he was urged by almost all the bishops of Asia then living, and by deputations from many Churches, to write more profoundly concerning the divinity of the Saviour, and to break through all obstacles so as to attain to the very Word of God (if I may so speak) with a boldness as successful as it appears audacious. Ecclesiastical history relates that, when he was urged by the brethren to write, he replied that he would do so if a general fast were proclaimed and all would offer up prayer to God; and when the fast was over, the narrative goes on to say, being filled with revelation, he burst into the heaven-sent Preface: "In the beginning was the Word, and the Word was with God, and the Word was God: this was in the beginning with God" (Schaff, The Principle Works of St. Jerome, p. 1068, found at https://ccel.org/ccel/schaff/npnf206/npnf206. (Note: a portion of this section was cited in an early chapter regarding Mark the Evangelist being the "amanuensis of St. Peter.)

10. See article, Dionysius "The Great" in *The Oxford Dictionary of the Christian Church.*

11. See again Colossians 4:10, where Paul identifies John-Mark as the cousin of Barnabas.

12. See Chapter Four, End Note 7.

13. Eusebius, *History of the Church,* p. 145.

14. See Appendix E for the citations of these letters, and more on the question of their authenticity

15. There are conflicting traditions about where Mary died, and where she was buried. One long-standing tradition says she died and was buried in Jerusalem. The Church of the Sepulcher of Mary is venerated there to this day (see: https://www.holylandsite.com/marys-tomb). But it is based only on apocryphal works of the second to the fourth century, such as the "Acts of St. John by Prochurus", written (160-70).

The competing tradition says Mary moved to Ephesus with John the Beloved Disciple, and that she died and was buried there. (A good many holding this view believe, of course, that this John "the Evangelist" was bar Zebedee.) According to an article published by New Advent, "Many scholars believe that she died in Jerusalem. But another tradition asserts

that Mary accompanied St. John to Asia Minor and settled in a small house outside of Ephesus, which was the most important and prosperous city of the region during that time" (Article at EWTN: https://www.ewtn.com/catholicism/library/marys-last-earthly-home-5608).
Some present-day scholars accept the Ephesus tradition, which is based in part on a letter that was sent from the members of the Council of Ephesus (431 AD) to the clergy of Constantinople which notified them that Nestorius had arrived in the city of Ephesus where "John the Theologian and the Mother of God, the Holy Virgin, were separated from the assembly of the holy Fathers," referring to the long-held local tradition that John the Evangelist and the Virgin Mary were both buried at Ephesus. (New Advent article at: https://www.newadvent.org/cathen/14774a.htm#:~:text=The%20tomb%20of%20the%20Blessed,and%20was%20buried%20at%20Ephesus).

16. Luke is the only gospel to give us details of the conception and birth of Jesus from Mary's perspective. Luke claims to have exhaustively researched his gospel with "eyewitnesses." Was Mary one of those? A meeting in Ephesus during these later years of her life, after she and John left Jerusalem, would answer a great deal of questions.

Ten

OVER THE COURSE of fourteen years of research for this study, after making repeated assessments of what actual evidence we have regarding the authorship of the Fourth Gospel and the other Johannine books, I settled on the theory that John-Mark may have been the author of John and the likely author of the three Johannie letters (though not Revelation).

In 2018, while doing further online research, I discovered a 1960 article in the *Journal of Biblical Literature* by Pierson Parker, then a professor at General Theological Seminary in New York. I found, to my amazement, that Parker's Article "John and John Mark" not only contained helpful analytical detail about the Fourth Gospel but landed squarely on my previous supposition that John-Mark was likely the Fourth Evangelist.[1]

Parker's article did not go into the historical evidence that I have assembled here; rather, it focused strictly on the internal evidence of the New Testament. Parker highlights what I laid out in the early chapters of this study: such details as the fact the John-Mark lived in Jerusalem, and the fact that settings in and around Jerusalem and Judea take up four-fifths of John's gospel. He likewise notes that John-Mark was probably of the Levitical (priestly) family, and emphasizes how much John's gospel focuses not only on Jerusalem, but on the Temple, the sacrifices conducted there, and the relationship of Jesus' sacrifice on the cross to killing of the Passover lambs. (Only John ties the crucifixion to the day of that slaughter in preparation for Passover.)

Parker suggests that this other John, John-Mark, may have been of a well-to-do family in Jerusalem (known to — and possibly related to — the high priest) and goes so far as to suggest that the "large upper room" where the Last Supper was held may have been in Mary and John-Mark's home. That, of course, would further explain how John-Mark, the Beloved Disciple, came to be *an actual eye-witness* to the crucial Passion events. It might also help explain some of the copious detail we find about the supper in the Fourth Gospel that is missing entirely in the Synoptics. Just two examples make the point: 1) that Jesus, during the supper, removed his outer garment, tied a towel around his waist, and washed the feet of his disciples, an event entirely missing from the other three gospels; and, 2) the statement from Jesus to the Beloved Disciple identifying his betrayer:

> So lying thus, close to the breast of Jesus, he said to him, "Lord, who is it?" Jesus answered, "It is he to whom I shall give this morsel when I have dipped it." So when he had dipped the morsel, he gave it to Judas, the son of Simon Iscariot (John 13:25-26).

Such details, of course, do not even begin to take into account the extremely long teaching narrative and prayer recorded through chapters 14-17, unmatched by anything in the Synoptics. Some modern scholars argue that the whole of these chapters are simply a "made-up" narrative to give later theological meaning to the brief events of what was a routine Passover supper. Consider, however, that if John-Mark was actually present that night, and considering the events that followed over the next day at the cross, the words of Jesus from that supper may have been quite literally burned into his memory. Also, we should not fail to recall Jesus' own promise in this regard (John 14:26; cf. 16:4).

The other central point of Parker's article is to draw out the fascinating relationships and correspondences that exist between the Third Gospel and the Fourth. He outlines no less than 120 points of similarity or contact between Luke and John, and challenges, as I have, the notion that John-Mark wrote the Second Gospel. Pierson's conclusions rest in part on the fact that Paul's later letters show John-Mark again working alongside Paul in Asia Minor, presumably during the timeframe that the physician Luke was also there. Parker specifically points out the obvious, which so many commentators miss: that each time Paul mentions Mark in concluding those letters, he mentions Luke, also (Col 4:10, 14; Philemon 24; II Tim 4:10).

Although he does not refer to the Peter and Peter's "son" argument that I presented above, Parker does develop the view that John-Mark wrote the Fourth Gospel, not the Second. If he was correct, as I believe he was, then we have a plausible explanation for the many significant commonalities that exist between the gospels of Luke and John. Those connections, Parker shows, are no accident. These two men would not only have known each other but had worked together and traveled with Paul for some length of time, during the timeframe when their gospels would have been in the formative stages. As Parker highlights:

> Both these Evangelists discuss their own writing tasks (Luke 1 1-3; John 21 24 f.). Both are interested, far more than the others, in Samaria and Judea, in Jerusalem and in the Temple. Both place the feeding of the five thousand on the eastern shore of the lake (Luke 9 1; John 6 1). Neither speaks of any extensive Galilean ministry after that feeding and, in both, Peter's confession follows it immediately. Both show special interest in Jesus' mother; describe the sisters Mary and Martha; and tell of someone named Lazarus, whose return from death would fail to convert the nation" ("John and John Mark," p. 99).

Parker enumerates many similar details between these two gospels. With the publisher's permission, I want to quote some of Parker's comparisons of Luke and John at length to make his detailed perspective clear:

In writing of John the Baptist, both stress his name and his divine commission, give far more of his teaching than the other Gospels do, tell of popular wonder as to whether he was the Messiah; yet are exceedingly sketchy about his imprisonment. Both stress, more than the other Gospels, the inclusiveness of the word "disciple." Both say that Satan entered into Judas Iscariot (Luke 22 3; John 13 27). In both, Jesus tells Peter of the latter's restoration and commands him henceforth to lead the young Church (Luke 22 31 f.; John 21 15 ff.). Both describe Passovers before the last one, are interested in chronology, and in Jesus' age. Each describes a miraculous catch of fish. Each details the charges against Jesus and, in each, Pilate three times declares Jesus innocent. Both Luke and John have two angels at the tomb, tell what Mary Magdalene said to the Eleven, and report the disciples' visit to the sepulchre. The earliest Resurrection appearances are in or near Jerusalem, and include one in the upper room. The disciples at first fail to recognize Jesus, and he asks them to verify his physical reality by touching him. Both authors refer to the Ascension (Luke 24 50 ff.;9 John 3 13; 6 62). As is often remarked, even John 14-16 would seem more appropriate to the pre-Ascension period: its content closely resembles Acts 1 4-8, though the wording is utterly different. In Christology, Luke has fewer signs of a Messianic secret than have the other Synoptics, while John has none at all. Both Luke and John use "son of man" frequently before Peter's confession, yet neither has nearly as much apocalyptic as have the other Gospels. Only in Luke and John is Jesus able to slip miraculously through a crowd (Luke 4 29 f.; John 8 59). Only in these are we told that his followers "saw his glory" (Luke 9 32; John 1 14). In fact, by the present writer's count, John has some 120 points of agreement with Luke against the first two Gospels. This is about five times as many as its contacts with Matthew alone, or with the Second Gospel alone, or with those two against Luke. While such a count is bound to be rough, it is nonetheless plain that the Third Gospel is related to the Fourth in a way completely unmatched by the other Synoptics. Yet these agreements are usually put in very different language, and set within totally different contexts and circumstances. The situation is precisely like that of two authors, of widely variant personality and education, who worked for a time in the same areas and shared a common oral tradition. That is what Luke and John Mark did (Parker, "John and John Mark," pp. 99-100; original footnotes omitted).

Parker lays out many further reasons to suppose that the Fourth Evangelist was John Mark, including these:

In the NT, of all the men named John, only John Mark is ever placed in Ephesus (I Tim 1 3; II Tim 1 18; 4 12). Mark's stay at Ephesus is asserted also by later writers. Certainly he would have been well-known there! *Therefore either Mark was one of the two Ephesian leaders named John, to whom Papias, Dionysius, and Eusebius refer; or, if there was only one such person, he was John Mark.* Yet none but the Fourth Gospel is ever called 'the Ephesian Gospel'" (John and John Mark, p. 103; *emphasis added*).

Finally, Parker adds this observation:

As every NT student knows, Papias' statement about Mark seems to bristle with difficulties. Yet the worst difficulty is seldom dwelt upon: Papias' words just do not fit our Second Gospel at all. *The fact is, they describe the Fourth*" (p. 103, *emphasis added*).

Suffice to say, Parker's article touches on, and supports, a number of the same points I have made in this study that bear on the identity of John the Evangelist. He supports, with great detail, my suggestion that John-Mark may have been that author.[2]

Endnotes

1. The Parker article can be purchased on line at: https://www.jstor.org/stable/3264460. All quotations are used by permission of the publisher.

2. I would commend the entire Parker article to any serious students of the Fourth Gospel. It is not a lengthy article and is well-worth the time.

Eleven

FROM THE OUTSET of this study, I have attempted to do one central thing: to examine not just traditional theories about the authorship of the Fourth Gospel but to carefully examine and assess what precious little evidence we actually have about the Johannine books and their origin. Here, I want to try to sum up what I believe the actual evidence tells us about the identity of John the Evangelist.

A Picture That Makes Sense

If we are willing to set aside the idea that the Fourth Evangelist was a humble Galilean fisherman whose command of written Greek was likely far less than what we find in John, we need to seek a different author. If we are willing to consider John-Mark instead, we may have an author, 1) who was raised from childhood in cosmopolitan Jerusalem, 2) who was intimately acquainted with the people and places in and about the Holy City, and 3) if he is the disciple mentioned in 18:15, he was even acquainted with the high priest of the Jewish faith — one of the most powerful persons in Israel. We then have a gospel written not by a fisherman, nor patched together by a committee of early-Christian theologians (as some would have it), but written by a man who may, like Paul (Acts 22:3), have been trained in one of the respected rabbinical schools of Jerusalem. We discover an evangelist who could have known not only Hebrew and Aramaic but also the literary Greek that was the language of the "educated" members of this part of the Roman Empire at this period. This John, John-Mark, could plausibly be seen as a writer who knew passages of both the Septuagint (Greek) translation of the Old Testament, the "Bible" in common use among faithful Jews of that period, and the Hebrew original. If he was raised and educated in Jerusalem instead of "Galilee of the Gentiles," we can easily understand how John-Mark would have been more knowledgeable of the Hellenized Jewish thought of his day, including the Hellenistic concept of the *"logos"* (the Word) of God that we find to be central to this gospel's Prologue. We also now have a man who was intimately knowledgeable of the city of Jerusalem and its glorious Temple, and the families that were central to carrying on the Jewish worship of the time.

What We Know

As soon as we shift perspectives to consider John-Mark as our author, a great deal that seems confusing about the origin of the Fourth Gospel makes sense and becomes less confusing. Many questions posed by scholars over the years began with a thought such as, "How could a fisherman from Galilee have . . . ," and we can complete the sentence in a dozen ways. If, instead, John the Evangelist actually grew up in the schools of Jerusalem, and was related to some of the priestly family, we see how some precise details long written off by scholars as essentially "make-believe" suddenly become readily believable (like John 18:15-18, and 18:25-27), and critically important. Further, if it was the case that this John later lived in Ephesus, along with bar Zebedee, and came to be distinguished as "the Presbyter John," "the (Beloved) disciple of the Lord," we will have little trouble accepting that the three Johannine letters came from this Presbyter's hand, the same hand, as many have long believed, that wrote the Gospel.

The evidence I have put forth in this study, along with the evidence cited in Pierson Parker's article (referenced in the previous chapter) presents a very plausible case for John-Mark as our candidate for the Fourth Evangelist.

Let me sum up some of the basic pieces of that evidence. When we begin from the assumption that John-Mark was the Evangelist, the Beloved Disciple, we discover a young man who could, in fact, have met Jesus — as John 1 tells us — during the time John the Baptist was still preaching and baptizing in that region (Matthew 3:1; Mark 1:5), long before the focus of Jesus' ministry moved to Galilee. We have now a responsible basis to believe that the period of early ministry by Jesus in and around Jerusalem that the Fourth Gospel describes is, in fact, accurate, that period of ministry of a year to year-and-a-half that predated the Galilean ministry reported in the Synoptics.

We should also note one easily missed detail: that John-Mark himself, a cousin of the Levite Barnabas, may have been of the Levitical tribe, as we know that John the Baptist was (Luke 1). As we add such details together, it becomes harder and harder to make the easy assumption that all these connections are mere accidents.

We understand, also, how John-Mark could have known another family who plays a very prominent role in the Fourth Gospel: Mary, her sister Martha, and their brother Lazarus, close friends of Jesus who lived in a village just two miles outside Jerusalem. Indeed, John-Mark could have been present near Bethany that day for the second most miraculous event recorded in the Fourth Gospel, the raising of Lazarus from the dead, the event that according to John was critical in leading to the arrest of Jesus, and an event completely missing from the Synoptic record. Perhaps John-Mark was sitting with Jesus and the others that evening, in the home at Bethany just before Passion week, when Mary bathed the Lord's feet in perfumed ointment, as the beautiful odor filled the air, an act ominously foreshadowing not only Jesus' burial one week later (John 12:3), but also Lazarus' betrayal (John 12:4-8; See Appendix B).

Who but an actual eye-witness would have remembered, and recorded, such fine detail about what probably seemed an insignificant event at the time?

If John-Mark was a member of the Levitical tribe, it explains how one of Jesus' closest disciples would have known both Jesus' close friends and also the high priest and his household, a person who could usher Peter past the gate into the very courtyard of the high priest's residence, a place normally guarded closely, and where Jesus was then being interrogated after his arrest. Indeed, John-Mark's kinship might have been the only thing that prevented Peter's arrest on the spot when he was challenged three different times.

As we look at such details, the "mystery man" behind the Fourth Gospel becomes much less mysterious. Consider John-Mark in the light of these other details about the Fourth Gospel:

1. The Beloved Disciple was, according to very early tradition, a fairly young man when he first met Jesus through John the Baptist — a relative of Jesus — shortly after Jesus' own baptism.

2. During this earliest period of Jesus' ministry in and around Jerusalem, when Jesus first inflamed the opposition of the Sanhedrin over "cleansing the Temple" (John 2:13-22), John-Mark could have spent time with other of Jesus' friends, including the family of Mary, Martha, and Lazarus at Bethany; but Jesus could also, conceivably, have spent time with a different Mary, John-Mark's mother, in their home in Jerusalem, a home to which he would later commend the care of his own mother (John 19:26-27).

3. If John-Mark developed a special kinship with Jesus as his Beloved Disciple, we can understand how he could have been present during events he would later record in his gospel. He could, for example, have been with Jesus that evening when Nicodemus, a member of the Sanhedrin, came secretly to speak to Jesus and ask him questions. It is believable that as an educated young man, John might have shortly after written down the fascinating conversation the two men had that night, a conversation that would become one of the best known of the entire New Testament. Was that conversation, as some scholars have claimed, merely a nice theological fabrication of one of several authors of a later-pieced-together gospel? Or were these "words of life" actual words John heard from the lips of Jesus?

4. John could have heard many other actual teachings of Jesus in Jerusalem during this time period, before most of the Twelve had even been chosen by Jesus. Those teachings included many in the Temple itself that we would not have, had not John recorded them.

5. If John-Mark was, as I believe, the other unnamed disciple of John the Baptist mentioned in John 1, then he was friends with Andrew and so, early on, would have become friends with Andrew's brother Peter. This would help us understand why he was close by with Peter when Mary Magdalene came rushing in with such astonishing news on Easter morning (John 20). This would also explain why, after an angel freed him from prison, Peter fled that night to the home of John-Mark and his mother Mary for sanctuary (Acts 12).

6. John-Mark's closeness to Jesus, as the young man Jesus had befriended to mentor in the New Covenant, explains why he was there at the Last Supper. (Parker, as noted in the previous chapter, even suggested the supper was held in an upper room in John's home.) John was there at Jesus' right side at their table, and leaned against his chest to ask about the impending betrayal by Judas.

7. John would have gone out with Jesus and the others to the Garden of Gethsemane before his arrest. John watched as Peter sliced off the ear of the high priest's slave, a man he knew as Malchus.

8. When all the others fled, John-Mark stayed with Peter, as they followed at a distance while Jesus was dragged back through the city gates and into the courtyard of the high priest's house for interrogation. John either knew the maidservant at the gate that night, or at least she knew who John was (John 18:16). So, he was able to persuade her to let Peter inside the courtyard, too. (I must mention here again the absolute unlikelihood of what the "traditional" view would suggest we believe at this moment: that the intermediary with the servant girl was John bar Zebedee, an unknown Galilean

fisherman who likely knew very few people in Jerusalem — let alone in the high priest's household.)

We can imagine John-Mark's sadness, having gotten his good friend Peter into the courtyard, having to watch Peter three different times deny that he even knew this man Jesus. We will recall, though, that John was fortunate to be there on a morning not many days or weeks hence by the Lake of Galilee when he witnessed Peter's restoration (John 21).

9. When Peter himself also fled, and Jesus had been condemned by his own countrymen before Pilate, John-Mark found Jesus' mother and faithfully — and apparently fearlessly — stood at the very foot of the cross with his master's anguished mother. When, just before his death Jesus looked down at them and placed his mother into John's care, he did not hesitate. "From that hour," he would later write, he took her into his own home, which was not, as the traditional view would tell us, in Galilee, but nearby in Jerusalem.

10. John-Mark was with Peter Easter morning, no doubt still grieving, when Mary Magdalene arrived with the unbelievable claim that Jesus had risen, that the tomb of Jesus was empty, and she had just seen Jesus alive. The younger John outpaced Peter running to the tomb. He saw the grave clothes, and believed. We can recognize certain fine details about the grave cloths as *authentic observations* of an actual eyewitness, such as the fact that the head wrapping was "not lying with the linen cloths but folded up in a place by itself" (20:7 ESV).

11. Although Thomas was missing, John-Mark was no doubt in the upper room that night when Jesus suddenly and inexplicably stood among them, alive. He was probably present, also, the following Sunday evening, when Jesus again appeared to the group of disciples and chastised Thomas for his unbelief (John 20).

12. We can safely assume that John-Mark would have been with the disciples, at least at times, during the forty days that Jesus continued to appear to his disciples to

teach them of the Kingdom, and their coming mission (Acts1:3-4). He was likely among the 120 disciples who remained gathered in Jerusalem after the resurrection (Acts 1:15), when they drew straws to replace Judas Iscariot. He himself, of course, was not considered, because of his young age. Yet even during these early days, John-Mark may have been diligently starting to write it all down, forming the framework for his gospel, organizing it into its early shape.

13. John-Mark would later travel with his cousin Barnabas and a new convert named Saul to the church in Antioch; and he would accompany the two men as the Antioch church sent them off on their first missionary journey into Asia Minor. He would depart back to Jerusalem; we don't know why. Did it have to do with the fact that he still felt responsible for Mary at Jerusalem? We can only speculate.

14. He continued to care for Mary in his home, but at some point, perhaps during a persecution and after the murder of James bar Zebedee, he and Mary left Jerusalem and moved to the city (or region) of Ephesus. There, now much older, he was known simply at John the Presbyter, who had been an especially close friend of Jesus. During those later years, he reconnected with Paul and eventually went to Rome to see Paul after Paul's arrest in Jerusalem and appeal to Caesar. During the time in Rome, or perhaps later when Luke returned to Asia Minor, Luke and John-Mark compared and discussed what they were writing to record Jesus' life, death, and resurrection. What they shared led to Luke learning the unique stories from Mary of the miraculous conception and birth of her Son, and Jesus' relationship with John the Baptist. Luke could have also learned, here, about later events like the trip to Passover in Jerusalem when Jesus was twelve.

15. If John knew such details were being set down by Luke, it might explain why he himself decided to omit any history of Jesus' childhood and begin his own account with

the baptism of Jesus by John the Baptist. Or it may be, as I suggested in an early chapter, that as an actual eyewitness, John chose to record only those things of which he had some immediate or personal knowledge.

Such connections and details begin not only to take shape and form a whole picture, but to make reasonable sense once we let go of the traditional view that John bar Zebedee was the Fourth Evangelist. While we cannot prove in any iron-clad manner that John-Mark was the actual author, he at least fits better with the realities of what evidence we *do* have from the gospel itself, from the three letters John wrote, and from early references to John the Evangelist. This is, perhaps, the most we can hope for until, and unless, some further new evidence surfaces for our consideration.

Twelve

WHEN WE SET OUT to solve a dilemma, we can easily create new ones in its place. I expect others reading this study may find new problems my John-Mark proposal may beget. I hope those are not insurmountable.

My goal has been to try to bring clarity to what has always been a muddy picture. As I have shown, a lot of confusion has arisen over many centuries about who wrote the Fourth Gospel, the three letters, and the Book of Revelation. Despite the fact that many today still land with both feet on the oversimplified suggestion that John bar Zebedee wrote all five books, the debates continue to percolate through Christian biblical studies and among many good scholars who think that solution is unsupportable and who are not averse to challenging the "climate of opinion."

It is certainly the case that a good many commentators still reject the views of Brown and others and continue to hold the traditional assumption that John bar Zebedee was the Beloved Disciple and Fourth Evangelist. Open many popular commentaries or study bibles today and you will probably find that claim expressed. You will also most likely find the claim that bar Zebedee also authored the three letters. Finally, many of the same study guides continue to assert that "John Mark of Acts" was, without any question or doubt, the author of the Gospel of Mark. Some claim this "fact" goes back to the very beginning of church history, and that "all" the early Christian writers agree. In actual fact, the belief that John-Mark wrote the Second Gospel only came to be common in the time of St Jerome in the mid-fourth century, and only after a great deal of question about that gospel's origin.

As I have demonstrated, such popular assertions are not iron-clad and are wide open to debate. It may be that some commentators cling to these traditional assumptions because they believe these are the only safe grounds upon which to maintain the claim of "apostolic" authority for books like Mark (who was not an original disciple) and John. As I have pointed out, however, such apprehension is misguided. "Apostolic" authority of works in the early church was not based solely on the writer's name, but rather upon whether or not the book came either from "an eyewitness" to the risen Jesus, or at least from a writer who recorded the teaching of such an eyewitness (cf. Acts 1:21-23). Authority also rested on whether or not the teaching of a particular book was, on the whole, *consistent* with all other accepted Christian scripture and theology. Apostolic authority never meant that a book was written by "one of the Twelve." Had that been the case, Mark, Luke, and perhaps even Matthew (which, like Luke, seems to embody much of Mark) would have been excluded from the canon.[1] The great apostle Paul was not of the Twelve, although he tells us he had, indeed, seen the risen Christ (1 Corinthians 9:1; cf. Acts 9). Likewise, James was a relative of Jesus, but not of the Twelve.

So, although I have challenged the common wisdom about the origin of four of the Johannine books, what I have suggested *in no way* brings into question the apostolic authority of the Fourth Gospel or the three companion letters. If anything, the John-Mark theory strongly *enhances* the eye-witness authority of all four books, placing them without question as a product of an important member of the apostolic generation. If John-Mark was the Beloved Disciple, one of the people closest to our Lord during his early ministry, we could not ask for greater authority.

Some may object that the few mentions of John-Mark in Acts are insufficient to point to him possibly being one of the evangelists. That is a fair point, but we would have to make the same objection about St. Luke, who is essentially unknown in scripture except for three vague mentions by St. Paul (unless one credits, as many do, the "we" sections of Acts as references to himself). Further, if I am correct that the author of the Gospel of Mark is a different Mark, the scribe of St. Peter at Rome, then we would have to level the same objection against him. As I discussed in Chapter Five, however, when we look through the New Testament for possibilities, there is simply no other man who is a possible candidate for "the other John." Knowing that John-Mark was John the Evangelist would have been reason enough to explain why Luke mentioned John-Mark in Acts at all. Of the hundreds of disciples who populated the infant Church, why else would John-Mark receive such prominent mention, linked not only to Paul and Barnabas, but to Peter himself, as we see the two linked in the late chapters of the Fourth Gospel itself?

We must admit, of course, this other possibility: that the John who wrote Fourth Gospel was simply never (otherwise) named or known in the New Testament record. We have to allow for that; but accepting that requires no less imagination than considering John-Mark as our evangelist. If he was, it means the Fourth Gospel is not only authoritative but that it is also reliable as actual history. While a number of 19th and 20th century scholars asserted that this gospel contained *no* eyewitness testimony, my view is exactly the opposite: that it contains a great deal, and that only when we treat it as such will we be able to judge it fairly in relation to the very different Synoptic record.

I fully realize that when long-held, popular views are challenged, some react negatively (even emotionally) and have a hard time considering any alternatives. I only ask readers to carefully consider what I present here as a reasoned alternative to the traditional view. As I stated at the beginning, final "certainty" has not been my goal; rather, I have sought to mine out, investigate, and compare what evidence is available on the questions of Johannine authorship, and reassemble them together into a reasonable proposal.

I do not pretend that the John-Mark proposal is final, set in concrete, or unassailable. There remain too many gaps in the evidence. What I do believe is that this proposal and the details that underlie it make sense, and the pieces of a very complex puzzle do, in fact, fit with one another.

My hope is that this study will be helpful to others students of Scripture going forward. I also hope that any new avenues for inquiry and study I have opened up may be both useful, and motivating, to others. I have discussed many details here that can generate further discussion, and some that will no doubt provoke strong resistance and refutation. That is how this type of endeavor proceeds, so I welcome responses from others. I hope, of course, that criticisms will come clothed in a spirit of Christian charity.

Conclusion

Much of what I have put forward under the John-Mark proposal rests on conjecture because of the meager evidence we have about the Fourth Evangelist. It is conjecture, however, which I believe is consistent not only with the details we find in the New Testament itself but also with the majority of evidence we find preserved in the earliest historical records of the Church regarding the John the Evangelist, and the author of Revelation.

The collective weight of the various pieces of evidence, placed on a balance scale, suggests that the John-Mark proposal could be correct. If it is, it could lay to rest much of the scholarly doubt that has been generated over the last 150 years about the "unreliability" of the Fourth Gospel. Too often in modern scholarship, the Fourth Gospel has been dismissed not only as unreliable, but entirely unhistorical. I hope I have been able to show that, to the contrary, what we have in this gospel is one of the most accurate histories we possess of the ministry, death, and resurrection of Jesus, the product of the eyewitness account of a man who was very close to Jesus, favored as the Beloved Disciple, and one who indeed cared for Jesus' mother after his departure from us. Were it not for his witness, indeed, we would know virtually nothing of Jesus' public ministry in Jerusalem and Judea before the arrest of John the Baptist, and before opposition there forced Jesus north to Galilee to avoid arrest and a premature end of his work among us.

So, I conclude that John-Mark, who we meet part way through Acts, is the most likely John we know of in the New Testament period who fits the qualifications of the man who wrote this gospel, and the companion letters. Further, based on what I have laid out, including the early testimony of Justin Martyr, I remain persuaded (as long tradition actually agrees) that John bar Zebedee wrote the Apocalypse, the Book of Revelation.

Perhaps the most persuasive argument on the overall question is this: once we accept this proposal and return to take a fresh look not only at the Fourth Gospel but the other three, we find we have overcome a whole rat's nest of problems that have plagued scholars, commentators, and students of scripture for generations.

If, as I have argued, the Fourth Gospel is a reliable history of Jesus, then it is insufficient to consider Jesus a "one-year Messiah" who preached for a short time in Galilee of the Gentiles, then got into trouble on one trip to Jerusalem. Instead, we have from John the all-important and true proclamation of Jesus as the one Good Shepherd and Savior of Israel, the very Son of God, the *logos* incarnate, who spent more time in the Holy City than in Galilee, and returned during the last portion of his ministry to the Temple to claim his full right to the crown of Messiah, as well as his true title, King of Israel (John 18:33-38), so that his glory might be fully revealed "to the world" (7:2-4).

Moreover, if my related argument is correct that the apostle John bar Zebedee wrote Revelation, then we have a source for the Apocalypse which explains the very different language, style, and content of that book when compared to the works of John the Evangelist. We have for Revelation an author whose personal history explains the style and thought world expressed in that book: a simple fisherman steeped in the Old Testament and Jewish apocalyptic hope, who tried to communicate mystical visions in a language not his own to the largely gentile members of the Asian churches in and around Ephesus. We have, then, an author who was an acknowledged leader of the early Church whose own brother was murdered by Jewish authorities under the auspices of Rome, and who himself was beaten down and imprisoned by the over-reaching and seemingly intractable power of "Babylon the Great," and who thus prayed fervently and looked forward with ecstatic visions to the day when God would set his creation to rights, and restore what had been lost since Eden.

Endnotes
1. See Appendix F.

Appendix A
Sequence and Location in John's Gospel

I SAID IN CHAPTER TWO that the principal difference between the Fourth Gospel and the Synoptics is not so much a matter of time-lines or theology, but *geography*. Following is an examination of some details that support this view.

If John-Mark was indeed the Fourth Evangelist, the explanation of why John seems to be the "Jerusalem Gospel" lays close at hand. As a young man brought up in Jerusalem, John-Mark would have been more familiar with the events that occurred there or near there, and with the people who lived there, than would the Synoptic writers; and he would have also been more familiar and connected with the Holy City than the traditional author, John bar Zebedee, would have been.

The proposal that John-Mark was John the Evangelist explains his familiarity, even perhaps direct acquaintance, with friends and disciples of Jesus in Jerusalem, Bethany, Bethlehem, and the surrounding region. We recall that John the Baptist likely grew up there in "a town of Judah" in the hill country of Judea, close enough to Jerusalem that his father was able to carry on duties as a priest in the Temple (Luke 1, especially 1:39).

If what is reported is based on actual eyewitness testimony, as this gospel itself implies, we can understand why so many events recorded in the Synoptics do not appear in John: not because John felt they were unimportant, but simply because he himself did not witness them. As previously suggested, it may be that the *only* events John-Mark recorded were those of which he had personal or direct knowledge.

That would mean that John-Mark must have traveled with Jesus on the several reported visits of Jesus to Galilee that we have in John. If the wedding at Cana, for example, involved relatives or close family friends of Jesus, and if John-Mark was somehow distantly related to Jesus (see Appendix B), this could explain why we have the wedding account at all, and the first public miracle of Jesus, an event unknown to the Synoptic writers, even though it took place in Galilee. If the wedding took place before John the Baptist was imprisoned and Jesus' main "public" ministry began, it explains Jesus' peculiar response to Mary, "O woman, what have you to do with me? My hour has not yet come" (John 2:4), and why the Fourth Evangelist calls this "the first of his signs."

The Cana wedding is not only the beginning of Jesus' public actions, it leads directly to a series of events and chronology unique in John.

John-Mark would have been along, for example, on the visit to Galilee when the Feeding of the 5000 took place (see below); and he returns to Galilee with several other disciples after the Resurrection (John 21).

From the beginning of this gospel, we have details that "fill-out" the Synoptic record. The Synoptics tell us that John the Baptist was preaching at the Jordon in Judea. John specifically tells us he was baptizing at "Bethany beyond the Jordan" (John 1:28), although modern scholars don't agree on precisely where that was. The importance of this becomes clear when we read 1:43, for we are given the impression that Jesus had been in or around Jerusalem for some time. Jesus first meets Andrew, a disciple of John the Baptist, and the second "unnamed" disciple of the Baptist (possibly the Beloved Disciple) as well as Andrew's brother Peter while they are *in Judea* (John 1:40-44; cf. Matthew 4:18 and parallels). In other words, although Andrew and therefore Peter were from Bethsaida in Galilee, Jesus first befriends them in Judea — not, as the Synoptics all imply, in Galilee. We are certain of this because just after Jesus meets these brothers we are told, "The next day Jesus decided to go to Galilee" (John 1:43). This earlier, original meeting of Jesus, Andrew, and Peter explains why they were so ready and willing to follow Jesus when he "called" them as disciples — in Galilee — perhaps some months later (Matthew 4).

Whether the similar call of Nathanael happened in Judea or after they arrived in Galilee is not clear in the text; but 2:1 tells us that "on the third day" after they arrive in Galilee they went to the wedding at Cana.

Here we find a very peculiar fact regarding John's overall sequence. Although most of the important events of his gospel take place in or near Jerusalem, this first miraculous "sign" of Jesus, an event which carries both baptismal and Eucharistic overtones, occurs not in Jerusalem but in Cana of Galilee. We see, then, the beginning of Jesus' later connection to cities in Galilee here in John's second chapter.

The next major event, however — one of the most significant events of his ministry, the so-called "cleansing of the temple" — takes us back to Jerusalem. This second "sign" is significant in John's unique sequence of events because it takes place during the *first* Passover John records, a visit unreported in the Synoptics. In contrast, all three Synoptic writers place "the cleansing of the temple" during Jesus' *final* Passover week in Jerusalem, and it is one of the events that leads directly to Jesus' arrest. John's account, placing it at the very beginning of Jesus' ministry, at least two full years before Passion week, might explain why there was such tremendous hostility already built up toward Jesus when he came to Jerusalem for his final Passover.

Now, we cannot dismiss the possibility that this "cleansing" of the Temple actually happened twice, as the four gospels, collectively, would imply. If so, this first cleansing no doubt provoked the same level of hostility as the second, and we see a clearer pattern of why the Sanhedrin so opposed Jesus when he arrived, on the donkey, that final Sunday before his arrest. If he threw all the money changers out and disrupted the Temple a second time, we see more clearly why the authorities were itching for an excuse to arrest him. (The failure of this

The Other John | 189

view, of course, is that if Jesus did "cleanse" the Temple twice, why did John not report the second occurrence during Passion week, which he otherwise reports in great detail?)

The key point is that, unlike the picture drawn by the Synoptic writers of one final, catastrophic trip to Jerusalem, John paints a picture that shows Jesus spending much more time in and around the Holy City long before his Passion. It is during this first reported Passover that Jesus has his visit from Nicodemus, a member of the Sanhedrin (John 3). As a member of the High Council, Nicodemus likely lived in or near Jerusalem (he was also on the scene just after the Crucifixion). His conversation with Jesus, so crucial for its theology of regeneration (rebirth) is, of course, absent in the Synoptics. Indeed, the Synoptics make no mention of Nicodemus at all, even the fact that he helped Joseph bury Jesus (John 19:39-40).

If John-Mark, a native of Jerusalem, was our evangelist, and chronicled only what he could personally testify to, this suggests he may have been present that evening when Nicodemus came to see Jesus. The elaborate detail of the whole dialogue between them certainly suggests (as much of John does) an eyewitness account of the conversation. If John-Mark was the second "unnamed" disciple of John the Baptist who followed Jesus with Andrew (John 1), then John-Mark was already a disciple of Jesus when Nicodemus came to visit.

After this encounter with a member of the Sanhedrin, Jesus does not, as we might assume from the Synoptic tradition, return to Galilee:

> After this Jesus and his disciples went into the land of Judea; there he remained with them and baptized. John also was baptizing at Aenon near Salim, because there was much water there; and people came and were baptized. For John had not yet been put in prison (John 3:22-24).

The last sentence is key: in the Synoptics, Jesus is not going about publicly until after the Baptist's arrest (though before his death); in John, Jesus has begun public ministry while John is also still active. Contrary to the Synoptics, we discover that Jesus spent a significant period of time *in Judea* after his own baptism, time enough that he was baptizing more disciples than his relative John. John (the Evangelist) then tells us something else that is crucial: it is early hostility to Jesus' ministry *in Judea* (John 4:1-3) that causes him to withdraw into Galilee for a longer time. In other words, it was the growing hostility to an already active time of ministry in and around Jerusalem that caused Jesus to move north and focus on his home region of Galilee, once opposition from the Pharisees and Temple authorities began to build.

If that sequence is correct, as I believe it is, it explains why, in the Synoptics, Jesus is so certain he will face arrest and death when he returns to Judea in the not-distant future.

It is also interesting that most of John 4 recounts not the ministry *in* Galilee, but an event that occurs on the way there: the theologically important conversation with the woman in Samaria at Jacob's well. Then, in keeping with John's general focus on Judea, Jesus' period of ministry *in* Galilee is summed up *in one verse* (4:45). We then have "the second" miraculous sign in Galilee (4:54) — which once again occurs *at Cana* — when Jesus heals the son of an official from Capernaum. (The miracle happens in Capernaum, but Jesus accomplishes it from Cana.) Notice this oddity, however: while Capernaum is such a major focus of the Galilean ministry in the Synoptics, here (John 4) Jesus *does not even go there;* he heals the official's son from a distance. In total, this event plus the brief stay of "a few days" described earlier in John 2:12, along with the brief stop after the feeding of the 5000 (the setting of the Bread of Life discourse, 6:24-59), are the *only* references to Capernaum in John at all.

The unique chronology continues. Chapter 5 begins with Jesus returning again to Jerusalem for another feast that includes the healing at the pool of Bethzatha (or Bethesda), another important miracle not reported in the Synoptics — because it happens in Jerusalem. As far as we can tell from the text, the long discourse that follows this healing is still in Jerusalem, because it is provoked when the man went immediately to the Jewish authorities to show that he had been healed.

"After this," John 6:1 says, "Jesus went to the other side of the Sea of Galilee" (6:1) where the feeding of the five thousand takes place. Jesus walks on the water of the lake that night, and gives the Bread of Life discourse in Capernaum the following day. In fact, this compressed series of events is the only sequence that almost exactly parallels the Synoptics (Matthew 14; Mark 6; cf. partial parallel of Luke 9) prior to the Passion. Indeed, the feeding of the 5000 is the only miracle event recorded in all four gospels; and in John, we find an incredibly detailed account. Consider this very intriguing detail. As the disciples are trying to figure out how to feed the mammoth crowd (6:2) we read this:

> One of his disciples, Andrew, Simon Peter's brother, said to him, "There is a lad here who has five barley loaves and two fish; but what are they among so many?" (John 6:8-9).

Who was this young lad (some translations have "boy")? Was he John-Mark, the Beloved Disciple, who knew of this miracle because he had come along on the journey — which began from Jerusalem? *Notice* who it is who brings the boy forward: Andrew, the same Andrew who was friends with the other "unnamed" disciple of John the Baptist in chapter 1. Is this "lad" another cryptic reference by John the Evangelist to himself? We have to wonder. As scattered pieces or bread are gathered up, perhaps we have some scattered pieces of information about the Evangelist coming together as well. We remember the tradition that the Beloved Disciple was a relatively young man when he became a disciple of Jesus. Does he make a key appearance here in his own gospel?

Some may object that John's account is not unique, since it appears in the Synoptics, too. True, but notice this important difference: *none* of the Synoptics mention the "lad" carrying the food. Matthew says only "*We* have only five loaves here and two fish." Mark and Luke are similar. Why is it *only John* who mentions the "lad" who is carrying a rather generous supply of food? Was he indeed the Beloved Disciple? I will let the reader judge. This is one of those "minor" details that seem to stick out in John.

If John-Mark was that lad, this would help explain why the Feeding of the 5000 in John (only) leads to the lengthy Bread of Life discourse, with all its overtones of the Last Supper? Remember that while John reports the Last Supper, he omits the detail of Jesus giving his Body and Blood to the disciples at that time. The Bread of Life discourse in John 6 seems to take the place of what may have been this Evangelist's intentional — though glaring — omission from his account of the Last Supper. If the Fourth Evangelist had been personally present during the feeding of the 5000 — particularly if he himself brought along the food — might that account for this oddity? Is he telling us that in addition to the necessity of Christians receiving Christ's Body and Blood (John 6:53-56) that it is through this act of worship in Holy Communion that the Church itself will miraculously multiply, as the bread and fish did that day?

Next, we learn from John 7:1 that "After this Jesus went about in Galilee; he would not go about in Judea, because the Jews sought to kill him." Once again, however, we find the Galilean ministry briefly summarized in *a single verse,* leaving the impression that Judea, from John's perspective, was the true center of Jesus' ministry. He only stays away from Judea because of the threat to his life. Yet having told us this, Jesus immediately — in the following verses —once again returns to Jerusalem, albeit "in secret" (7:10).

The unique picture in John is clear and focused: throughout his gospel, Jerusalem, and in particular the Temple, is like a magnet that constantly draws Jesus back as the focus of his work. He is the true High Priest.

While in Jerusalem this time (John 7), another confrontation with the Jewish authorities is detailed (we know it almost certainly occurs in Jerusalem because of the presence of the chief priests in 7:44-46). Next follows the Light of the World discourse. Where? In the Temple (8:2, 8:59). Then comes the healing of the blind man (John 9), including detailed conversations that again bear the mark of an eyewitness; and since we have no textual evidence to the contrary, we must presume that the Good Shepherd discourse that follows (John 10) also occurs in Jerusalem (possibly again in the Temple). All these discourses, of course, are unique to John.

After the Good Shepherd discourse, there is a lapse of time until the Feast of the Dedication (10:22-24), but the geography does not change. If Jesus left the region of Jerusalem during that gap, we are not told. But the next events again take place in the Temple, the constant central focus, ever since Jesus' cryptic statement about himself (John 2:18-22). Whatever else we may say, it is clear that the narrator of all these events was not only very familiar with the Temple and its precincts, but was always focused on it as the true center of life in and around Jerusalem.

This continues to be the case in the next chapter which records the raising of Jesus' close friend Lazarus who lived at Bethany, a village just two miles from Jerusalem (11:18). We must notice that detail: this close friend, for whom he weeps, is from *Judea,* not Galilee. The whole scene, including details of Jesus' conversations with Martha and Mary, is very personal, painful and real, bearing again the impression of an eyewitness account of that famous two word observation: "Jesus wept" (11:35).

Note again that Jesus and his disciples had apparently left Judea (11:7), but between that unmentioned departure and the Lazarus account we are told nothing about where they were, or what they were doing; but after the raising of Lazarus, Jesus withdraws from the immediate area of Jerusalem again, *not* to Galilee but to Ephraim. John keeps his geographical focus near Jerusalem. This is followed by the supper at Bethany (John 12) where we find the moving account of Mary anointing Jesus' feet with precious oil and wiping his feet with her hair, including the beautiful aroma of the ointment. Only John gives us some key details. Only he identifies the woman as Mary, the sister of Lazarus and Martha, even though many incorrectly identify her as Mary Magdalene, based on a misreading of Luke 7:37-38, which described a very similar event in the home of a Pharisee (but even with that does *not* identify that woman as Mary Magdalene, who is first mentioned in Luke 8).

It is a curious and interesting parallel, however, that the incident with the woman washing Jesus' feet in Luke follows closely on the resurrection of the widow's son at Nain; and while the site of Nain has traditionally been supposed to be in southern Galilee, Luke 7:17 concludes that resurrection at Nain by saying "And this report concerning him spread through the whole of *Judea* and all the surrounding country." Is this similar to the many points of contact between Luke and John that Parker pointed out? Are these two events in John and Luke based on the same historical event? If, as I have argued, John the Evangelist was the true eyewitness, though Luke was not, it is possible the Fourth Evangelist's sequence and account is actually the more historical (compare Mark 14:1-3, which says this supper shortly before Jesus' final week in Jerusalem took place in the house of "Simon the leper" in *Bethany*; is this Simon the same man John calls Lazarus?)

During the supper at Bethany (John 12), John also gives us other key details that we do not learn from the Synoptics. Not only do we nearly smell the rich aroma of the ointment filling the room, but John tells us of Judas' angry reaction and what lay behind it:

> But Judas Iscariot, one of his disciples (he who was to betray him), said, Why was this ointment not sold for three hundred denarii and given to the poor?" This he said, not that he cared for the poor but because he was a thief, and as he had the money box he used to take what was put into it (John 12:4-6).

Does this reveal a central reason why Judas betrayed Jesus, a motivation we are never given in the Synoptics? John includes the other detail not known from the Synoptics: that Judas used to steal from the common purse of the disciples. (Compare Mark 14:4 and 14:10 which says some of those present were upset over the waste of the perfume, and that it was this event that sent Judas to the authorities to betray Jesus.) We learn from this moment also that the chief priests sought not only to kill Jesus, but Lazarus (12:10). We learn this only from John because, of course, the Synoptics do not record the raising of Lazarus from the dead — even though the parable in Luke 16 that focuses on resurrection has "Lazarus" as the poor beggar. Again, we have an interesting but indirect "link" between Luke and John, a link that could have come from a possible acquaintance between Luke and John-Mark.

The following day, according to John, the week of the Passion begins: Jesus' Messianic entry into Jerusalem, the Last Supper, the Crucifixion, and the Resurrection, all, of course, in Jerusalem. Here again, John's account of that entry into the city provides important details about how easily Jesus secured the animal that he rode into Jerusalem that day. One approach to Jerusalem from the east was through Bethany near the Mount of Olives. If John's history is correct, but unknown to the Synoptic writers, it solves the enigma about locating the donkey. The Synoptics each report that on his way to Jerusalem, Jesus sent disciples into Bethany to get the ass (or, according to Matthew, both an ass and a colt). Knowing nothing more than the Synoptic tradition, this story seems very odd. How would Jesus know where a particular colt would be tied, and how could he be so sure those at that house would allow it to be taken only on his word? The Synoptics don't help us. Matthew's reads thus:

> And when they drew near to Jerusalem and came to Bethphage, to the Mount of Olives, then Jesus sent two disciples, saying to them, "Go into the village opposite you, and immediately you will find an ass tied, and a colt with her; untie them and bring them to me. If any one says anything to you, you shall say, 'The

Lord has need of them,' and he will send them immediately" (Matthew 21:1-3).

How can we be certain it was in Bethany that they found the ass? The exact location of Bethphage is not certain but it may have been along the valley at the western foot of the Mount of Olives. Bethany lies just a short distance "opposite," along the eastern slope the Mount of Olives. That it was to Bethany they went is clearer in Mark's account:

> And when they drew near to Jerusalem, to Bethphage and Bethany, at the Mount of Olives, he sent two of his disciples, and said to them, "Go into the village *opposite you,* and immediately as you enter it you will find a colt tied, on which no one has ever sat; untie it and bring it. If any one says to you, 'Why are you doing this?' say, 'The Lord has need of it and will send it back here immediately.'" And they went away, and found a colt tied at the door out in the open street; and they untied it. And those who stood there said to them, "What are you doing, untying the colt?" And they told them what Jesus had said; and they let them go. And they brought the colt to Jesus, and threw their garments on it; and he sat upon it....And he entered Jerusalem, and went into the temple; and when he had looked round at everything, as it was already late, he went out to Bethany with the twelve (Mark 11:1-11, *emphasis* added).

Mark says they approached Bethphage, so "the village opposite" would of course be Bethany. Mark does not report that Jesus had close friends in Bethany, as John does; but John's record explains why the residents there, obviously acquaintances of Jesus, allowed the disciples to take the colt without further question.

For those scholars and critics who wish to argue that John is largely "made up" and historically unreliable, I suggest they must grapple with details like this which completely explain seeming mysteries in the Synoptics, mysteries for which John has a very simple answer.

Did that colt come from the home of Mary, Martha and Lazarus? If not them, it was from other friends. John tells us Jesus was in Bethany the night before, and his account simply states that the next morning, "Jesus found a young ass and sat upon it" (12:14).

Given that in the Synoptic tradition Jesus' ministry is so largely confined to Galilee, it is interesting that Bethany is even mentioned at all. What is more amazing, however, is that knowing of Jesus' connection to this town, the Synoptic writers do not seem to know of the miraculous resurrection of Lazarus that took place there.

If we knew only the Synoptic gospels, we would have no idea that Jesus had many close friends in Bethany and Jerusalem. Knowing these details from John's "Jerusalem Gospel" helps us understand why during that week Jesus already knew a family and household in Jerusalem he could call on to host his Passover meal with his disciples. We also realize the basis of the other Synoptic information, that Jesus and his disciples routinely went out and stayed at Bethany overnight (Matthew 21:17; Mark 11:11; cf, Mark 11:19; Luke 21:37).

Reliable Details

All the unique details noted, in my opinion, lend solid weight to the belief that John the Evangelist was indeed an eyewitness to the events he records. If John-Mark was that Evangelist, are there any other pieces of evidence in the gospel to support the view that the Fourth Evangelist was actually a resident of Jerusalem?

There is one that is quite obvious. I mentioned it in the body of this study: it was the Evangelist (the Beloved Disciple) who comforted Mary at the foot of the cross. Only John tells us that Jesus commended his mother to this disciple's care at that moment. John then says, "And *from that hour* the disciple took her to his own home" (John 19:26-27). Those who wish to argue that the Beloved Disciple was John bar Zebedee are hard pressed to explain this away. If the Beloved Disciple is John-Mark, no explaining is necessary.

Throughout, we see again and again how John's Gospel rings with the clarity of eyewitness testimony, and we can accept as reliable such statements as this:

> Since it was the day of Preparation, in order to prevent the bodies from remaining on the cross on the sabbath (for that sabbath was a high day), the Jews asked Pilate that their legs might be broken, and that they might be taken away. So the soldiers came and broke the legs of the first, and of the other who had been crucified with him; but when they came to Jesus and saw that he was already dead, they did not break his legs. But one of the soldiers pierced his side with a spear, and at once there came out blood and water. He who saw it has borne witness — his testimony is true, and he knows that he tells the truth — that you also may believe (John 19:31-35).

None of these details, including the breaking of the legs of the others and the stabbing of Jesus, are recorded in the Synoptics. And as already noted, only the Fourth Gospel places one of the male disciples, the Beloved Disciple, at the foot of the cross with Jesus' mother. So, it is completely plausible, in my view, that "He who saw it has borne witness," and that his testimony is historical, reliable, and true.

Because the Beloved Disciple was still right there at the foot of the cross when Jesus died, he witnessed the brutal lancing of Jesus's side; and only John gives us this one, fascinating detail: he saw "blood and water" pour out. Apart from the mixture of baptismal and eucharistic imagery this holds, this crucial detail tells us of something that was, without question, seen by an actual eyewitness. It could not have been made up by someone not there, because it was the result of a medical condition that was completely unknown at the time.[1]

John then gives a very detailed account of the burial by Joseph, so it is likely John remained there through the sealing of the tomb. (He certainly knew where to run Sunday morning.) John again gives us several specific details unknown in the Synoptics:

After this Joseph of Arimathea, who was a disciple of Jesus, *but secretly, for fear of the Jews*, asked Pilate that he might take away the body of Jesus, and Pilate gave him leave. So he came and took away his body. *Nicodemus also,* who had at first come to him by night, came bringing a mixture of myrrh and aloes, about a hundred pounds' weight. They took the body of Jesus, and bound it in linen cloths with the spices, as is the burial custom of the Jews. Now in the place where he was crucified there was a garden, and in the garden a new tomb where no one had ever been laid. So because of the Jewish day of Preparation, as the tomb was close at hand, they laid Jesus there (John 19:38-40, *emphasis* added).

John not only knows of Nicodemus' prior acquaintance with Jesus, but reports, unlike the Synoptics, that Nicodemus assisted Joesph with the burial. John also tells us that Joseph of Arimathea was a "secret" disciple of Jesus "for fear of the Jews," no doubt his fellow members of the Sanhedrin (cf. Mark 15:43; Luke 23:50). Joseph's home, Arimathea, was in Judea only about 25 miles from Jerusalem. Again, if we know only the Synoptic records, we would have no clear idea why it was Joesph who came to claim the body of Jesus.

Here again, John simply contradicts the viewpoint of those scholars who argue that simply because the three Synoptic traditions largely "agree," they must be more historically reliable than John. The Synoptics often leave us perplexed; John often clears up the confusion. If we accept the fact that John the Evangelist was John-Mark, a native of Jerusalem, we can understand how he could learn so much "insider" information, including details of discussions that were held among the Sanhedrin (John 11:47-52). In one such meeting, it is Caiaphas, the high priest that year, who declares it is better for one man "to die for the nation" (11:50). If John-Mark is the "unnamed" disciple of 18:15 who was "known to the high priest," we have a clue as to how John could have later found out the substance of this angry discussion in the high council.

One final thing is worth noting: in chapter 21, the likely "editorial addition" to John, Peter is very interested in the ultimate fate of John, the Beloved Disciple. Recall that John links himself and Peter not only in the account of the Last Supper, and through the arrest. We see a similar linking at the Resurrection (20:2-10). Through the course of months, they had probably become close friends. In fact, if the Beloved Disciple was the unnamed disciple in 1:35-42, then Peter and John had become friends from the very beginning of Jesus' ministry. Perhaps after Jesus ascended, Peter, in Jesus' place, took the Beloved Disciple, who was still a young man, under his wing. The fact that John was now caring for Mary would have made this even more important. This could certainly explain why John-Mark went up to Galilee with Peter and the others after the Resurrection, and was with them that morning by the lake when Jesus appeared there, and it would help us understand the special interest Peter showed in the fate of "the Beloved Disciple."

Endnotes

1. Neither John, nor the soldiers, nor his readers would have understood the medical basis for what he and the soldiers witnessed. During severe cardiac and respiratory trauma, of the kind that would happen during beating and crucifixion, a condition called pericardial tamponade can develop where a clear, watery fluid and blood builds up in the pericardial sack around the heart, which compresses the heart, making it impossible to beat and leading to death. When the soldier pierced his side, the bloody, watery fluid burst out. This, by the way, is clear evidence Jesus was actually dead, for those who wish to say he only "swooned" and recovered in the tomb.

Appendix B
John The Evangelist in the New Testament

BEYOND THE MENTIONS in Acts, do we know anything more of value about of John-Mark from the New Testament itself in terms of his friendship, or relationship, to Jesus? The most interesting question is John's possible link to the Levitical tribe. What was that link?

First, John-Mark and Jesus may have shared at least a distant kinship. If the reference to "Mark, the cousin of Barnabas" in Colossians is a reference to John-Mark (I believe it is), based on Acts 15:39, then one of John-Mark's parents may have been of the tribe of Levi.

Second, if the unnamed disciple of John 18:15 was John-Mark, the Evangelist, we have another possible link with the Levitical tribe because he was "known to the high priest." This may only mean they were acquainted, so it is a long stretch to assume from this that John was *related* to the high priest; but it is possible.

Third, we know that the family of Jesus was connected to the Levitical tribe also. Mary's relative Elizabeth who lived in Judea was married to one of the Temple priests, all of whom were of the tribe of Levi. Further, Luke's genealogy of Jesus names "Matthat, the son of Levi" as a forefather of Mary herself (3:24), which implies a kinship of her own with the Levitical tribe.

Then there is this: If, as I believe, John-Mark was first a disciple (with Andrew) of John the Baptist (John 1), we have another possible connection, for The Baptist was either a half- or full-blooded Levite. That means Jesus, through his mother and her kinship to Elizabeth, was at least distantly related to the Levites, if not himself an actual member of that Tribe. (We do not know the exact relationship of Mary and Elizabeth. They are sometimes called "cousins," but Luke's account is not that specific.)

These various links suggest that the friendship between Jesus and John-Mark may have been based in part on kinship. As I suggested before, this might help explain Jesus' special fondness for this young disciple.

John-Mark was from Jerusalem, so certainly had other kin and many friends in the region, perhaps as far as Bethlehem, situated only 5 or 6 miles from Jerusalem. We know that Jesus' parents remained in Judea for some period of time, perhaps a year or more, after his birth, so they doubtless had close friends there.[1,2] Wherever Mary's kinswoman Elizabeth and her husband Zechariah lived, they were close enough to Jerusalem for Zechariah to carry out his duties as a priest of the temple. We also have one early apocryphal tradition that Mary herself had served as a maiden in the Temple as a girl.[3]

Of course, Joseph was originally from Bethlehem (and of the tribe of Judah and the lineage of David), so he must have had family there. So, Jesus himself was "kin" to some in that region. Perhaps this explains his close connection to the family of Lazarus of Bethany.

All of these small details suggest that John-Mark may have had some connection to Jesus other than being one of his first disciples. That connection, in part, was through John the Baptist, a relative of Jesus.

We have looked at many interesting perplexing questions through this study. I would like to add one more. Throughout, I have said John-Mark and his mother Mary were residents of Jerusalem, or its immediate environs, based on Acts 12:12. In reality, though, all Acts actually tells us is that after Peter's miraculous escape from the prison *in* Jerusalem, "he went to the house of Mary, the mother of John whose other name was Mark, where many were gathered together and were praying." Since the prison was in Jerusalem, we naturally assume this house was, too. But was it?

If we remember that Bethany was just a short distance away, and how often Peter, along with Jesus and the other disciples had made frequent trips to stay the night there during Passion Week, is it possible that the "house of Mary" to which Peter went that night was the house of Mary, Martha, and Lazarus at Bethany? In other words, was John-Mark the son of this same Mary, the dear friend of Jesus? That would make John the nephew of Lazarus.

We have to remember that Luke, in Acts, is providing second-hand information. So, we should be careful not to push the implications of these details too far. Some are facts, some mere inferences.

If true, though, we see another example of the type of connection Pierson Parker found between Luke and John. For example, when we hear that when Peter arrived at that house "many were gathered together and were praying" (Acts 12), we might recognize an echo of John 11:18-19: "Bethany was near Jerusalem, about two miles off, and many of the Jews had come to Martha and Mary to console them concerning their brother." We also might put more credence in the authenticity of the Johannine-like detail Luke shares: "And when he knocked at the door of the gateway, a maid named Rhoda came to answer" (Acts 12:13).

Did Peter take refuge that night within the city, from where he had just escaped prison? Or did he, perhaps, follow once again that well-worn footpath of Jesus toward the Mount of Olives, and back to the house of his Lord's dear friends at Bethany? Do we, in fact, find here one more "connection" between Jesus' family, friends, and the Beloved Disciple?

Endnotes

1. According to the Matthean tradition, Mary and Joseph were living in Bethlehem in Judea, not Galilee, for a period of time after Jesus' birth. Contrary to Luke's infancy narrative which has Joseph and Mary leaving Nazareth to travel to Bethlehem just before the birth of Jesus, Matthew's account begins with Joseph and Mary living in Bethlehem, in a house (Matthew 2:11). Further, Matthew's account implies that they only later moved to Nazareth upon their return from Egypt to escape the grasp of Herod's son:

> But when he [Joseph] heard that Archelaus reigned over Judea in place of his father Herod, he was afraid to go there, and being warned in a dream he *withdrew* to the district of Galilee. And he went and dwelt in a city called Nazareth, that what was spoken by the prophets might be fulfilled, "He shall be called a Nazarene" (Matthew 2:22-23; emphasis added).

Returning from Egypt, Matthew implies that Joseph and Mary were headed "home" to Judea, and only "withdrew" to Nazareth to protect Jesus from further attempts on his life (see note 2, below).

Luke's account tells us they came *from* Nazareth to Bethlehem for the census. Regardless, Matthew makes clear they were still living in Bethlehem, for a year or more, when the wisemen arrived in Judea. This is implied by the fact that Herod later ordered the murder of all boys in Bethlehem who were two years old or younger (cf. Matthew 2:7, 2:16).

If Joseph and Mary did not make a brief visit to Bethlehem but lived there for some months after Jesus was born, they clearly had had friends and possibly other relatives in the area. Bethlehem was, after all, Joesph's home town.

2. It is possible to harmonize Matthew's chronology with Luke's, thus: although Matthew tells of Mary and Joseph in a "house" in Bethlehem when the wise men from the East arrive, this is likely a year or more after the birth of Jesus (based on the age of the children Herod orders murdered). After that, Joseph took Mary and Jesus into hiding in Egypt. Luke's account can still fit, that before the birth, Joesph and Mary were in fact living north in Nazareth, and went to Bethlehem on mandate of the census and stayed for a time.

The stumbling block to fully harmonizing the accounts is that Luke's version, particularly 2:39-40 implies that they returned to Nazareth shortly after they performed the infancy rites at the Temple. The other difficulty in this harmonization is that Matthew's account certainly implies that they are "moving" to Nazareth, rather than simply "returning."

3. This tradition contains the ancient legend that as a young girl Mary was a maid-servant in the Temple until she reached the age of about fourteen, at which point she was betrothed to Joseph. If that legend preserves any shred of historical truth, it strengthens the possibility that Mary was of the priestly tribe of Levi herself, to be considered for that role. (The account is found in *The Protoevangelion of James the Lesser*, in *The Lost Books of the Bible*, pp. 24-30.)

Appendix C
The Evidence of Justin Martyr

JUSTIN MARTYR WAS AN EARLY Christian writer who lived about 100-165 AD. In his "Dialogue with Trypho" written about 135-160 AD we find this reference to "John":

> For as Adam was told that in the day he ate of the tree he would die, we know that he did not complete a thousand years. We have perceived, moreover, that the expression, 'The day of the Lord is as a thousand years,' is connected with this subject. And further, there was a certain man with us, whose name was *John, one of the apostles of Christ*, who prophesied, by a revelation that was made to him, that those who believed in our Christ would dwell a thousand years in Jerusalem; and that thereafter the general, and, in short, the eternal resurrection and judgment of all men would likewise take place. Just as our Lord also said, 'They shall neither marry nor be given in marriage, but shall be equal to the angels, the children of the God of the resurrection.' (*Justin Martyr's Dialogue With Trypho*, Chapter LXXXI; emphasis added)

In this reference, Justin certainly means the author of Revelation. Calling him "John, one of the apostles of Christ" clearly points to John bar Zebedee (although, as we've seen throughout, many besides the Twelve were known as apostles). In such an early writer, writing not long after the time of Papias and Polycarp, is this significant? Irenaeus knew of Justin's work, yet he is always careful to refer to the Evangelist as "John, the disciple of the Lord." (We must take care to remember, though, that Irenaeus apparently believed the same John also wrote Revelation.) So, is the man Papias called "the Presbyter John" the same man Justin not long after calls "one of the apostles of Christ," or are they referring to two different men? Do we have here mere glomming together of titles, or do we have different writers using specific titles to distinguish different men?

On this issue, I would highlight an interesting observation from R. P. C. Hanson in his Introduction to Justin's *Dialogue With Trypho* regarding the source of Justin's Christology:

> Did Justin learn this doctrine from the Fourth Gospel? . . . When he wrote, this Gospel had not yet won full recognition as worthy to be ranked with the other three; and though he often in both *Dialogue* and *Apology* refers to the "memoirs of the apostles," *he never uses this phrase of a quotation which can be traced to the Fourth Gospel* (Hanson, *Justin Martyr's Dialogue With Trypho*, p. 10; emphasis added).

This is very significant. Hanson reminds us that the Fourth Gospel was not always accepted early on because it was thought some other John, not bar Zebedee, had written it. If Justin mistrusted the authority of the Fourth Gospel, this is a strong argument that he believed that gospel came from someone other than John bar Zebedee, whose authority would have to be taken for granted.

Justin is one of the earliest Christian writers and apologists just outside the New Testament, so we should give particular attention to his views. He never equated John bar Zebedee with John the Evangelist, yet he referred quite unequivocally to the author of Revelation as "John, one of the apostles of Christ." This is in agreement with the overall proposal I have put forward in this study. It does not address the John-Mark proposal directly, but it clearly reinforces the view that the Fourth Gospel came from someone other than John bar Zebedee.

Appendix D
The Evidence of Tertullian

ONE OTHER EARLY SOURCE that bears examination is the early Christian father Tertullian who lived about 160-220 AD, about the same time as Irenaeus. While notorious for starting out as an orthodox Christian who later became a follower of the man he spent most of his life condemning (the heretic Marcion), Tertullian's works do contain many references to "John," sometimes referring to the Evangelist, sometimes to the author of 1 John, and sometimes to the author of Revelation. Here is a summary of those references:

Against Marcion (five part work)
Book 3:
- Ch. 3.8: refers to heretics "whom the Apostle John designated as antichrists." (possibly a reference to 1 John).
- Ch. 3.13: refers to author of Revelation simply as "John."
- Ch. 3.14: "which the Apostle John, in the Apocalypse…"
- Ch. 3.25: again identifies author of Revelation as "the Apostle John."

Book 4:
- Ch. 4.2: "Of the apostles, therefore, John and Matthew first instill faith into us; while of apostolic men, Luke and Mark renew it afterwards." Here "John" must mean John the Evangelist, and Tertullian places him alongside Matthew "of the apostles," while Luke and Mark he calls "apostolic men." Tertullian may mean John bar Zebedee was the Evangelist; or, since he refers to Paul as an "apostle," too, he may mean Matthew and John were "apostles" in the sense that they

were eyewitnesses to Jesus, while Luke and Mark were not. In that case, John could be some John other than bar Zebedee. We should note the sequence: he implies Matthew and John were the original gospels, and Luke and Mark came later (See Appendix F).
- Ch. 4.3: Refers to Peter, James and John as a group, but not in reference to John the Evangelist.
- Ch. 4.5: "We have also [St.] John's foster Churches. For although Marcion rejects his Apocalypse, the order of the bishops (thereof), when traced up to their origin, will yet rest on John as their author." Notice the reference to John's "foster churches," which suggests, as I argued in Chapter Eight, that John was not necessarily the leader of the seven churches addressed in Revelation.
- Ch. 4.5: "I mean the Gospels of John and Matthew — while that which Mark published may be affirmed to be Peter's whose interpreter Mark was. For even Luke's form of the Gospel men usually ascribe to Paul." Here he does not use the term "the apostle" of John. Also notice the reference to Mark as Peter's interpreter, who is not identified as John-Mark of Acts. We should read this as we did the reference to the "apostle" in 4.2.: "apostle" may mean bar Zebedee, or some John who was an eyewitness disciple.
- Ch. 4.35: refers to the Gospel of John, but does not identify him here as an "apostle."

Book 5:
- Ch. 5.16: Refers to author of 1 John clearly as "the apostle John": "According indeed to our view, he [Marcion] is Antichrist; as it is taught us in both the ancient and the new prophecies, and especially by the apostle John, who says that 'already many false prophets are gone out into the world,' the fore-runners of Antichrist, who deny that Christ is come in the flesh, and do not acknowledge Jesus (to be the Christ), meaning in God the Creator."

Against Praxaeus
- Ch. 15: refers to writer of 1 John only as "John."
- Ch. 17: Mentions "The Revelation of John," with nothing to clarify the identity of John.
- Chs. 21 & 25: The titles include "St. John's Gospel."
- Ch. 23: "Now, in what way these things were said to him, the Evangelist and Beloved Disciple John knew better than Praxeas; and therefore he adds concerning his own meaning . . ." He does not identify John the Evangelist here as "apostle" or bar Zebedee, but he does not exclude him.
- Ch. 26: the title is: "Chapter XXVI. — A Brief Reference to the Gospels of St. Matthew and St. Luke. Their Agreement with St. John, in Respect to the Distinct Personality of the Father and the Son."
- There is no direct reference to John as an "apostle" or to John bar Zebedee in this work.

Treatise On The Soul
- Ch. 8: Refers to author of Revelation simply as "John."
- Ch. 18: refers to author of 1 John simply as "John."

On Baptism
- Ch. 16: refers to author of 1 John simply as "John."

On The Resurrection of the Flesh
- Ch. 23: refers to author of 1 John simply as "John."
- Ch. 25: The title: "Chapter XXV. — St. John, in the Apocalypse, Equally Explicit in Asserting the Same Great Doctrine."
- Ch. 25: Text: "In the Revelation of John, again, the order of these times is spread out to view . . ."
- Ch. 27: "Thus in the Revelation of John . . ."

Summary

Tertullian, like Irenaeus, gives the overall impression that he believed the same man wrote both the Fourth Gospel and Revelation (and 1 John). In the one passage, he places this John alongside Matthew where they are called "apostles," but it is not certain if he means John bar Zebedee. We face once again the problem that many apostolic figures other than the Twelve were known as "apostles." Since Tertullian does not give a specific reference to John bar Zebedee, we cannot rule out that he may have meant a different John (he does call him the Beloved Disciple).

Further, we do not know if Tertullian was familiar with "the two Johns" tradition regarding Ephesus, as Irenaeus was. Tertullian himself could have been confused about the identity of "John" because of earlier traditions. We have no way to be certain.

All we can say for certain is that he calls the author of both the Gospel and Revelation an "apostle." Irenaeus consistently called the author of both books "John, the disciple of the Lord." Did they both mean the same man, or two different men?

Appendix E
The Supposed Letters of Ignatius

I REFERRED TO FOUR purported letters of St. Ignatius in the study because of the reference to "John the Presbyter." The body of letters attributed to St. Ignatius were unknown to scholars until they were found and translated in the early-to-middle 16th century. From the time the group of fifteen letters was first published, however, they sparked a fair amount of controversy, some scholars believing all fifteen letters were genuine while others argued all fifteen were forgeries.

The debate heated up during the 19th century, but by the 20th century, scholars who studied the known manuscripts in their various original languages came to a consensus that only seven of the letters were genuine and the other eight — including those four I referenced — were probably pseudonymous forgeries attributed to Ignatius.

Some of the letters considered genuine, however, existed in two versions, one longer, one shorter. Some commentators put forward the theory that where duplicates appear, the longer versions must have been elaborations of a shorter original; while other scholars argued it was equally possibly that the shorter version was actually an abridgment of the longer (authentic) original.

I am certainly not qualified to suggest of definitive conclusion on those questions, but I will share one observation. In looking at all fifteen letters, I notice that several of those judged forgeries have something in common: they contain a large number of scriptural quotations (either direct, or paraphrases) which seem, where they appear, either superfluous or a break in the train of thought. That causes me to ask: are the "forgeries" perhaps not forgeries in total, but "enhanced" versions of authentic, shorter letters than some scribe or editor decided to embellish with appropriate scripture quotations? In other words, is there a genuine "core" in some of these "forgeries" to which an editor added what we would call scriptural "proof texts" to elucidate or clarify the original letter?

If that were the case, we find something interesting: if we simply edit *out* these scriptural quotations, we discover then a text that seems a lot more like the letters which have been judged genuine.

Here is an example of one such a passage. The full reading is this:

> Chapter III.—The true doctrine respecting Christ. Mindful of him, do ye by all means know that Jesus the Lord was truly born of Mary, being made of a woman; and was as truly crucified. For, says he, "God forbid that I should glory, save in the cross of the Lord Jesus."[A] And He really suffered, and died, and rose again. For says [Paul], "If Christ should become passible, and should be the first to rise again from the dead."[B] And again, "In that He died, He died unto sin once: but in that He liveth, He liveth unto God."[C] Otherwise, what advantage would there be in [becoming subject to] bonds, if Christ has not died? what advantage in patience? what advantage in [enduring] stripes? And why such facts as the following: Peter was crucified; Paul and James were slain with the sword; John was banished to Patmos; Stephen was stoned to death by the Jews who killed the Lord? But, [in truth,] none of these sufferings were in vain; for the Lord was really crucified by the ungodly.[1]
> A. Galatians 6:14
> B. Acts 26:23
> C. Romans 6:10

When we edit out the possibly interpolated scriptures, we have:

> Chapter III.—The true doctrine respecting Christ. Mindful of him, do ye by all means know that Jesus the Lord was truly born of Mary, being made of a woman; and was as truly crucified.

> And He really suffered, and died, and rose again. Otherwise, what advantage would there be in [becoming subject to] bonds, if Christ has not died? what advantage in patience? what advantage in [enduring] stripes? And why such facts as the following: Peter was crucified; Paul and James were slain with the sword; John was banished to Patmos; Stephen was stoned to death by the Jews who killed the Lord? But, [in truth,] none of these sufferings were in vain; for the Lord was really crucified by the ungodly.[2]

I show this example simply to point out another interesting fact: of the four letters I referred in this study, all read like one of these shorter "edits." That is, they contain almost no quotations of scripture, are brief and to the point, and seem much more like an actual letter of correspondence. Does that prove these four letters are genuine? I cannot say that. I only raise the question.

Following are the links to the CCEL.org website for the four letters that I referenced with a portion of the text. (The full text is available at the website.) I quote only a portion of the first three.

> a. First, from Ignatius to "John the Presbyter":
> https://ccel.org/ccel/ignatius_antioch/epistles_of_ignatius/anf01.v.xx.html
> [NOTE: the Editors title this "Ignatius to John the Apostle," but that is not what the text itself reads. It reads in part]:
>
> Ignatius, and the brethren who are with him, to *John the holy presbyter.* We are deeply grieved at thy delay in strengthening us by thy addresses and consolations. If thy absence be prolonged, it will disappoint many of us. Hasten then to come, for we believe that it is expedient. There are also many of our women here, who are desirous to see Mary [the mother] of Jesus, and wish day by day to run off from us to you, that they may meet with her, and touch those breasts of hers which nourished the Lord Jesus, and may inquire of her respecting some rather secret matters (*emphasis* added).
>
> b. A second letter from Ignatius to John the Presbyter:

https://ccel.org/ccel/ignatius_antioch/epistles_of_ignatius/anf01.v.xxi.html

[NOTE: The editors title this one "Ignatius to St. John," not specifying "the Apostle." It reads in part]:

His friend Ignatius to *John the holy presbyter*. If thou wilt give me leave, I desire to go up to Jerusalem, and see the faithful saints who are there, especially Mary the mother, whom they report to be an object of admiration and of affection to all. For who would not rejoice to behold and to address her who bore the true God from her own womb, provided he is a friend of our faith and religion? And in like manner [I desire to see] the venerable James, who is surnamed Just, whom they relate to be very like Christ Jesus in appearance, in life, and in method of conduct, as if he were a twin-brother of the same womb. They say that, if I see him, I see also Jesus Himself, as to all the features and aspect of His body. Moreover, [I desire to see] the other saints, both male and female. Alas! why do I delay? Why am I kept back? Kind teacher, bid me hasten and fare thou well. Amen (*emphasis added*).

[NOTE: This letter might have been objectionable to some later scholars, as it could seem to call into question the idea of the perpetual virginity of Mary.]

c.   The third letter if from Ignatius to the Mary, the mother of Jesus.

https://ccel.org/ccel/ignatius_antioch/epistles_of_ignatius/anf01.v.xxii.html

[It reads in part]:

Her friend Ignatius to the Christ-bearing Mary. Thou oughtest to have comforted and consoled me who am a neophyte, and a disciple of thy [beloved] John. For I have heard things wonderful to tell respecting thy [son] Jesus, and I am astonished by such a report. But I desire with my whole heart to obtain information concerning the things which I have heard from thee, who wast always intimate and allied with Him, and who wast acquainted with [all] His secrets. I have also written to thee at another time, and have asked thee concerning the same things. Fare thou well; and let the neophytes who are with me be comforted of thee, and by thee, and in thee. Amen.

[NOTE: The CCEL editor notes that the Greek translation calls Mary χριστοτόκος {Christ-bearer} rather than the later common θεοτόκος {God-bearer} which, he suggests, makes this letter a Nestorian forgery. It could instead suggest a fairly early forgery.]

d. The fourth letter referred to is a supposed reply of Mary to Ignatius titled by the editors "Reply of the Blessed Virgin to this Letter":

https://ccel.org/ccel/ignatius_antioch/epistles_of_ignatius/anf01.v.xxiii.html

[It reads in full]:

The lowly handmaid of Christ Jesus to Ignatius, her beloved fellow-disciple. The things which thou hast heard and learned from John concerning Jesus are true. Believe them, cling to them, and hold fast the profession of that Christianity which thou hast embraced, and conform thy habits and life to thy profession. Now I will come in company with John to visit thee, and those that are with thee. Stand fast in the faith, and show thyself a man; nor let the fierceness of persecution move thee, but let thy spirit be strong and rejoice in God thy Saviour. Amen.

As I suggest, compared to several of the letters deemed forgeries, these letters read like actual correspondence. Of course, that does not prove them genuine. It does suggest, however, that the earliest recipients of these letters, like the original 16th century translators, certainly may have thought them genuine. Would their acceptance have been in part based on the fact that they knew of "the Presbyter John" later known to Papias?

Again, I am not vouching for their authenticity, simply making the point that pseudonymous letters staked their hope for authority on the use of genuine, known names and facts. So even if forgeries, they may embody a few jewels of authentic history that would have made them seem authentic to those who originally received them, and we should, therefore, not reject them out-of-hand without consideration of what those hidden jewels might be.

Endnotes
1. Quotations are from the CCEL.org website.
2. If the letter is genuine, all of these deaths would have taken place by the time Ignatius would have written. Naming much later deaths would, of course, been clearer evidence of a forgery; but we do not find that.

Appendix F
The Development of the Gospels

BASED ON THE EVIDENCE, findings, and resulting inferences of this overall study, I want to set forward some provisional suggestions about the origins of the four gospels and how they may have developed in relation to each other.

The development of the gospels during the New Testament period (roughly 30-100 AD) began to be debated not long after they began to widely circulate in the Church across the Roman Empire, for the simple reason that clear records about the writers were not preserved; or, at least, we do not have them.

Over the last century, many of scholars have accepted the view that Mark is the oldest, the "original" gospel of the four. Some believe its current form is essentially its original form, while others suggest that even Mark may be based on an earlier source-gospel that was longer (more like Matthew and Luke) but was pared down, perhaps to make it more precise, or simply to fit the common length of a papyrus scroll of the time.

From this assumption, the further assumptions grew that the writers of Matthew and Luke in their final form must have used the earlier Mark as the basis for their chronology and much of their content. This theory always includes the addition to both Matthew and Luke of material from an unknown but common source (identified as "Q"), as well as unique material they each added to their work which is not in the other two Synoptics.

This overall theory makes a certain amount of sense with Luke. We assume he learned the gospel orally from Paul, but he tells us he also researched the teaching and records of others to create his gospel (Luke 1:1-4). For Matthew, one of the Twelve, however, it seems odd that he would have had to rely on the work of someone like Mark, who was not eyewitness of any of the events he records, since he was not (as I believe, with Jerome and others) an actual disciple of Jesus.

A further-unanswered question relates to the fact that there is a great deal of material in Luke, including some of Jesus' most beloved parables, that is not in Matthew or Mark. Where did Luke get this material? The teaching of Jesus he records is so detailed that it seems unlikely that he just made it all up.

Finally, of course, where does John fit into this picture, or does it fit at all? Was the Fourth Gospel, as some claim, a very late work, perhaps not written until around 110-120 AD, created entirely by a "Johannine community" of disciples of this John. If that were so, how do we credibly account for the large amount of fine detail that I have highlighted throughout this study?

Finally there is Acts. Though not one of the gospels, it is certainly a continuation of one, where Luke continues his account of the Church from the Resurrection forward to around 62 AD when Paul arrives in Rome. Where did Luke find such records and so much detail?

Where does this lead? It leaves us with a muddy picture and a great deal of uncertainty, especially about the Fourth Gospel. So, let us consider different options that grow out of this present study.

I. JOHN

If John-Mark was the Fourth Evangelist, an actual eyewitness to the ministry of Jesus and his Resurrection, then, contrary to recent scholarly theories, the Fourth Gospel may well be the first, or one of the first, at least in its formative state. If John was as well-educated as his writing testifies, he could have started recording details of Jesus' ministry very early. I have no objection to the supposition that he could even have made "scribal" notes while spending time with or traveling with Jesus, of such discussions as took place one night with Nicodemus. In that time, and even in more recent times until the invention of recording devices (and even now with those), having a secretary make contemporary notes of a talk or conversation was very common, especially when the speaker was someone worth documenting. It seems most probable to me, however, that since none of the disciples had a clear understanding of where the ministry was leading — to the cross — that not very much would have been written down before the Resurrection.

Certainly, though, after the Resurrection, during the forty days Luke tells us that Jesus spent with various disciples before his Ascension, it seems very likely to me that John and others would have begun furiously writing down whatever they could as it happened; and may have begun, with Jesus' help, to write details of many of the events and his teaching prior to his Crucifixion. If so, John's gospel may embody some of this early written material that he kept to preserve the life-altering events they had all witnessed. Ask yourself: wouldn't you?

Some of this very early material would have become the basis for John's gospel. We know from reading it, however, that John developed a very intentional, structured outline of events and "signs" that formed the framework for his written gospel. It is quite apparent that the synoptic writers all took some liberty with sequencing events to highlight certain events or teachings at a particular point, usually for theological reasons. We cannot rule out that John did the same as he wrote out what would become the "original" Fourth Gospel (which I assume never contained chapter 21.) "History" in that time — and still today — was often organized thematically more than chronologically, so this should not surprise us.

Since I believe John, of the four evangelists, was the only disciple "on the scene" during the first two years of Jesus' ministry, which began while John the Baptist was still preaching, what John recorded in his original "notes" or records could have been as early as 30-35 AD. (Peter was present during that period as well, so as to antiquity of the record, Mark may contain genuine, early material through Peter; but Mark includes nothing of this first two years of the ministry.) Scholars often complain that no person could actually remember such detailed conversations as John records if they were written (as those scholars presume) fifty to sixty years later. If John's notes were written down within a few years, or even a few months, we find a very different picture of authenticity, and reliability.

It is likely, though, that John continued to remember details, to write, and to add material as time passed, in particular through discussions which undoubtedly took place with other disciples. On this point, we recall that the Muratorian Canon alleges there was a specific discussion between John and some of his fellow disciples (some bishops, which, at that point, John himself may have been) about John composing a gospel "in his own name." His friend Andrew (allegedly) was part of that discussion. If that actually happened, did it happen early on, while Andrew and others of the disciples were still in Jerusalem, or perhaps Antioch? That is the most likely; but tradition tells us the Fourth Gospel was "the Ephesus gospel," so this discussion with John could have happened after his move there, perhaps on an occasion when Andrew was traveling in the region. (We know little of what became of Andrew, so we cannot be sure.) If so, the bishops who were part of urging John on could have included such men as Papias and Polycarp.

If what I suggest here is close to what happened, then those modern scholars who believe John's gospel was a very late composition of a "Johannine community" are very far afield, not only not in the ballpark, but not even in the parking lot of the ballpark. On the contrary, I would estimate that if John began to write things down quite early, he could have composed the original, main body of his Gospel by 40-50 AD, during the same time period, in other words, that the three synoptics were also in development.

II.   LUKE

We do not know at what date Luke first met and became a co-worker with Paul. If the "we" sections of Acts refer to Luke's presence, then he was with Paul from around 50-52 AD. From the Roman prison letters, we know Luke probably stayed near Paul until his death.

From near the beginning of their acquaintance, though, Luke would have begun to learn details of the gospel events. He also probably learned from other disciples in their travels, not only in Greece and Asia Minor, but back in Jerusalem itself just before Paul's arrest there. While Paul insists that he did not learn his "gospel" from men, referring apparently to the core theology he taught everywhere (Galatians 1:11-12), he most certainly must have learned details of Jesus' actual ministry from other disciples who were present with the Lord when Paul had not been. Some of this information he would certainly pass on to Luke, especially once Luke began to write things down. So, the Third Gospel could have been in early stages by the mid-50s to about 60 AD.

An important question, of course, is where did Luke get all the unique material found only in his work: in particular, the infancy/child narratives of Luke 1-2, and the many unique parables? If some of the details I shared about Pierson Parker's article are correct, then we have a possible answer. Luke may have met John-Mark in later years, after John and Jesus' mother Mary had moved to Ephesus (if not before).[1] If so we have a credible source for the infancy and childhood accounts in Luke. Did John know many of the parables of Jesus that Luke includes? If so, why we he not include them in his own gospel? The only explanation might be that the parable style teaching, which he knew was reported elsewhere, did not fit his own structure and purpose, which was based on much longer discourse-style teaching.

If John and Luke knew each other, is it possible Mary herself, having been with Jesus through much of his work — up to his final week in Jerusalem, not to mention the 40 days following — knew many of the parables and passed them along to Luke, parables either forgotten, or simply not used, by Matthew and Peter? We can only speculate, but we cannot rule out John and Mary as sources for Luke. Luke assures us he spoke to eyewitnesses, "those who from the beginning were eyewitnesses and ministers of the word have delivered them to us . . ." (1:2).

Luke's gospel, then, was probably being developed over a period of years before Paul's execution at Rome. It was likely finished either shortly before, or shortly after, Paul's death. Luke may already have been working on Acts during this same period.

III. MARK

Mark, as this study has shown, may have been a gentile convert who became Peter's secretary, either during Peter's (presumed) travel through Asia Minor or Greece, or perhaps after Peter arrived in Rome. This explains why Mark gets names and places in and around Judea sometimes wrong, or mixed up. It was a foreign place to him; he probably never saw Jerusalem until perhaps passing through Judea enroute to Alexandria, after his gospel was written.

As mentioned in the study, there is valid debate about when Peter arrived at Rome to combat the heretic Simon Magus. Eusebius thinks it was in the 50s, but Schaff in his commentary on Eusebius argued that Peter did not likely arrive in Rome until around 60 AD or later, not long before his death. Since the chronology I developed shows that Peter's secretary Mark was in Alexandria by at least 57-58 AD, I accept, with Eusebius, the earlier date of Peter's arrival in Rome, probably in the very late 40s or early 50s. If so, then the gospel he taught, which Mark his "son" wrote down, was written by 55-58 AD.

Did Luke use the Second Gospel for much of the material of his own, including the passion account? Luke certainly could have read a copy of Mark's gospel while at Rome with Paul (and Peter?). He could have met, in person, with John-Mark, the Fourth Evangelist, also in Rome during this time; or, as suggested above, with John-Mark and Mary at a later time in Ephesus. As hinted above, though, and elaborated below (under MATTHEW), I tend to believe that Matthew was probably Luke's principle written source of material found in common between the three Synoptics, which would explain a lot of the material attributed (by modern scholars) to the theoretical "Q" source.

IV. MATTHEW

The Gospel of Matthew is perhaps the most interesting in terms of development. While it was possibly the first published of the four, at least in its original form, it also probably underwent the most changes early in its existence. This conclusion is based on the fact that several early, credible Christian writers refer repeatedly to a Gospel of Matthew that was written in Hebrew (or possibly Aramaic?). Papias referred to it, and in the study above, we saw the quotation from Irenaeus: "Matthew published a written gospel for the Hebrews in their own tongue . . ." (Eusebius, *History,* pp. 210-11). In *Against Heresies,* Irenaeus also writes about one of the heretical groups in his time that had preserved this Hebrew version: "For the Ebionites, who use Matthew's Gospel only, are confuted out of this very same, making false suppositions with regard to the Lord" (*Ag. Her.* III.11.7).

Jerome makes many references to this early "Hebrew" Gospel of Matthew, all or part of which was still intact and in use in his time by two heretical Christian sects, the Nazoreans and the Ebionites. Jerome, in fact, claimed to have read a copy of the Hebrew original in the library at Caesarea (the library created by Eusebius). In his work *Of illustrious men,* chapter II (on James the Lord's brother), Jerome writes:

> "The Gospel also which is called the Gospel according to the Hebrews, and which I have recently translated into Greek and Latin and which also Origen often makes use of, after the account of the resurrection of the Saviour says . . ." (https://ccel.org/ccel/schaff/npnf203/npnf203.v.iii.iv.html).

In chapter III of the same work, he adds:

> Matthew, also called Levi, apostle and aforetimes publican, composed a gospel of Christ at first published in Judea in Hebrew for the sake of those of the circumcision who believed, but this was afterwards translated into Greek though by what author is uncertain. The Hebrew itself has been preserved until the present day in the library at Cæsarea which [Eusebius] Pamphilus so diligently gathered. I have also had the opportunity of having the volume described to me by the Nazarenes of Berœa, a city of Syria, who use it. In this it is to be noted that wherever the Evangelist, whether on his own account or in the person of our Lord the Saviour quotes the testimony of the Old Testament he does not follow the authority of the translators of the Septuagint but the Hebrew. Wherefore these two forms exist "Out of Egypt have I called my son," and "for he shall be called a Nazarene." [Note: at "Berœa," some manuscripts read "Veria," the modern Aleppo.]
> (https://ccel.org/ccel/schaff/npnf203/npnf203.v.iii.v.html)

One curious quirk in the record of this Hebrew version of Matthew is that the writer Epiphanius, in his own work titled (like Irenaeus') *Against Heresies* (xxix.9.4, Nazoraeans) writes:

> They have the Gospel according to Matthew quite complete, in Hebrew: for this Gospel is certainly still preserved among them as it was first written in Hebrew letters. I do not know if they have even removed the genealogy from Abraham to Christ (https://www.earlychristianwritings.com/gospelhebrews.html).

The quirk is how to interpret the statement that this gospel was written "in Hebrew letters." Was the gospel in the Hebrew language, or possibly just written in the Hebrew script? A possible answer lies elsewhere in Jerome. For writing not long after Epiphanius (his near-contemporary) Jerome in his *Dialogue against Pelagius* (iii.2.) says:

> In the Gospel according to the Hebrews which is indeed in the Chaldaean and Syrian speech but is written in Hebrew letters, which the Nazarenes use to this day, called 'according to the

apostles', or, as most term it, 'according to Matthew', which also is to be seen in the library of Caesarea . . . (https://www.earlychristianwritings.com/gospelhebrews.html).

This raises a difficult question still under debate: did the Apostle Matthew originally write a genuine *Hebrew language* version of his gospel (in Hebrew script), or did one of these sectarian groups take a copy of an original Greek version of Matthew and translate it into the "Chaldaean and Syrian" language, using Hebrew script? The answer is, we cannot be sure. Both views have been argued.[2]

Whichever was the case, Jerome assures us he had his hands on a copy of it in the library at Caesarea, and that he translated all, or a portion, of it himself. Sadly, that translation does not now exist, so we have no actual, complete text of this "Gospel of the Hebrews." We have only short quotations from the work in Jerome and several other writers.

One further piece of information that has survived about this document is in a biblical chronology developed by Nicephorus, the Patriarch of Constantinople from 806-815 AD. His *Stichometery* lists several apocryphal New Testament books and includes "The Gospel of the Hebrews" which it shows was composed of 2200 lines (of Greek text, either the original or a translation of the Hebrew original), whereas the Greek text of our canonical Matthew is about 2500 lines (http://www.ntcanon.org/Stichometry_of_Nicephorus.shtml).

This tells us that the two versions (Hebrew, and Greek), if they are indeed two versions or editions of the authentic Matthew, were not identical. If both were genuine, that means that the Greek canonical version that we have includes material that was not in the Hebrew version. How or when the assumed changes were made, whether additions to the Greek or cuts from the Hebrew, we have no way of knowing.

At some point, according to Jerome, a Greek translation was made of the original Hebrew. (Some think Jerome backed away from this view later in life and decided the Hebrew version was in fact an altered translation of the Matthew's Greek. Since Epiphanius says he did not know if Nazoreans "have even removed the genealogy from Abraham to Christ," the latter may be the case.)

This information about the Hebrew Matthew, taken in summary, suggests that of the four gospels, *some version* of Matthew may indeed have been the first completed and circulated in the Church. If, as Jerome says, Matthew first "composed a gospel of Christ at first published in Judea in Hebrew *for the sake of those of the circumcision who believed,"* this suggests a fairly early date, when a large number of the Church were Jewish converts in Judea itself. Commentators have always noticed that Matthew (the canonical version) clearly caters toward a Jewish-background audience, beginning with the focus on Joseph rather than Mary in the infancy narratives and using (as Jerome suggests) quotations from the original Hebrew Old Testament rather than from the Septuagint translation for his many "proofs" to show that Jesus was their Messiah.

Did Peter's secretary Mark, then, know of Matthew's gospel and have access to it? If Matthew's "original" gospel was fairly early and predates Mark, would that account for the many nearly verbatim parallels in Mark? Does this suggest that Matthew, as well as Peter, were together in Rome at some time in the 50s, and that Matthew and Mark collaborated? Or is it possible Matthew's original gospel was shorter (the reputed Hebrew version was about 300 lines shorter than our canonical version)? If it was that shorter version that came into the hands of Mark at Rome, this could explain some of the parallels still intact in Mark's shorter gospel. If that was the case, then Matthew, or some later editor, may have "filled out" the shorter Matthew into its eventual (present) form.

Which of these scenarios may have actually happened we simply don't know; but if, as some suggest, Mark used abridged material from an earlier Matthew to create his own gospel, then Mark could no longer be considered the original "proto-gospel" on which the other two Synoptics were built, as has long been argued. If this last was the case, it means Luke, too, ended up — through Mark — with essential parts of Matthew in his own gospel, again explaining some of the obvious parallels in the three.

The major stumbling block to sorting all this out is that we have no intact copy of this (supposed) early Hebrew version of Matthew's gospel. One legend says that Cyril of Jerusalem, on finding a copy that a monk had been studying, seized it and had the entire book burned as containing heresy. Earlier writers, though, indicate that this Hebrew version contained most of what is now in our canonical Matthew. If the Hebrew original was in fact written by Matthew, and copies made, it is tragic we no longer have an intact copy for comparison.

One other supposition is possible: did this early Hebrew version of Matthew contain much (or all?) of the material that scholars believe made up the hypothetical "Q" or "M" documents which they believe were sources for our canonical Matthew (and "Q" for Luke?) No such documents have actually been found; they were postulated on the *assumption* that Mark was the original of the Synoptics, so Matthew and Luke must have had sources for their additional material (not in Mark). If, however, the Hebrew Matthew (or its translation) was indeed the original of the three Synoptics, then Matthew needed no "Q," and already contained all the postulated "M" material (material in Matthew not in either Luke or Mark); and, of course, Luke could have simply utilized large parts of Matthew, rather than Mark, with the addition of material Luke himself researched.

This last suggestion means that Luke — likely in Rome — would have had access to this early version of Matthew (the original Hebrew, or more likely the Greek version) and simply incorporated into his gospel-in-progress those sections of Matthew which fit his plan. That would include the lengthy discourse of Jesus which makes up the "Sermon on the Mount" in Matthew (5-7) and the "Sermon on the Plain" in Luke (6:20-49, and parts of Luke 9-11). The possible sources of the unique materials in Luke 1-2 were already discussed above. If Luke had access to a version of Matthew that was older than Mark, he may not, then, have utilized Mark at all.

Summary

Taken together, these suppositions would point to the following line of development for our four canonical gospels:

> 1. JOHN was as early in composition as the Synoptics, based perhaps on written records John-Mark kept from just after the Resurrection (if not before). We have no evidence that John was written in any version other than Greek as we have it (in which it shines), with the likely editorial addition of chapter 21. Chapters 1-20 of the gospel were likely completed by 50-60 AD.
>
> As John aged, he may have added to or refined his gospel. After he died, a close friend added a new chapter, describing Peter's restoration by Jesus after the Resurrection, and answering a difficult question about why John himself had died before Jesus' promised return.
>
> 2. MATTHEW was written and in Judea (or possibly Antioch of Syria?) and published in that region before the Gospel of John, but in a Hebrew version that was long preserved, perhaps in an "edited" version that suited the two sectarian groups who favored its use only. It was at some point translated by some other person into Greek, and that version, or an edit of it, became the canonical version we have today (a gospel that is longer than the Ebionite/Nazorean version).
>
> 3. MARK was written at Rome by Peter's secretary Mark sometime around 55 AD, and Mark himself carried a copy of his gospel to Alexandria where he founded the Christian community. Mark may have worked in part from a copy (either Hebrew but more likely Greek) of Matthew that had reached Rome.
>
> 4. LUKE was the last gospel completed. At Rome, he had access to Mark, or the Greek text of Matthew, or both. If he

had Matthew, then he had no need of material from the supposed "Q" document. Both the First and Second Gospels may have been part of his sources, along with traditions and teaching from Paul. The "L" material unique in Luke may have come in part from Paul; but Luke also likely spent time with John-Mark either in Rome or later in Ephesus, where he learned unique details of Jesus' ministry directly from John-Mark, and possibly (at Ephesus) from Jesus' mother Mary, that he incorporated into his gospel, thus accounting for the many points of contact noted by Parker between the Third and Fourth Gospels.

Endnotes

1. Some speculate that Luke may have been the Lucius of Cyrene in the church at Antioch (Acts 13:1), so he would have known Paul much sooner. If so, he could have met John-Mark, and Mary, early on as well (see Appendices B and E). We have, though, no real evidence to connect Lucius and Lucas (Luke). In his parting greeting in Romans (16:21) Paul mentions a Lucius with him; but it would be odd to call Luke by a different name here. Of course, Lucias could be a copy error from Lucas. Lucius is a name distinct from Lucas, the latter being the source of our English Luke.

2. Fuller references to this version of Matthew and comments from early writers are found at
https://www.earlychristianwritings.com/gospelhebrews.html

Bibliography

Barker, Kenneth (General Editor), New American Standard Study Bible. Grand Rapids, MI: Zondervan, 1999.

Barton, John, and Muddiman, John: *The Oxford Bible Commentary*. Oxford: Oxford University Press, 2001.

Bettenson, Henry, *Documents of the Christian Church*. London: Oxford University Press, 1963.

Brown, Raymond E. *An Introduction to The Gospel Of John*, (Francis J. Moloney, Editor). New York: Doubleday, 2003.

Brown, Raymond E. *The Gospel and Epistles of John*. Collegeville, MN: The Liturgical Press, 1988

Caird, G. B., *The Revelation of Saint John*. Peabody, MA: Hendrickson Publishers. First published by A & C Black Limited London, 1966.

Christian Classics Ethereal Library. Found at http://www.CCEL.org

Crane, Frank, *The Lost Books Of The Bible*. New York: Alpha House, Inc., 1926.

Eusebius, *The History of the Church from Christ to Constantine*. Translated by G. A. Williamson. Baltimore, Maryland: Penguin Books, 1967.

James, M.R., Translation of fragments regarding the Gospel of the Hebrews, at: https://www.earlychristianwritings.com/text/gospelhebrews-mrjames.html

Lewis, C. S. *The Problem of Pain.* New York: Macmillan Company, 1962.

Martyr, Justin, *Dialogue With Trypho.* Translated and edited by R. P. C. Hanson. Association Press, New York, 1964.

Parker, Pierson. "John and John Mark." *Journal of Biblical Literature*, vol. 79, no. 2, 1960, pp. 97–110.*JSTOR*, https://doi.org/10.2307/3264460.

Richardson, Cyril C., *Early Christian Fathers, Volume I.* Philadelphia: The Westminster Press, 1953.

Schaff, Philip, *Eusebius Pamphilius: Church History, in Nicene and Post-Nicene Fathers, Series II, Volume 1,* found at CCEL, Grand Rapids, MI: Christian Classics Ethereal Library.

Schaff, Philip, *The Principle Works of St. Jerome, , in Nicene and Post-Nicene Fathers, Series II, Volume 6,* found at CCEL, Grand Rapids, MI: Christian Classics Ethereal Library.

Schaff, Philip, Irenaeus, *Against Heresies, in Anti-Nicene Fathers*, Volume 1, found at CCEL, Grand Rapids, MI: Christian Classics Ethereal Library.

Barton and Muddiman, *The Oxford Bible Commentary,* John Barton and John Muddiman, Editors. New York: Oxford University Press, 2001.

Cross, F. L., *The Oxford Dictionary of the Christian Church*, F. L. Cross, Editor. London: Oxford University Press, 1971.

Early Christian Writings, Various Works, at:
https://www.earlychristianwritings.com

A Note On Sources: In cases where a title is out of print and attempted contacts with the author or publisher received no response, quotations have been used under the Fair Use Doctrine of the US Copyright Act, Section 107.

About The Author

JOHN R. SPENCER holds a degree in English Literature from the University of Northern Colorado, where he was editor-in-chief of the campus literary magazine *NOVA,* and a Master of Divinity degree from Nashotah House Seminary near Milwaukee. He is a retired priest of The Anglican Church in North America.

His diverse career has included parish ministry, diocesan leadership, and 20 years in secular professions as a police officer, criminal investigator, coroner's investigator, emergency medical technician, social services worker, and community corrections supervisor.

He is the author of two other non-fiction works, *New Heavens, New Earth* (2002), and *Interrogating God: Seven Questions That Cause You To Doubt His Goodness* (2020), as well as the fictional *Solarium-3 Trilogy (Solarium-3, Haeven, and ReGeneration).*

He lives with his wife Candice in Wisconsin.

DeerVale Publishing

DeerVale™ is an independent publisher created to help new or independent authors bring their work into the marketplace of ideas. DeerVale books are available for order world-wide through most major booksellers.

Faced with the obstacles of self-publishing, the high costs of many subsidy publishers, and no one to "get them in the door" of a traditional publisher, many writers feel stuck and simply give up.

DeerVale can help. We tailor services to fit your needs. Since authors can handle some production work themselves (like hiring an editor or proofreader), we don't sell pricy "packages." We charge only for the services you actually need.

Unlike a vanity press, we don't publish everything submitted. We look for quality books we can support.

Visit our Submissions tab to learn more.

www.DeerValePublishing.com

www.ingramcontent.com/pod-product-compliance
Lightning Source LLC
Chambersburg PA
CBHW030547080526
44585CB00012B/297